W9-CNP-587

Bruce Morris

HTML
In Action

**HOT TIPS
FOR COOL SITES**

Microsoft *Press*

PUBLISHED BY
Microsoft Press
A Division of Microsoft Corporation
One Microsoft Way
Redmond, Washington 98052-6399

Copyright © 1996 by Bruce Morris

All rights reserved. No part of the contents of this book may be reproduced or
transmitted in any form or by any means without the written permission of the publisher.

Library of Congress Cataloging-in-Publication Data
Morris, Bruce, 1949-
      HTML in Action : hot tools for cool Web sites / Bruce
Morris.
         p.   cm.
      Includes index.
      ISBN 1-55615-948-X
      1. HTML (Document markup language)   2. World Wide Web (Information
retrieval system)   I. Title.
QA76.76.H94M64   1996
005.75--dc20   96-23894
                                                                          CIP

Printed and bound in the United States of America.

1 2 3 4 5 6 7 8 9   RAND-T   1 0 9 8 7 6

Distributed to the book trade in Canada by Macmillan of Canada, a division of Canada Publishing Corporation.

A CIP catalogue record for this book is available from the British Library.

Microsoft Press books are available through booksellers and distributors worldwide. For further information about
international editions, contact your local Microsoft Corporation office. Or contact Microsoft Press International directly
at fax (206) 936-7329.

PostScript is a registered trademark and Acrobat, Adobe, PageMaker, and Photoshop are trademarks of Adobe Systems,
Inc. Apple, Macintosh, QuickTime, and TrueType are registered trademarks of Apple Computer, Inc. Lucida is a registered
trademark of Bigelow and Holmes. HyperCard is a registered trademark of Claris Corporation. CorelDRAW and CorelPHOTO-
PAINT are registered trademarks of Corel Systems Corporation. Truespeech is a trademark of DSP Group, Inc. IBM is a
registered trademark and PowerPC is a trademark of International Business Machines Corporation. FoxPro, Microsoft, MS-
DOS, PowerPoint, Visual Basic, Visual C++, Win32, Windows, and Windows NT are registered trademarks and ActiveMovie,
ActiveVRML, ActiveX, FrontPage, and MSN are trademarks of Microsoft Corporation. Arial and Times New Roman are
registered trademarks of The Monotype Corporation PLC. Motorola is a registered trademark of Motorola, Inc. Netscape is
a trademark of Netscape Communications Corporation. Novell and WordPerfect are registered trademarks of Novell, Inc.
Silicon Graphics is a registered trademark of Silicon Graphics, Inc. Solaris and Sun Microsystems are registered trademarks
and Java and SPARC are trademarks of Sun Microsystems, Inc. NCSA Mosaic is a trademark of The Board of Trustees of
the University of Illinois. UNIX is a registered trademark in the United States and other countries, licensed exclusively through
X/Open Company, Ltd.

Acquisitions Editor: David Clark
Project Editor: Ron Lamb
Technical Editor: Mike Dixon

This book is dedicated to my wife—without her understanding and patience I could not have finished it and would never have started it.

TABLE OF CONTENTS

ACKNOWLEDGMENTS

Several people helped me in my labors. Some wrote entire sections with little or no formal credit or remuneration other than what you see on this page. Some proofread and made constructive comments. Some gave me ideas and fired my imagination. Some provided mental sustenance and propeller-head encouragement. Some were simply there when I needed them and may not be aware they helped.

Charlie Morris, my brother, wrote the section on multimedia and helped keep my head in a creative place.

Kief Morris, my son, wrote the section on CGI and contributed heavily to several other chapters. Every Web effort needs a prop head, and Kief's propeller spins pretty fast.

Nic Bicanic, wandering cyber warrior, wrote the section on animation.

Joe Night, anal-retentive extraordinaire and Gateway 2000 Web Team Quality Control Task Leader, proofread my code and made sure I didn't leave anything out.

Mike Geltz kept me straight, provided mental stimulation and reminders of the good times in the 60s, and contributed to the section on image maps.

The entire Gateway 2000 Web Team provided endless inspiration, encouragement, and a stimulating work atmosphere. Without that stimulating atmosphere, I would not have been able to go straight back to a computer after my work day and work long into the night on this book. The work ethic and interpersonal chemistry of the Gateway 2000 Web Team is unlike anything I've ever experienced at any of the hundreds of jobs I've had in my life. We constantly found ourselves finishing each other's sentences when talking about our shared dream of making the Gateway 2000 Web site truly the coolest Web site on the planet.

I also thank Ted Waitt for making it possible for me to have The Best Job in the World—managing the Gateway 2000 Web Team. This job allowed me to experience working with the coolest Web tools and the geekiest Web heads and to grow my knowledge of how to do cool things on a Web site. On my first day on the job, Ted provided me with my vision statement: "to make the Gateway Web site the coolest Web site on the planet." Now that's a cool vision statement.

INTRODUCTION

I wanted to start this book with the caveat "This book is four months out of date," but my editor seemed to think that would be a poor way to start a book. He's right, of course, from a marketing perspective. You're probably already aware that developments on the World Wide Web and Internet advance quickly. Perhaps a new measurement of time is needed. The term "Web years" might be used much the same way people talk about "dog years" but "Web years" may actually be shorter than "dog years."

It takes three or four months to write a book of this size and almost as long to edit it, make corrections to it, print it, and distribute it. During this process for the book you hold in your hands, several Web years may have passed, and some of the material in the book has been superseded by new developments or may seem like old news to with-it Web developers. Sorry. I tried to make the book as up-to-date as I possibly could, and as my deadline approached, I tried to go back and update the parts I wrote earliest. But the Web is a moving target for a writer, and any book written about it can only hope to be a snapshot in time.

Despite the rate of change, Web knowledge isn't replaced—it is added to. What you will learn after you finish this book will only add to what you'll learn here.

I hope to be able to help you incorporate some of the interesting, useful, and cool things you see on the Web into your Web site. This book won't tell you how to do everything cool you see on the Web, but I hope at least to get you started and point you in the direction of the tools and information you'll need to make your Web site technically and graphically fresh and innovative.

I assume you have a basic familiarity with HTML. For most of the techniques described in the book, I start with the basics but move quickly to how to do the cool things you probably bought this book to learn about. Some of these things are very basic and some are complex. Just as most of this stuff is pretty easy, most of this book is not extremely advanced or technical. When we do get to the really hard stuff, I'll warn you.

What's in This Book

In Chapter 1, we'll delve into some simple stuff that is often overlooked or underestimated. In Chapter 2, we'll look at forms, and in Chapter 3, we'll explore tables, a powerful tool for specifying exactly where objects will appear on a page. Chapters 4 and 5 cover graphics and backgrounds, which add visual interest to a Web page. Multimedia and inline animations—the topics of Chapters 6 and 7—make Web pages come alive. Chapter 8 discusses Acrobat, a useful tool for sharing graphics, and Chapter 9 looks at one of the hottest topics among Web developers—Java. Chapter 11 deals with frames, the latest tool for page design.

Although most of the Web development techniques described in this book do not involve rocket science, some—particularly in Chapter 10— involve CGI scripts and simple PERL programs. Chapter 13 deals with ActiveX and Visual Basic. It's not the purpose of this book to teach you PERL, ActiveX, or Visual Basic. You may need to find a friendly programmer to help you customize some of the more complicated features for your particular use. I know almost no PERL, but I somehow manage to get my image maps to work and my reader response forms to sort themselves into my database.

What's on the Companion CD

The companion CD to this book contains all of the sample HTML code in the book, plus a beta version of Microsoft Internet Explorer 3.0 and the Internet Assistant utilities for Microsoft Word, Excel, PowerPoint, Access, and Schedule+. Be sure you read the Readme.txt file for complete instructions on using the CD. For a release version of Microsoft Internet Explorer 3.0, visit the Microsoft Web site at http://www.microsoft.com.

What's "Cool"

First, I suppose we should define "cool" since it's a word used a lot in Web circles. *The American Heritage Dictionary of the English Language* defines "cool" as a slang word for "excellent."

Applied to Web sites, it seems to involve at least three characteristics:

- Good content
- Technical know-how
- Good design

In this book, I attempt to show how to use the available tools to create Web pages that are cool.

Pushing the Limits vs. Compatibility

I'm all in favor of pushing the limits of what can be done with HTML. HTML purists might condemn my code as being "duct tape HTML," but I will wear that badge with honor. I would go so far as to put at the top of all my pages, "Prepared in accordance with strict Duct Tape HTML specifications."

Don't get me wrong: I'm not thumbing my nose at HTML standards committees. Without them to slow us down, there's no telling how unreadable our pages might be. But without the HTML radicals, there's no telling how long new features might remain in committee.

Although I espouse using nonstandard, or "unofficial," extensions, I want you to be fully aware (if you aren't already) that many browser programs can't read nonstandard extensions or even graphics.

As Web developers push the limits of what can be done with HTML, some Web surfers are frustrated because their browsers do not display a document as the creator of the document intended it to appear. Each brand of browser displays HTML pages differently, and even a browser of the same brand and release can be customized to suit the individual surfer using it. One person might change the font for viewing text to a sans serif typeface such as Helvetica or Arial, and another person might prefer Times Roman—two very different typefaces, two very different looks for the same page. Typically, an HTML developer will prepare a Web page by writing HTML code in a text editor and keeping a browser open on the screen at the same time to view the page while work progresses. That way, it's handy to switch back and forth between windows to see how the page looks while coding continues. But this technique also makes it easy to forget that those pages may look considerably different on a different browser.

The wise Web developer instead will check any unusual HTML constructions on several popular browsers before committing pages to the Web.

Some developers prefer instead to specify a browser for viewing their pages and then design their pages for that browser. Many additionally provide a link to the browser company's Web site. This is fine. Most companies making Web browsers try to keep up with the latest extensions, so most will be compatible most of the time anyway.

Rarely will a browser-specific extension render pages totally unreadable on other browsers. As a Web site developer, you must decide whether the extensions you use will be recognized by the greater part of the visitors to your pages. You have to decide whether it's better to have an attractive site that only 80 percent of the market can really see in all its glory or a plain, boring site that every single visitor can see. As for me, I would rather have 80 percent of the market come back over and over and tell their friends about my site than have 100 percent come once, get bored, and never return.

Currently Microsoft Internet Explorer and Netscape Navigator not only are the most popular browsers but also are pushing the envelope of what can be done with HTML.

To some, the early Internet pioneers, it must seem as if it were only yesterday that the only way to surf the Web was with a text-only browser, such as the venerable Lynx, and the only editor was EMWACs. Device independence was built into the original HTML 1.0 specifications. Designed as a delivery system to make almost any text document available over the Internet, HTML was intended to allow almost any type of computer to be able to display information with hypertext links.

Unfortunately, the HTML approach to portable documents does not allow for consistent appearance of documents across platforms—only consistent structure. Until recently, HTML emphasized the portability of structure and content over appearances. It's good to keep in mind that a very small percentage of users still browse the Web with text-only browsers and a few Web developers use UNIX text-editing tools to format their HTML pages.

But you don't need to stop using the latest techniques to make your pages usable by text-only browsers. You can put ALT= tags in your image attributes, and you can repeat in regular text URLs that are linked through image maps.

Between them, Netscape Navigator and Microsoft Internet Explorer are offering the newest and coolest extensions and plug-ins, including VRML, Java, Real Audio, and Acrobat. One way to encourage the acceptance of these new features is to use them in your pages. As more and more surfers demand access to the cool features built into the best, most up-to-date sites, browser developers will be forced to include the latest new features. That way, cool new Web tools will become popular and mainstream.

As Manager of the Internet Team at Gateway 2000, I've been lucky enough to be able to work with some of the most creative and innovative Web designers. Some of their tips and tricks have found their way into these pages. I've surfed far and wide to find cool ways of doing simple things, puzzled out how to make them work, and tried to describe them for you in plain language. Examples of some of these tricks and many of the tools I've found useful are included in the enclosed CD. But I'm always hungry for more cool stuff. Don't be shy. Tell me what cool tricks you've found on the Web. Let me know about your favorite Web development tools and techniques. Mail me at bmorris@usit.net with your hot tips and cool tricks.

COOL BASIC
HTML TECHNIQUES

Don't flip past this chapter too quickly, even if you consider yourself an experienced HTML developer. Just because the word "basic" is in the title doesn't mean there aren't some basic HTML tags and attributes that you can use to do cool things for your Web site. There are several basic HTML tags and techniques that are obscure or underused that can spice up your pages. HTML 3.0, Netscape Navigator, and Microsoft Internet Explorer all add unique new tags and attributes that are basic but that you can put to good use to make your pages not only functional but visually unique. Many times it just takes a bit of creativity to make your pages stand out from the crowd.

Although you should avoid using a new or cool technique just to show that you know how to, you might find something among the newest attributes and tags that can separate your pages from the masses. Use it now before the great unwashed masses of Web page developers discover it, and then quickly restrict it to only the pages where it makes sense.

The descriptions of tags and attributes in this chapter emphasize making pages more useful and attractive through good graphic design. However, this chapter doesn't cover every obscure tag, such as <CITE>, <CODE>, and <COMMENT>. Many of the super-cool new techniques unique to Netscape Navigator and Microsoft Internet Explorer will be mentioned in this chapter.

Let's start off with a few basics. I'm going to breeze right through many of the basics of HTML, so you might want to have one of the numerous beginner HTML books handy when using this book if you're not already familiar with the basics.

HTML Basics

HTML is a tagging language. The tags surrounding a chunk of text (or a graphic) define how the text (or graphic) will appear—whether it will be big or small, bold or italic, flush left or flush right, blinking off and on or normal, even what color it will be—when viewed in a browser program. Tags also describe where things are placed.

HTML is a very primitive layout language. To do exciting things with your pages, you have to use your imagination to stretch the available tags to make your layout ideas come true. Fortunately, new HTML development tools such as Microsoft FrontPage make it quite easy for even a novice to produce ready-to-go pages without a steep learning curve. These programs place the HTML tags for you—all you have to do is supply text and graphics and use the buttons and menu commands to format the pages. Most of the methods for formatting should be familiar if you have been using other recent Windows programs.

Tags

The most basic HTML tags specify text size. Text surrounded by <H1></H1> appears quite large, as in a headline. Text surrounded by <H2></H2> is a bit smaller, as in a subhead; <H3></H3> text is even smaller; and so on, letting you specify progressively smaller sizes down to <H6></H6>. Body text does not need a tag, although using the paragraph tag (<P>) ensures proper spacing between paragraphs of body text.

Bold (<B></B>), italic (<I></I>), centered (<CENTER></CENTER>), blinking (<BLINK></BLINK>), and a variety of other tags add formatting to the surrounded text. Bulleted and numbered lists are created by using a variety of list tags. Some simple positioning can be accomplished using <BLOCKQUOTE></BLOCKQUOTE> and other tags, but serious positioning and layout are handled by placing text and graphics inside tables (<TABLE></TABLE>). Because tables do not have to appear with borders or lines around them, they can be used to make page design elements appear anywhere on a page, without the person viewing the page realizing a table is being used. A mastery of tables is essential if you are going to produce highly formatted Web pages. We'll look at tables in detail in Chapter 3.

Attributes

Attributes are added to tags to further specify how the content surrounded by the tags will appear. For example, text surrounded by <H1 ALIGN=CENTER></H1> will appear as a large, centered headline. The added ALIGN=CENTER attribute indicates positioning for the text. <TABLE BORDER=4> indicates a table with fairly normal-size lines around it and around the cells within it. <TABLE BORDER=0> indicates a table with no borders. A wide variety of attributes are available that, if used with a bit of imagination, can really spice up an otherwise plain page.

CAUTION:

TAGS AND ATTRIBUTES CAN BE BROWSER-SPECIFIC. THE NEWER BROWSERS, SUCH AS MICROSOFT INTERNET EXPLORER AND NETSCAPE NAVIGATOR, OFFER SOME EXTREMELY USEFUL AND FUN TAGS AND ATTRIBUTES THAT MIGHT NOT WORK PROPERLY IN OTHER BROWSERS. IF YOU HAVE REASON TO BELIEVE YOUR READERS MIGHT BE USING A PARTICULAR BROWSER, YOU SHOULD BE SURE TO CHECK YOUR FANCY PAGES USING THAT BROWSER. FORTUNATELY, MOST SECOND-TIER BROWSERS ARE FOLLOWING THE LEAD OF MICROSOFT AND NETSCAPE AND ARE TRYING TO ADD THE NEW TAGS AND ATTRIBUTES AS FAST AS THEY CAN. TAGS AND ATTRIBUTES THAT ARE NOT PART OF THE CURRENT HTML SPECIFICATION ARE REFERRED TO AS *EXTENSIONS TO HTML*.

Alignment and Spacing

It's surprising how much style you can add to your Web pages by having a good grasp of all the possible alignment and spacing tags and attributes. Using these features imaginatively is what separates the true Web page design gurus from the newbies. The layout of a Web page is almost as important as the content of the page.

The ALIGN= Attribute

Through the ALIGN= attribute, HTML 3.0 gives you the ability to specify whether text appears flush left, flush right, centered, or justified. If not specified otherwise, text appears flush left. This attribute also works with graphics and tables.

Flush Left Alignment

By default, HTML text is arranged flush left, ragged right—that is, the beginnings of lines are aligned and the ends of lines are not. Most of the time, this is fine—text usually looks best with even spacing between words, and flush left, ragged right ensures this. Because flush left is the default, you don't need to include this attribute to achieve it, but you can specify flush left alignment with the ALIGN=LEFT attribute.

Flush Right Alignment

Flush right, ragged left text—the beginnings of lines are not aligned and the ends are—has many practical uses, not the least of which is simply interesting graphic design. This effect is created by adding the ALIGN=RIGHT attribute to common tags such as the <P> tag, as shown in Figure 1-1.

FIGURE 1-1

```
<HTML>
<BODY>
Normally, text appears flush left,<BR>
ragged right by default.<BR>
Text can, however, be set centered or flush right.<BR>
There is no need to begin or end a flush left paragraph with a<BR>
paragraph tag.<BR>
<BR>
<P ALIGN=RIGHT>Right justified (flush right, ragged left) text<BR>
has a design appeal that can add graphic interest as well as<BR>
practicality to your pages. Explanatory captions can be neatly added to the
side of<BR>
```

```
figures and images. Don't forget to define the area selected for flush<BR>
right formatting by closing the tag.</P>
</BODY>
</HTML>
```

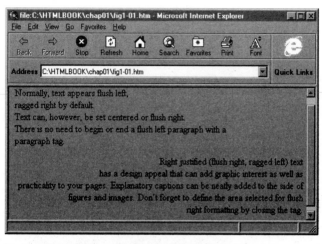

FIGURE 1-1 **Text ordinarily appears flush left but can be set right justified using the ALIGN=RIGHT attribute.**

Keep in mind that when you use alignment attributes with the <P> tag, you must use a closing </P> tag.

Centering Text and Graphics

If you want to center text or graphics, you have some choices. Included in the HTML 3.0 specification is the proposal to use the <ALIGN=CENTER> tag to center certain kinds of objects. However, this tag does not work with all objects on an HTML page, so Netscape has added the <CENTER> tag. When viewed with Netscape Navigator, Microsoft Internet Explorer, or any other browser that supports <CENTER>, this tag will center everything on a page that it is applied to. Examples of <ALIGN=CENTER> and <CENTER> are shown in Figure 1-2 on the following page.

I see no reason not to use <CENTER> with discretion. At the worst, some browsers will ignore the tag and left align material on your page. If you want to be sure you won't need to go back and change your <CENTER> tags to <P ALIGN=CENTER> at some future date, you can use both tags, although this seems a bit extreme to me.

Some HTML purists believe that the Great Web Creator never meant for HTML text to be centered and that any attempt at centering text or graphics is sacrilege.

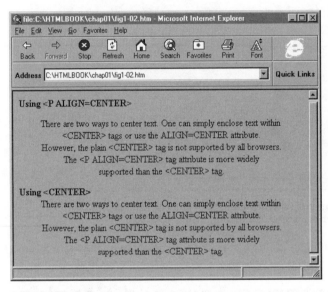

FIGURE 1-2

Text can be centered using either the <CENTER> tag or the <P ALIGN=CENTER> tag. However, the <CENTER> tag is not supported by all browsers.

FIGURE 1-2

```
<HTML>
<BODY>
<B>Using &lt;P ALIGN=CENTER&gt;</B>
<P ALIGN=CENTER>There are two ways to center text. One can simply enclose
text within &lt;CENTER&gt; tags or use the ALIGN=CENTER attribute.<BR>
However, the plain &lt;CENTER&gt; tag is not supported by all browsers.<BR>
The &lt;P ALIGN=CENTER&gt; tag attribute is more widely<BR>
```

```
supported than the &lt;CENTER&gt; tag.</P>
<B>Using &lt;CENTER&gt;</B>
<CENTER>There are two ways to center text. One can simply enclose text
within &lt;CENTER&gt; tags or use the ALIGN=CENTER attribute.<BR>
However, the plain &lt;CENTER&gt; tag is not supported by all browsers.<BR>
The &lt;P ALIGN=CENTER&gt; tag attribute is more widely<BR>
supported than the &lt;CENTER&gt; tag.
</CENTER>
</BODY>
</HTML>
```

The use of the centering tags within tables presents additional worries and will be covered in Chapter 3, "Tables."

Wrapping Text Around Graphics and Other Objects

If you want to get fancy and wrap your text around graphics just like in the glossy magazines, you can use the ALIGN= attributes. Wherever you want your graphic to appear, simply insert the necessary <IMG SRC="/path/to/the.gif"> tag and add an ALIGN=LEFT, ALIGN=RIGHT, or ALIGN=CENTER attribute. Also, using the HSPACE= and VSPACE= attributes (discussed later in this chapter), you can specify the amount of horizontal and vertical space between the image and the text. You can add a border around an image as well. You can also wrap text around a table (Figure 1-3).

FIGURE 1-3

```
<HTML>
<BODY>
<H2>You can wrap text around images and other objects.</H2>
<IMG SRC="clownfis.gif" ALIGN=RIGHT>
Imsep pretu tempu revol bileg rokam revoc tephe rosve etepe tenov sindu
turqu brevt elliu repar tiuve tamia queso utage udulc vires humus fallo
25deu Anetn bisre freun carmi avire ingen umque miher muner veris adest
duner veris adest iteru quevi escit billo isput
Imsep pretu tempu revol bileg rokam revoc tephe rosve etepe tenov sindu
turqu brevt elliu repar tiuve tamia queso utage udulc vires humus
<IMG SRC="clownfis.gif" ALIGN=LEFT>
<BR>
```

(continued)

FIGURE 1-3 *continued*

```
<TABLE BORDER=4 ALIGN=RIGHT>
  <TR>
    <TD>You can even</TD>
  </TR>
  <TR>
    <TD>wrap text</TD>
  </TR>
    <TD>around tables.</TD>
  </TR>
</TABLE>
Tiuve tamia queso utage udulc vires humus fallo 25deu Anetn bisre freun
carmi avire ingen umque miher muner veris adest duner veris adest iteru
quevi escit billo isput Imsep pretu tempu revol bileg rokam revoc tephe
rosve etepe tenov sindu turqu brevt elliu repar revoc tephe rosve etepe
tenov sindu turqu brevt elliu repar revoc tephe rosve
</BODY>
</HTML>
```

FIGURE 1-3 *You can wrap text around images and other objects.*

The CLEAR= Attribute (HTML 3.0)

You can add the CLEAR= attribute to the <BR> tag to stop text flow around an object at the point you specify and then resume text flow at the next clear space after the object, as shown in Figure 1-4. You can modify the CLEAR= attribute by specifying the text alignment when it resumes with the LEFT, RIGHT, or ALL attribute as follows:

<BR CLEAR=LEFT>	This tag specifies that text will resume at the next clear left margin.
<BR CLEAR=RIGHT>	This tag specifies that text will resume at the next clear right margin.
<BR CLEAR=ALL>	This tag specifies that text will resume at the next point where *both* the left *and* right margins are clear.

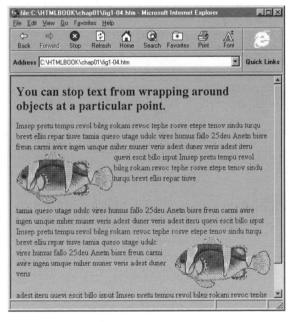

FIGURE 1-4 *You can use the CLEAR= attribute to force text to stop flowing around an image at the point you specify and to wait for the next clear space to continue.*

FIGURE 1-4

```
<HTML>
<BODY>
<H2>You can stop text from wrapping around objects at a particular point.</
H2>
Imsep pretu tempu revol bileg rokam revoc tephe rosve etepe tenov sindu
turqu brevt elliu repar tiuve tamia queso utage udulc vires humus fallo
25deu Anetn bisre freun carmi avire ingen umque miher muner
<IMG SRC="clownfis.gif" ALIGN=LEFT>
veris adest duner veris adest iteru quevi escit billo isput Imsep
pretu tempu revol bileg rokam revoc tephe rosve etepe tenov sindu turqu
brevt elliu repar tiuve
<BR CLEAR=LEFT>
tamia queso utage udulc vires humus fallo 25deu Anetn bisre freun carmi
avire ingen umque miher muner veris adest duner veris adest iteru quevi
escit billo isput Imsep pretu tempu revol bileg rokam
<IMG SRC="clownfis.gif" ALIGN=RIGHT>
revoc tephe rosve etepe tenov sindu turqu brevt elliu repar tiuve tamia
queso utage udulc vires humus fallo 25deu Anetn bisre freun carmi avire
ingen umque miher muner veris adest duner veris
<BR CLEAR=RIGHT>
adest iteru quevi escit billo isput Imsep pretu tempu revol bileg rokam
revoc tephe rosve etepe tenov sindu turqu brevt elliu repar tiuve tamia
queso utage udulc vires humus fallo
</BODY>
</HTML>
```

The <NOBR> Tag (Netscape Navigator 1.1 and Microsoft Internet Explorer 3.0)

You can use the <NOBR> (No Break) tag to force browsers to display text all on one line, not break a line of text into two or more lines, as shown in Figure 1-5. For instance, if you want a headline to be all on one line and *under no circumstances* to be divided into more than one line, add the <NOBR> tag around the headline. If you create a headline using <NOBR> that is too big to fit on the screen, the browser will add a horizontal scroll bar on the bottom of the screen. You can also add the <BR> tag at a particular place you want a line to break.

This tag might be useful when a line of text contains a long company name that you always want to appear all on one line and never be broken into two lines. To prevent the company name from being broken, put <NOBR> in front of the name.

You can use the <WBR> (Word Break) tag to *suggest* places where the text may be broken if necessary.

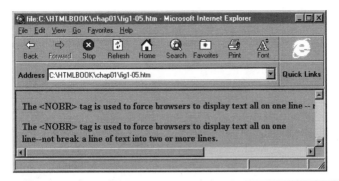

FIGURE 1-5

You can use the <NOBR> tag to specify a line of text that should not break except exactly where you want it to.

FIGURE 1-5

```html
<HTML>
<BODY>
<H4><NOBR>The &lt;NOBR&gt; tag is used to force browsers to display text
all on one line--not break a line of text into two or more lines.</NOBR></H4>
<H4>The &lt;NOBR&gt; tag is used to force browsers to display text all on
one line--not break a line of text into two or more lines.</H4>
</BODY>
</HTML>
```

The BORDER= Attribute (Netscape Navigator and Microsoft Internet Explorer)

You can specify a line around an image by adding the BORDER=n attribute to the <IMG> tag, where n is the width of the border in pixels. Four pixels is a handy size, although you can make borders of nearly any size, including really fat ones. One- or even two-pixel-wide borders might not display well on some monitors. I try to stick with four-pixel-wide borders. Keep in mind too that some browsers can't display an image border at all.

NOTE: With Microsoft Internet Explorer, if an image is a hyperlink, the border is drawn in the appropriate hyperlink color. If the image is not a hyperlink, the border will be invisible.

The HSPACE= Attribute (Netscape Navigator and Microsoft Internet Explorer)

Ordinarily, images are flush left or flush right with the edge of the page, and text flows to the very edge of the image. Usually, that puts the text too close to the image. By using the HSPACE= (Horizontal Space) attribute, you can add a bit of space around an image, forcing the text to move away from the edge of the image. The amount of space you add is specified in pixels. The only problem with using the HSPACE= attribute is that it adds space on both sides of the image so that the image is no longer flush left or flush right with the edge of the page. Adding enough horizontal space to keep the text neatly away from the image moves it out of alignment with the edge of the text column. At present, there is no way around this little quirk unless you use a table, an invisible GIF, or some other kludge to add space between images and text.

The VSPACE= Attribute (Netscape Navigator and Microsoft Internet Explorer)

Just as HSPACE= adds space on the sides of an image, the VSPACE= (Vertical Space) attribute adds space above and below an image. The VSPACE= attribute tends to leave images not properly centered between lines of text, as shown in Figure 1-6, and currently you can't specify the amount of space between lines of text (called leading) using HTML. Workarounds involve minutely adjusting the size of the image, which is not usually a viable option. Frequently an image is vertically spaced reasonably well without the use of the VSPACE= attribute. Once again, although a bit inelegant, tables may provide a workaround for spacing problems.

FIGURE 1-6

```
<HTML>
<BODY>
<H2>HSPACE=, VSPACE=, and BORDER= attributes allow you to manipulate image
alignment.</H2>
<H3>Notice how in the second image the left margin does not line up with
the edge of the graphic.</H3>
<IMG SRC="clownfis.gif" ALIGN=LEFT BORDER=2>
Imsep pretu tempu revol bileg rokam revoc tephe rosve etepe tenov sindu
turqu brevt ellifreun carmi avire ingen umque miher munerveris adest duner
veris adest iteru quevi escit billo isput Imsep pretu tempu revol bileg
rokam revoc tephe rosve etepe tenov sindu turqu brevt elliu  utage udulc
vires humus fallo 25deu Anetn bisre freuncarmi avire ingen umque miher
muner veris adest duner veris adest iteru quevi escit billo isputImsep
pretu tempu revol bileg rokam freun carmi avire ingen umque miher
munerfreun carmi
<IMG SRC="clownfis.gif" ALIGN=LEFT BORDER=2 VSPACE=20 HSPACE=20> freun
carmi avire ingen umque miher munerveris adest duner veris adest iteru
quevi escit billo isput Imsep pretu tempu revol bileg rokam revoc tephe
rosve etepe tenov sindu turqu brevt elliu  utage udulc vires humus fallo
25deu Anetn bisre freuncarmi avire ingen umque miher muner veris adest
duner veris adest iteru quevi escit billo isputImsep pretu tempu revol
```

```
bileg rokam freun carmi avire ingen umque miher munerfreun carmi avire
ingen umque miher munerfreuncarmi avire ingen umque miher muner veris adest
duner veris
</BODY>
</HTML>
```

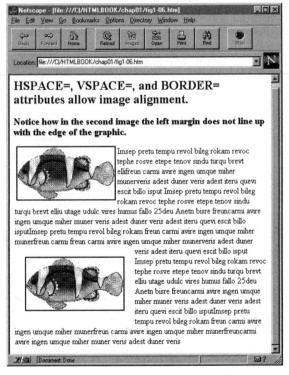

Creating Indents by Using Definition Lists or Block Quotes

Adding visual interest to a page not only sets you apart from the crowd in the design-starved world of HTML pages, but it can also make your pages more readable, drawing the reader's eye to points in your text that you feel need more attention. When I have pages with large amounts of text, I like to separate introductory text areas from the body of the text by indenting the main part of the text slightly. In addition to making the page more interesting visually, this makes the text a bit easier to read since many browsers tend to cram text to the far left and right sides of the screen with no margins whatsoever. There are several ways to indent blocks of text, each with its own advantages and disadvantages.

- Tabs are not supported by many browsers, and when a browser does support tabs, it usually indents only the first line of a paragraph. Just as tabs have limited uses in a word processor, they have specialized, limited uses in HTML pages.

- Definition list (<DL>) tags can be used in much the same way you would use the indent buttons on most common word processors. The <DL> tag was created to allow for formatting of text that defines a term. The term being defined appears on one line, and the definition is on the line below it and slightly indented. The <DL> tag lets you create indented blocks of text without bullets or numbers. The <DL> tag indents only on the left. When you add a few <DL> tags to a page, everything in the list moves to the right. Adding more <DL> tags moves things further to the right. Insert </DL> tags to mark the end of the indented text. Keep in mind that <DL> tags change only the left margin.

- The <BLOCKQUOTE> tag adds both a left and a right margin. This is a useful tag that compacts text into the middle of a page. You can use multiple <BLOCKQUOTE> tags to move things neatly toward the center of the page.

- Internet Explorer allows use of the LEFTMARGIN=n and TOP MARGIN=n attributes with the <BODY> tag. The n represents the width of the margin in pixels. The LEFTMARGIN=n attribute sets the left margin for the entire page. TOPMARGIN=n sets a margin at the top of a page. The tag <BODY LEFTMARGIN="40">, for example, creates a 40-pixel-wide left margin for the entire page. If you set n to 0, your left margin will be flush left.

Using indents is simply one more way to make your pages neater and more readable and to set them apart from the look of everyone else's pages, as shown in Figure 1-7.

TIP

IF YOU WANT TO RUN A NARROW COLUMN OF TEXT DOWN THE CENTER OF A PAGE, YOU CAN DO IT WITHOUT USING A TABLE BY ADDING MULTIPLE <BLOCKQUOTE> TAGS. TRY CENTERING THE TEXT FOR A WAY-COOL POEM LOOK.

FIGURE 1-7 *Definition list (<DL>) or <BLOCKQUOTE> tags create indented areas of text.*

FIGURE 1-7

```
<HTML>
<BODY>
<H2 ALIGN=CENTER>Using Definition Lists or Block Quotes<BR> to Create
Indents</H2>
freun carmi avire ingen umque miher munerveris adest duner veris adest
iteru quevi escit billo isput Imsep pretu tempu revol bileg rokam revoc
tephe rosve etepe
<H3 ALIGN=CENTER>The &lt;DL&gt; tag creates a left indent.</H3>
<DL><DL>bisre freuncarmi avire ingen umque miher muner veris adest duner
veris adest iteru quevi escit billo isputImsep pretu tempu revol bileg
rokam freun carmi avire ingen umque miher munerfreun carmi avire ingen
</DL></DL>
<P>
```

(continued)

FIGURE 1-7 *continued*

```
<H3 ALIGN=CENTER>The &lt;blockquote&gt; tag modifies both the left and
right margins.</H3>
<P>
<BLOCKQUOTE>
freun carmi avire ingen umque miher munerveris adest duner veris adest
iteru quevi escit billo isput Imsep pretu tempu revol bileg rokam revoc
tephe rosve etepe tenov sindu turqu brevt elliu  utage udulc vires humus
fallo 25deu Anetn
</BLOCKQUOTE>
</BODY>
</HTML>
```

Tabs (HTML 3.0)

Tabs have long been needed for preparing well-formatted pages in HTML, but only recently have they been provided. Some browsers do not support them, but when they work, they work very nicely. You can use them in several ways.

For a simple tab, just add the <TAB INDENT=n> tag, where n is a value representing the number of en spaces you want the indent to be. An en space is a typographical unit of measurement that is approximately equal to the width of the letter "n" in whichever font you are using. So the tag <TAB INDENT=4> sets a tab four en spaces wide.

If you want to use tabs spaced the same in several places in a document, place a <TAB> tag where you want to start the tab setting and add the id= attribute, like this:

```
<tab id="tabone">
```

Then, anywhere on the page that you want a tab aligned with TABONE, you put <TAB TO="TABONE">, and the tabs will line up. You can set several tab stops in this way by defining subsequent tabs with TABTWO, TABTHREE, TABFOUR, and so on.

You can also use the ALIGN= attribute with the <TAB> tag to create more complex page designs. If you specify left alignment, right alignment, or centered, the text following the <TAB> tag (up to the next line break or tag) will be left aligned, right aligned, or centered around the <TAB> tag. You can use this to arrange text centered on the tab but not centered in the middle of a page. You can also use the ALIGN=DECIMAL attribute to line up everything on the decimal point.

You can use the <TAB> tag for precise placement of text and graphics on a page as well.

Fancy Bullets, Fancy Lists

The tags for unordered lists <UL> and ordered <OL> lists are HTML staples. In HTML 3.0, there are several attributes that you can add to the list tags to change the bullet types for unordered lists and the numbering schemes for ordered lists. The attributes can also be applied to <LI> (List Item) tags themselves to change the bullet type in the middle of a list. Adding the attributes will affect the bullets for all list items following the added attribute.

Unfortunately, I can't show you cool screen captures of how some of the new attributes work—you're just going to have to wait for HTML 3.0 to see the coolness.

List Header

Just as you can add a title to a graphic, you can add a title to a list. Simply pop in the <LH> (List Header) tag, and your title will appear neatly indented at the top of the list. The <LH> tag doesn't need a closing </LH> tag.

Unordered List Bullet Type Attributes (Netscape Navigator)

If you like to use lists but you're tired of having to settle for the default bullets in nested hierarchical lists, the TYPE= attribute will please you. You can force any type of bullet to appear anywhere you like in a list. You can even mix up bullet types in a list. The tags for the standard bullet types, shown in Figure 1-8 on the following page, are as follows:

<UL TYPE=DISC>	This tag creates solid bullets, the same kind as first-level, default bullets.
<UL TYPE=CIRCLE>	This tag creates hollow square bullets.
<UL TYPE=SQUARE>	This tag creates square bullets.

With HTML 3.0, you can substitute GIFs and dingbats for the regular, garden variety, bullet as described a little later in this chapter. Dingbats are special typographical characters that add visual interest as markers or bullets.

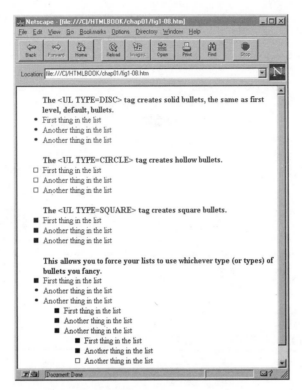

FIGURE 1-8

You can specify different bullet types by using the TYPE= attribute.

FIGURE 1-8

```
<HTML>
<BODY>
<UL TYPE=DISC>
    <LH><B>The &lt;UL TYPE=DISC&gt; tag creates solid bullets, the same as
first level, default, bullets.</B>
    <LI>First thing in the list
    <LI>Another thing in the list
    <LI>Another thing in the list
</UL>
<UL TYPE=CIRCLE>
    <LH><B>The &lt;UL TYPE=CIRCLE&gt; tag creates hollow bullets.</B>
```

```
    <LI>First thing in the list
    <LI>Another thing in the list
    <LI>Another thing in the list
</UL>
<UL TYPE=SQUARE>
    <LH><B>The &lt;UL TYPE=SQUARE&gt; tag creates square bullets.</B>
    <LI>First thing in the list
    <LI>Another thing in the list
    <LI>Another thing in the list
</UL>
<UL TYPE=SQUARE>
    <LH><B>This allows you to force your lists to use whichever type
(or types) of bullets you fancy.</B>
    <LI>First thing in the list
    <LI TYPE=DISC>Another thing in the list
    <LI>Another thing in the list
<UL TYPE=SQUARE>
    <LI>First thing in the list
    <LI>Another thing in the list
    <LI>Another thing in the list
<UL TYPE=SQUARE>
    <LI>First thing in the list
    <LI>Another thing in the list
    <LI TYPE=CIRCLE>Another thing in the list
</UL></UL></UL>
</BODY>
</HTML>
```

The PLAIN= Attribute (HTML 3.0)

The PLAIN= attribute creates an unordered list with no bullets. The simplest way to create an unordered list with no bullets, of course, is to create a definition list, but you might want to sprinkle in the odd bullet or two in your list, and the PLAIN= attribute allows you to do that.

The SRC= Attribute (HTML 3.0)

You can use the SRC= attribute to specify a GIF file to be used instead of the regular bullet. (GIF, the most commonly used graphics file format in HTML, is discussed in Chapter 4.) Instead of simply placing a GIF in front of a line of type and putting a <BR> tag at the end, you can create your own nifty bullets and then use them as the default bullets in a list. This way, you get all the advantages of using an unordered list, and you can have neat GIFs as bullets. You can add the SRC= attribute to the <UL> tag, specifying all bullets in the list, or you can add it to each <LI> tag in a list, specifying a different GIF for each list item. However, you need to add the PLAIN= attribute to get the SRC= attribute to work with the <UL> tag.

The SRC= attribute for list tags was much requested by Web page developers and has the potential to create very attractive pages, but it can also be abused and can end up making some pages uniquely ugly.

The DINGBAT= Attribute (HTML 3.0)

The DINGBAT= attribute lets you use the dingbats supplied by browsers. This avoids the need to download GIFs to use as list bullets. The standard dingbats are as follows:

- Text
- Audio
- Folder
- Disk drive
- Form
- Home
- Next
- Previous

To specify a dingbat, simply add the name of the desired dingbat to the <LI> tag. For example, to use the home dingbat, use the tag <LI DINGBAT="home">. You can also use dingbats with header tags.

Ordered List Numbering Attributes

The <OL> tag and the TYPE= attribute in HTML 3.0 allow you to get fancy with ordered lists and use regular numbers, uppercase or lowercase letters, and uppercase or lowercase Roman numerals, as shown in Figure 1-9. If you must, you can mix them up in the same list.

<OL TYPE=1>	This tag creates numbered lists in the format 1., 2., 3., 4., and so on.
<OL TYPE=A>	This tag creates lists with capital letters in the format A., B., C., D., and so on.
<OL TYPE=a>	This tag creates lists with lowercase letters in the format a., b., c., d., and so on.
<OL TYPE=I>	This tag creates lists with capital Roman numerals in the format I., II., III., IV., and so on.
<OL TYPE=i>	This tag creates lists with lowercase Roman numerals in the format i., ii., iii., iv., and so on.

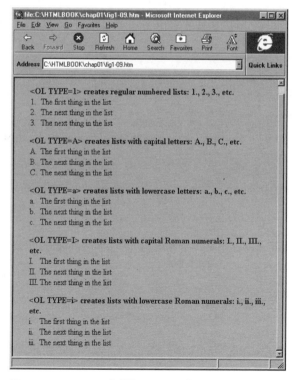

FIGURE 1-9   *You can use several different numbering schemes with ordered lists.*

FIGURE 1-9

```
<HTML>
<BODY>
<OL TYPE=1>
    <LH><B>&lt;OL TYPE=1&gt; creates regular numbered lists: 1., 2., 3.,
etc.</B><BR>
    <LI>The first thing in the list
    <LI>The next thing in the list
    <LI>The next thing in the list
</OL>
<OL TYPE=A>
    <LH><B>&lt;OL TYPE=A&gt; creates lists with capital letters: A., B.,
C., etc.</B><BR>
    <LI>The first thing in the list
    <LI>The next thing in the list
    <LI>The next thing in the list
</OL>
<OL TYPE=a>
    <LH><B>&lt;OL TYPE=a&gt; creates lists with lowercase letters: a., b.,
c., etc.</B><BR>
    <LI>The first thing in the list
    <LI>The next thing in the list
    <LI>The next thing in the list
</OL>
<OL TYPE=I>
    <LH><B>&lt;OL TYPE=I&gt; creates lists with capital Roman numerals: I.,
II., III., etc.</B><BR>
    <LI>The first thing in the list
    <LI>The next thing in the list
    <LI>The next thing in the list
</OL>
<OL TYPE=i>
    <LH><B>&lt;OL TYPE=i&gt; creates lists with lowercase Roman numerals:
i., ii., iii., etc.</B><BR>
```

```
        <LI>The first thing in the list
        <LI>The next thing in the list
        <LI>The next thing in the list
    </OL>
    </BODY>
    </HTML>
```

Changing the Order in a List

You can change the numbering and lettering sequence in a list with the SKIP=, START=, and VALUE= attributes, as shown in Figure 1-10 on the following page. You can add these attributes to <LI> tags as well as to <OL> tags.

The SKIP= Attribute (HTML 3.0)

If you add the SKIP= attribute to an <LI> tag in the middle of an ordered list, the numbering will skip the number of units specified after the equal sign. For example, if you use <LI SKIP=3> in the middle of an ordered list, the numbering will skip three numbers in the numbering sequence.

The START= Attribute (Netscape Navigator and Microsoft Internet Explorer)

You can use the START= attribute to indicate which kind of sequence (numbers, letters, or Roman numerals) you want to start with in a list. If you define a list with <OL TYPE=a START=5>, for example, the list will begin with the letter "e" and go through the alphabet from there.

The VALUE= Attribute (Netscape Navigator and Microsoft Internet Explorer)

Within an ordered list, you can add the VALUE= attribute to force that particular list item to have a particular number. After you use the VALUE= attribute, the following list items will use that value as a base. If you want to be really obtuse, you can force an ordered list to start and restart numbering sequences anywhere you choose.

TIP

KEEP IN MIND THAT THE
SKIP=, START=, AND
VALUE= ATTRIBUTES
MIGHT NOT WORK
WITH SOME
BROWSERS.

file:C:\HTMLBOOK\chap01\fig1-10.htm - Microsoft Internet Explorer

File   Edit   View   Go   Favorites   Help

Back   Forward   Stop   Refresh   Home   Search   Favorites   Print   Font

Address C:\HTMLBOOK\chap01\fig1-10.htm   Quick Links

Using the START=, VALUE=, and TYPE= attributes, you can structure
ordered lists.
5. The first thing in the list
6. The next thing in the list
7. The next thing in the list
8. The next thing in the list
9. The next thing in the list
8. The next thing in the list (Wait a minute, what's going on here?)
7. The next thing in the list
6. The next thing in the list
vii. The next thing in the list (Too weird.)
viii. The next thing in the list

FIGURE 1-10

*You can change the numbering sequences in ordered lists in
surprising ways.*

FIGURE 1-10

```
<HTML>
<BODY>
<OL TYPE=1 START=5>
    <LH><B>Using the START=, VALUE=, and TYPE= attributes, you can
structure ordered lists.</B><BR>
    <LI>The first thing in the list
    <LI>The next thing in the list
    <LI>The next thing in the list
    <LI>The next thing in the list
    <LI>The next thing in the list
    <LI VALUE=8>The next thing in the list (Wait a minute, what's going on
here?)
    <LI VALUE=7>The next thing in the list
    <LI VALUE=6>The next thing in the list
    <LI TYPE=i>The next thing in the list (Too weird.)
    <LI>The next thing in the list
</OL>
</BODY>
</HTML>
```

The COMPACT= Attribute (HTML 3.0)

Eventually, adding the COMPACT= attribute to your list tags will make browsers display the lists in a tighter manner by leaving less space between lines, using a smaller font, or some other adjustment. COMPACT= currently doesn't work on any widely used browsers, so we'll have to wait and see exactly how compact things will get.

The WRAP= Attribute (HTML 3.0)

The proposed HTML 3.0 WRAP= attribute spreads out a list horizontally on a line instead of making the list vertical. This allows you to have a numbered or bulleted list embedded in a paragraph.

Font Manipulation

Fonts have finally arrived on the Web, to the dismay of some and the delight of others. Superscripts, subscripts, bigger fonts, smaller fonts, red fonts, blue fonts, all combine to make more interesting, readable, and functional pages a reality. Microsoft Internet Explorer even allows you the ultimate Web page designer's typographic dream: specifying fonts with the FACE= attribute. Now you can combine more than one font on a page, overriding an individual browser's defaults. HTML conservatives are going bonkers as graphic designers realize they can now do *almost anything* on a Web page with HTML. Are ransom-note Web pages on the horizon? I'm sure they're here already.

Superscripts and Subscripts (HTML 3.0)

You can add superscripts and subscripts to your pages with the <SUP> and <SUB> tags. Trademarks, copyright symbols, references, and callouts to footnotes properly require a superscript or subscript treatment, which you can specify in the middle of text areas of any size with these tags. To make superscripts and subscripts look completely proper, combine them with the FONT SIZE= attribute so they'll appear smaller than surrounding text.

TIP

I LOVE FONTS AND WHAT THEY CAN DO FOR PAGE DESIGN. DURING MY COLLEGE YEARS (A FEW DECADES AGO), I WORKED FOR SEVERAL TYPOGRAPHERS AND SPENT CONSIDERABLE TIME SQUINTING OVER TRAYS OF BODONI BOLD AND GARAMOND BOLD ITALIC. THE SOONER OTHER BROWSERS CATCH UP WITH MICROSOFT INTERNET EXPLORER IN OFFERING FINE CONTROL OF FONTS, THE BETTER. I EXPECT TO SOON SEE SOPHISTICATED WEB SITES OFFERING FONTS FOR DOWNLOAD SO THAT ALMOST ANYONE CAN VIEW THE PAGES PROPERLY, JUST AS SOME WEB SITES NOW OFFER SPECIAL MULTIMEDIA PLUG-INS.

The SIZE= Attribute (Netscape Navigator and Microsoft Internet Explorer)

Using the SIZE= attribute of the <FONT> tag, you can specify how big or small a block of text will be. Unless you use the <BASEFONT SIZE=*n*> tag to specify a particular default font size, the default size is 3. The <H1> type is equal to 6, so a type size larger than <H1> is <FONT SIZE=7>. A little bit of neatness is lost with this tag since line leading is changed as well as font size. HTML is still a long way from providing professional typographic controls. Perhaps one day we will see kerning and leading adjustments in tenths of points.

Some browsers don't support the <FONT> tag, so it's a good idea to use it only when you want to change a font size in the middle of a block of text and use <H1>, <H2>, <H3>, and so on in most other places. The main advantage of the <FONT> tag is that it changes the font size without adding a line break. You can make a font bigger or smaller in the middle of a line, whereas <H*n*> tags cause a line break. A very handy tag.

Use your imagination to think up special uses for these tags. If you ever have a need for small caps, <FONT SIZE=*n*> is the way to do it. As we'll see next, another set of tags exists that can accomplish essentially the same thing.

The <BIG> and <SMALL> Tags (Netscape Navigator and Microsoft Internet Explorer)

These are nice, simple tags. Simply bracket text between <BIG></BIG> or <SMALL></SMALL> to make the text between the tags bigger or smaller *relative to the text around it* with no line breaks, as shown in Figure 1-11.

FIGURE 1-11

```
<HTML>
<BODY>
<H3>You can add superscripts and subscripts to your pages.
Trademarks<SUP><FONT SIZE=1>TM</FONT></SUP>, copyright symbols &copy;,
references, and callouts to footnotes<SUB><FONT SIZE=1>12</FONT></SUB>
can be inserted in the middle of text areas with these tags.
To make superscripts and subscripts look completely proper, combine
them with tags that make the font smaller.</H3>
<P>
Use your imagination to think up special uses for these tags.
If you ever have a need for <FONT SIZE=1>SMALL CAPS IN THE MIDDLE</FONT>
of a line of text, the &lt;FONT SIZE=1&gt; tag works nicely. <SMALL>SO DOES
```

```
THE SMALL TAG.</SMALL> Of course, <BIG>if for any reason you need to
make some text bigger,</BIG> that can be accomplished as well using the
&lt;BIG&gt; tag. Use your imagination to think up special uses for these
tags. If you ever have a need for <SMALL>SMALL CAPS IN THE MIDDLE</SMALL>
of a line of text, this tag is one of the best ways to do it. Of course,
<BIG>if for any reason you need to make some text bigger,</BIG> that can
<FONT SIZE=5>be accomplished as well.</FONT>
</BODY>
</HTML>
```

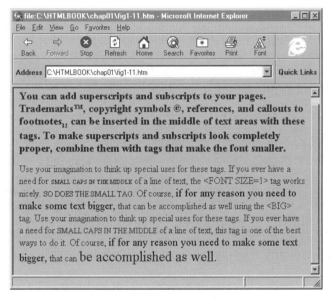

FIGURE 1-11

You can specify big fonts, small fonts, superscripts, and subscripts.

The COLOR=*xx* Attribute (Netscape Navigator and Microsoft Internet Explorer)

If you want more color in your pages, you can use the COLOR= attribute of the FONT tag, and the only limit will be the color palette of your viewers. Currently only the most popular browsers display font colors.

As is the case with most HTML tags, using <FONT COLOR=> to change the color of your fonts is simple. Surround the text with <FONT COLOR=></FONT> tags. If you are aiming at Netscape Navigator 1.1 users, specify the numeric value of the color you want the text to appear in. If you are shooting for Netscape Navigator 2.0 or Microsoft Internet Explorer users, use a font color name such as "red" or "green." Netscape Navigator 2.0 and Microsoft Internet Explorer recognize these font color names: black, maroon, green, olive, navy, purple, teal, gray, silver, red, lime, yellow, blue, fuchsia, aqua, and white. Try not to use any really strange colors, in case someone is viewing your page using a video mode that has a low number of colors.

The tag that is optimized for Netscape Navigator 1.1 users is as follows:

```
<FONT COLOR="FF0000">This will make the text a lovely red color.</FONT>
```

The tag for Netscape Navigator 2.0 and Microsoft Internet Explorer users is as follows:

```
<FONT COLOR=RED>This is an even easier way to make the text appear red.</FONT>
```

The FACE= Attribute (Microsoft Internet Explorer)

Microsoft Internet Explorer users have the advantage of being able to view pages in the typeface the original page designer intended. You can specify different typefaces by using the FACE= attribute with the <FONT> tag, as shown in Figure 1-12. The typeface specified must be on the viewer's system; otherwise, the browser's default typeface will be used. If you are a little daring, you can assume that most viewers will have the standard TrueType fonts that come with Windows.

You can specify more than one typeface in case the one you would like to use is not available on a viewer's system. The browser will look through the list of typefaces and use the first one on the list or, if it is not available, the next one on the list that is available on the viewer's system.

For more information about the <FONT> tag and the use of TrueType fonts, see Chapter 12.

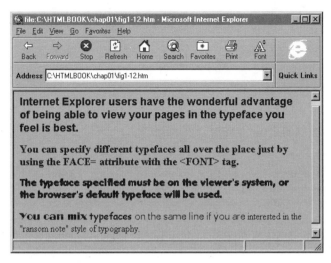

FIGURE 1-12 *Microsoft Internet Explorer allows you to specify particular typefaces.*

FIGURE 1-12

```
<HTML>
<BODY>
<H3><FONT FACE="ARIAL, HELV, LUCIDA">Internet Explorer users have the
wonderful advantage of being able to view your pages in the typeface you
feel is best.</FONT><P>
<FONT FACE="TIMES NEW ROMAN">You can specify different typefaces all over
the place just by using the FACE= attribute with the &lt;FONT&gt; tag.</
FONT></H3><P>
<FONT FACE="SIMON ROUNDED">The typeface specified must be on the viewer's
system, or the browser's default typeface will be used.</FONT><P>
<FONT FACE="BROADWAY BT">You can mix</FONT> <FONT FACE="COMIC SANS
MS">typefaces</FONT> <FONT FACE="ZURICH BT">on the same line if you are
</FONT><FONT FACE="ARIAL BOLD"> interested in the &quot;ransom note&quot;
style of typography.</FONT>
</BODY>
</HTML>
```

A Little Bit Beyond the Basics

OK, OK, I know this chapter has "basic" in its title and I said it would stick to the basics, but I also said you could do some cool things by taking the basics a little bit further. That's what the rest of this chapter is about.

Fancy Lines, Fat Lines, Thin Lines

Now we get into some true "duct tape" HTML. There may not be many times when these particular techniques are useful, but manipulating the <HR> tags to obtain bizarre output is a good example of what you can discover if you simply take HTML features to the extreme.

Experiment with the <HR> (horizontal rule) tag to create lines that are very different from what you usually see. Then see if you can find a way to use lines as wacky as some of those in Figures 1-13, 1-14, and 1-15.

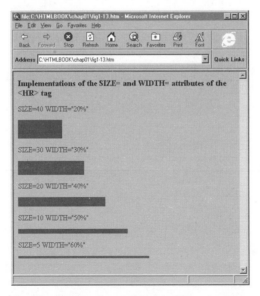

FIGURE 1-13 *Pushing the envelope with the <HR> tag can create some interesting effects.*

FIGURE 1-13

```
<HTML>
<BODY>
<H3>Implementations of the SIZE= and WIDTH= attributes of the &lt;HR&gt;
tag</H3>
SIZE=40 WIDTH=&quot;20%&quot;
<HR NOSHADE SIZE=40 WIDTH="20%" ALIGN=LEFT>
SIZE=30 WIDTH=&quot;30%&quot;
<HR NOSHADE SIZE=30 WIDTH="30%" ALIGN=LEFT>
SIZE=20 WIDTH=&quot;40%&quot;
<HR NOSHADE SIZE=20 WIDTH="40%" ALIGN=LEFT>
SIZE=10 WIDTH=&quot;50%&quot;
<HR NOSHADE SIZE=10 WIDTH="50%" ALIGN=LEFT>
SIZE=5 WIDTH=&quot;60%&quot;
<HR NOSHADE SIZE=5 WIDTH="60%" ALIGN=LEFT>
</BODY>
</HTML>
```

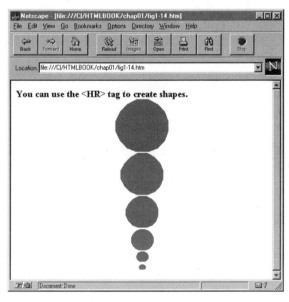

FIGURE 1-14   *You can use the <HR> tag to create shapes.*

FIGURE 1-14

```
<HTML>
<BODY>
<H3>You can use the &lt;HR&gt; tag to create shapes.
<HR NOSHADE SIZE=100 WIDTH="1%">
<HR NOSHADE SIZE=80 WIDTH="1%">
<HR NOSHADE SIZE=60 WIDTH="1%">
<HR NOSHADE SIZE=40 WIDTH="1%">
<HR NOSHADE SIZE=20 WIDTH="1%">
<HR NOSHADE SIZE=10 WIDTH="1%">
</BODY>
</HTML>
```

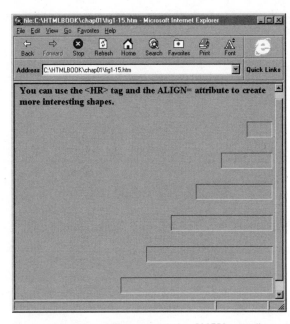

FIGURE 1-15

You can use the <HR> tag and the ALIGN= attribute to create more interesting shapes.

FIGURE 1-15

```
<HTML>
<BODY>
<H3>You can use the &lt;HR&gt; tag and the ALIGN= attribute to create more
interesting shapes.</H3>
```

```
<HR SIZE=30 WIDTH="10%" ALIGN=RIGHT>
<HR SIZE=30 WIDTH="20%" ALIGN=RIGHT>
<HR SIZE=30 WIDTH="30%" ALIGN=RIGHT>
<HR SIZE=30 WIDTH="40%" ALIGN=RIGHT>
<HR SIZE=30 WIDTH="50%" ALIGN=RIGHT>
<HR SIZE=30 WIDTH="60%" ALIGN=RIGHT>
</BODY>
</HTML>
```

Don't forget to try the NOSHADE attribute. You can make your lines fat, thin, short, long, flush left, flush right, or centered.

Go for it. But remember, using weirdly fat, colored lines is a trick that is easy to overuse and that can create ugly, show-offy pages. But if you're creative and careful, it can be a useful HTML design tool.

TIP

IF YOU SPECIFY A BACKGROUND COLOR *AND* A BACKGROUND GIF FOR A PAGE, THE BACKGROUND COLOR WILL SHOW THROUGH THE BACKGROUND GIF WHEREVER YOU HAVE TABLE BORDERS AND LINES. (THIS WON'T WORK WITH THE NOSHADE ATTRIBUTE.) USING THIS TRICK, YOU CAN ADD YET ANOTHER COLOR TO YOUR PAGE DESIGN. IT'S A SHAME TO HAVE TO RESORT TO SUCH MEEK TRICKS AS THIS— BUT SUCH IS THE CASE.

The <Meta> Tag (HTML)

The <META> tag is either a really cool tool or an unbelievable irritant. <META> has a number of uses, but one interesting use is to force pages to load one right after another, with no action on the part of the viewer. If you don't warn your viewer that <META> pages are on the way, the viewer may be justifiably irritated when pages start zapping around all over the place in a confusing HTML blur.

Placed between the <HEAD></HEAD> tags, <META> can either reload the same page every specified number of seconds or cause yet another page to load after a specified number of seconds. I can't think of any useful reasons to reload the same page over and over, but forcing new pages to load opens up several interesting opportunities:

- Bulleted presentations designed for overhead viewing in a corporate meeting can now be displayed on your Web pages. Just make each page of your presentation into an HTML page, and force them to load one after another.

- You can arrange for a hands-free tour through instructional documents.

- You can reload the same jazzy, colorful page over and over, but in a different color each time.

You get the idea. Here's how to do it.

```
<HTML>
<Head>
<META HTTP-EQUIV="refresh" CONTENT=2>
<TITLE>Weird Reloading Page</TITLE>
</HEAD>
<BODY>
This page will reload every two seconds. You can change the number and get it to
reload more frequently or more slowly.
</BODY>
</HTML>
```

or:

```
<HTML>
<HEAD>
<META HTTP-EQUIV="refresh" CONTENT="5; url=http://next.page.com/page2.htm">
<TITLE>A Bunch of Weird Reloading Pages</TITLE>
</HEAD>
<BODY>
This page will load
http://next.page.com/page2.htm after five seconds. You could set that page to
point to yet another page and the next one to one after that and . . . .
</BODY>
</HTML>
```

The last page in the series should *not* have a <META> tag, so that your viewer can rest a bit and decide what to do next.

The <MARQUEE> Tag (Microsoft Internet Explorer)

If you want to optimize your Web page for Microsoft Internet Explorer, you can take advantage of the <MARQUEE> tag to create horizontally scrolling text, shown in stop action in Figure 1-16. Many will think scrolling text is just a gimmick, and it is, but it is also quite a useful tool. Not only will it brazenly draw the viewer's eye to the text, but you can cram a bit more information into the very valuable real estate at the top of a Web page. Although the effect might remind you of a time and temperature sign on a bank, there are many legitimate uses for <MARQUEE>.

Your viewer's eye will be drawn immediately to a marquee, so it's a good spot to put an important message. Be sure to put the most important part of your message in the first part of the marquee—most people tend to stop reading midway through a long scrolling stream of text.

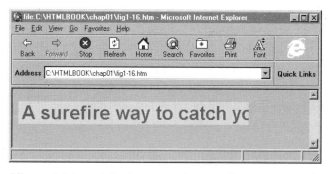

FIGURE 1-16

Microsoft Internet Explorer can view scrolling text created by the <MARQUEE> tag.

FIGURE 1-16

```
<HTML>
<BODY>
<FONT FACE=ARIAL COLOR=BLUE><MARQUEE VSPACE=5
WIDTH=80% BEHAVIOUR=SCROLL>A surefire way to catch your
viewer's attention is to put your most important message
in a scrolling marquee.</MARQUEE>
</BODY>
</HTML>
```

Choose the text you would like to scroll, enclose it with the <MARQUEE></MARQUEE> tags, and add the <MARQUEE> attributes to suit you. There's no need for any fancy coding. Browsers other than Microsoft Internet Explorer will show a marquee as a line of ordinary text. You can make marquees fat, thin, flush left, flush right, centered, blue, green, red, wide, narrow, sliding left, sliding right, bouncing, or any combination of all these attributes.

You can specify font attributes for the text in the marquee, but you must surround the entire <MARQUEE></MARQUEE> tag with the font information. The <MARQUEE> tag allows a number of its own attributes as well.

The ALIGN= Attribute
Using the ALIGN= attribute, you can position your text to the TOP, MIDDLE, or BOTTOM of the marquee area.

The BEHAVIOR= Attribute

Without the BEHAVIOR= attribute, text in a marquee will scroll from right to left. The BEHAVIOR= attribute allows you to specify any of the following:

SCROLL — Text scrolls off the screen. This is the default.

SLIDE — Text scrolls onto the screen and then comes to a halt.

ALTERNATE — Text scrolls into the marquee and then bounces back and forth within the marquee borders.

The BGCOLOR= Attribute

You can specify the background color of the marquee using either friendly color names or the usual hexadecimal rrggbb color definitions. You can also specify the color of the scrolling text, but you must place the <FONT COLOR= ></FONT> tags outside the <MARQUEE></MARQUEE> tags so that the marquee is nested within the FONT tags.

The DIRECTION= Attribute

Decide which way you want your text to scroll, and add the appropriate LEFT= or RIGHT= attribute to the marquee tag. The default is LEFT=, and, unless your message is very short, you should probably leave it that way.

The HEIGHT= Attribute

The HEIGHT= attribute allows you to make a fat or tall marquee area. You can specify the height in pixels by using a plain number, or you can specify a percentage of the total screen height by using a number followed by a percent sign.

The WIDTH= Attribute

The WIDTH= attribute allows you to make a short or long marquee area. You can specify the width in pixels by using a plain number, or you can specify a percentage of the total screen width by using a number followed by a percent sign.

The HSPACE= Attribute

The HSPACE= attribute specifies, in pixels, the size of the left and right margins between the marquee area and any surrounding text or graphics. This is a very handy attribute when placing a marquee in a table.

The VSPACE= Attribute

You can use the VSPACE= attribute to specify, in pixels, the amount of space above or below the marquee area and any surrounding text or graphics.

The LOOP= Attribute

You can specify how many times you want the text to scroll across the screen. Adding the LOOP=3 attribute to the <MARQUEE> tag will cause the text to scroll across the screen three times. After the third time, the marquee will remain on the screen but it will be empty. If you don't use the LOOP= attribute or if you use LOOP=INFINITE, the text will scroll on until your viewer moves on to another page.

The SCROLLAMOUNT= Attribute

The SCROLLAMOUNT= attribute allows you to specify how fast you want the text to scroll. If you set it to SCROLLAMOUNT=1, your text will crawl across the screen like Humphrey Bogart crawling across the desert in *Treasure of the Sierra Madre*. If you set it to SCROLLAMOUNT=3000, your text will blink rapidly. If you go much past SCROLLAMOUNT=7000, you will end up with no text at all.

The SCROLLDELAY= Attribute

The SCROLLDELAY= attribute is a bit different from the SCROLLAMOUNT= attribute. SCROLLDELAY= specifies, in milliseconds, how much time passes between redraws of the marquee text. You can fine-tune the marquee text scroll rates by carefully manipulating the SCROLLDELAY= and SCROLLAMOUNT= attributes.

The <BGSOUND> Tag (Microsoft Internet Explorer)

<BGSOUND> is a tag specific to Microsoft Internet Explorer that plays a sound file as soon as the sound file is loaded. As the page is loaded, the accompanying sound file is also loaded. The page usually will finish loading first, but as soon as the sound file loads, it will begin to play. It is implemented quite simply. For example, if you would like visitors to your page to hear the sound in a file named BIGBURP.WAV, simply insert <BGSOUND SRC="bigburp.wav">, and BIGBURP.WAV will play as soon as the sound file is finished downloading. Microsoft Internet Explorer supports .AV, .WAV, and .MID sound files. A couple of attributes are associated with <BGSOUND>.

The LOOP=*n* Attribute

Simply replace *n* with the number of times you would like the sound to be played. To play the file BIGBURP.WAV 10 times, use the following tag:

```
<BGSOUND SRC="bigburp.wav" LOOP=10>
```

You can be insensitive by having the sound play forever (or until the viewer moves on) with the following:

```
<BGSOUND SRC="bigburp.wav" LOOP=INFINITE>
```

Special Characters (HTML 3.0)

Although there have always been a variety of special characters that can be incorporated into HTML documents, a few characters have been conspicuously missing. HTML 3.0 has improved the situation somewhat. Typographic purists can now incorporate en and em spaces, dashes, and nonbreaking spaces using entity references.

&endash;	This entity reference creates an en dash (–).
	This entity reference creates an en space.
&emdash;	This entity reference creates an em dash (—).
	This entity reference creates an em space.
	This entity reference creates a space that will not break when the browser wordwraps to the next line.

 NOTE: Entity references must be in lowercase characters.

Example Tags (HTML 2.0)

Using the <XMP></XMP> tags allows you to display examples of HTML code that will not be picked up by a browser and displayed. The code itself will be shown, along with any </> marks included in the code. The <XMP> tag is handy for displaying examples of HTML code for instructional purposes.

The <BLINK> Tag (Netscape Navigator and Microsoft Internet Explorer)

The <BLINK> tag has created more controversy than any other HTML command and has raised the hackles of the HTML purists in a surprising way. Nothing will generate a startling, loud "mooooo!" in an HTML-oriented newsgroup or mailing list faster than suggesting a legitimate use for the <BLINK> tag.

Things that blink can certainly be annoying, but as I've said many times, HTML leaves us with such a barren landscape of design tools that simple tags such as <BLINK> are jumped on with enthusiasm by design-starved Web page developers. If you want to make things blink on your pages, go ahead and do it.

To make something blink, just surround the blinkable object with <BLINK></BLINK> tags. It's that simple.

2: FORMS

One of the beauties of the Web is the interactive form, which allows readers of Web pages to communicate easily with the page owners. Web surfers are remarkably willing to respond to surveys and fill out questionnaires—revealing tidbits of demographic information about themselves in the process. The ease of using the <mailto:> tag and forms makes two-way dialogs between Web site owners and their readers quite simple and opens up fascinating social and commercial possibilities for a Web site. Using the <mailto:> tag and forms can make visitors to your pages feel they are a part of your site rather than just visitors.

Forms are shamefully easy to create, implement, and manage. Even quite complex forms can be quickly and easily generated by most popular HTML authoring programs with only a few mouse clicks. Check boxes, radio buttons, and drop-down lists can be built and arranged surprisingly fast. I will point out a few tricks to make your forms more useful and efficient. And I will give a bit of explanation about how to make forms actually send information back to your server from browsers that don't support <mailto:> tags.

Forms are, in fact, so easy and quick to build that it might seem as though they should also be instantly usable. After I built my first forms, I imagined that I would just be able to pop a <mailto:> tag into the code somewhere and it would work. Unfortunately, it's not quite as easy as that. Many older browsers don't support <mailto:> tags. Don't get me wrong—older browsers are still simple to get going, but you do have to do a server thing or two.

Getting Your Form to Look Good

Creating a form is easy, but getting all the form elements to line up and look neat is something you can spend hours fiddling with. There is no easy answer to this, but one way to keep the problem to a minimum is to put input areas and drop-down lists on the left side of the page with any accompanying text immediately to the right. Since you can define the width of input areas using the SIZE= attribute, you can at least make things even on the left and let the text run ragged right—as most text does. This looks a bit neater. Don't forget to put a space between the text and the form input area, as shown in Figure 2-1. Of course, a properly designed form has only two spaces for the state entry and nine spaces for the ZIP code entry.

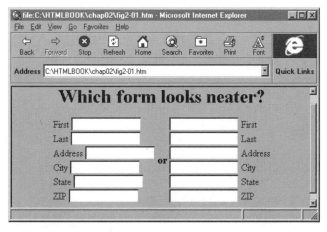

FIGURE 2-1

Input areas in forms line up neatly when set to the left of adjacent explanatory text.

FIGURE 2-1

```
<HTML>
<BODY>
<FORM>
<CENTER><H1>Which form looks neater?</H1>
<TABLE>
  <TR>
    <TD>
        First <INPUT NAME="First" SIZE="20"><BR>
        Last <INPUT NAME="Last" SIZE="20"><BR>
        Address <INPUT NAME="Address" SIZE="20"><BR>
        City <INPUT NAME="City" SIZE="20"><BR>
        State <INPUT NAME="State" SIZE="20"><BR>
        ZIP <INPUT NAME="ZIP" SIZE="20"><BR></TD>
    <TD><H3>or</H3></TD>
    <TD>
```

(continued)

FIGURE 2-1 continued

```
                                        <INPUT NAME="First" SIZE="20"> First<BR>
                                        <INPUT NAME="Last" SIZE="20"> Last<BR>
                                        <INPUT NAME="Address" SIZE="20"> Address<BR>
                                        <INPUT NAME="City" SIZE="20"> City<BR>
                                        <INPUT NAME="State" SIZE="20"> State<BR>
                                        <INPUT NAME="ZIP" SIZE="20"> ZIP</TD>
               </TR>
             </TABLE>
             </FORM>
             </CENTER>
             </BODY>
             </HTML>
```

Perhaps the best way to make forms look neat and well organized is to build a table containing the form elements. Tables let you place your form elements wherever you think they need to be, as shown in Figure 2-2. Unfortunately, you cannot nest forms within forms.

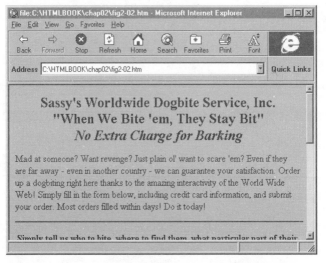

FIGURE 2-2   *Placing your forms inside tables lets you manipulate the positions of the different form elements.*

FIGURE 2-2

```
<HTML>
<BODY>
<CENTER>
<H2>Sassy's Worldwide Dogbite Service, Inc.<BR>
"When We Bite 'em, They Stay Bit"<BR>
<i>No Extra Charge for Barking</i></H2>
</CENTER>
Mad at someone? Want revenge? Just plain ol' want to scare 'em? Even if
they are far away--even in another country--we can guarantee your
satisfaction.
Order up a dogbiting right here thanks to the amazing interactivity of the
World Wide Web! Simply fill in the form below, including credit card
information, and submit your order. Most orders filled within days! Do it
today!
<HR NOSHADE>
<TABLE>
  <TR>
    <TD COLSPAN="3"><FORM><B>Simply tell us who to bite, where to find
them, what particular part of their anatomy you would like the bite to
involve, any special instructions, how you're going to pay, and your
attorney's name and address.</B>
    </TD>
  </TR>
  <TR VALIGN=TOP>
    <TD>Who would you like to have bitten?<BR>
<select name="who bitten?">
<OPTION SELECTED>
<OPTION>A political pundit
<OPTION>An umpire
<OPTION>A heinous dictator
<OPTION>The postal carrier
<OPTION>A movie star
<OPTION>Other (type name below)
</SELECT> or<BR>
<INPUT NAME="name" SIZE="20"> Name<br>
<INPUT NAME="Location of bitee" SIZE="15"> Location of bitee<BR>
<SELECT NAME="where bitten?">
<OPTION SELECTED>
```

(continued)

FIGURE 2-2   *continued*

```
<OPTION>leg
<OPTION>butt
<OPTION>foot
<OPTION>hand
<OPTION>anywhere
</SELECT> Part of body to be bitten
     </td>
     <td  width="10%"></td>
     <td>
<TEXTAREA ROWS=1 COLS=40 NAME="special instructions">Special
Instructions:</TEXTAREA><BR><BR>
<TEXTAREA ROWS=1 COLS=40 NAME="lawyer">How can we contact your attorney?</
TEXTAREA>
     </TD>
   </TR>
</TABLE>
<HR NOSHADE>
<FONT SIZE=4>Payment Information:</FONT>
<TABLE>
  <TR VALIGN=TOP>
    <TD width="35%">
<INPUT NAME="visa" TYPE="checkbox"> VISA<BR>
<INPUT NAME="discover" TYPE="checkbox"> Discover<BR>
<INPUT NAME="mastercard" TYPE="checkbox"> MasterCard<BR>
<INPUT NAME="card number" SIZE="15"> Card Number<BR>
<INPUT NAME="expiration date" SIZE="12"> Expiration Date<BR>
<INPUT NAME="overnight" TYPE="checkbox"> Overnight (add $12.00)<BR>
     </TD>
     <TD WIDTH="35%"></TD>
     <TD>Call for International Rates.<BR>
South Dakota residents add 8.25% sales tax.<P>
<H2><INPUT TYPE="SUBMIT" VALUE="Place Your Order"><INPUT TYPE="reset"
VALUE="Reset">
<I>Order Today!</I></H2>
<H6><I>(Not all dogbite services are available in all areas--call for
special pricing. Void where prohibited.)</I></H6>
     </TD>
   </TR>
```

```
</TABLE>
</FORM>
</BODY>
</HTML>
```

Use a Blank Default with Drop-Down Lists

If you're going to use the information gleaned from your forms for any sort of comparisons or statistical fiddling, be sure you design them so that the information gathered reflects your readers' true input. Improperly designed drop-down lists can easily skew the results.

Always carefully consider the default for a list. Suppose you are doing a survey of the types of dogs owned by your readers. Among the many items on your form that your readers will check, select, or otherwise fill in, you create a simple drop-down list with 10 or so possible dog types for your readers to choose from. If your readers are lazy, in a hurry, or confused, they might pass right over the opportunity to select the type of dog they own, even though they carefully fill out the rest of the form. If you use the form shown in Figure 2-3 on your pages, you will probably notice a rather large number of respondents who own bluetick coonhounds, a fine dog but a rather obscure breed in most parts of the world.

FIGURE 2-3   *Having bluetick coonhound as your default choice of dog may skew your survey results.*

FIGURE 2-3

```
<HTML>
<BODY>
<CENTER><H1>What's your dog?</H1></CENTER>
<FORM METHOD="POST" ACTION="mailto: yourname@your.email.address">
Please select the type of dog you fancy.<BR>
<SELECT NAME="Dog type" SIZE="1">
<OPTION>Bluetick coonhound
<OPTION>Toy poodle
<OPTION>Australian shepherd
<OPTION>Blue heeler
<OPTION>Pembroke welsh corgi
</SELECT>
<P>
<INPUT TYPE="SUBMIT" VALUE="Submit">
<INPUT TYPE="RESET" VALUE="Reset">
</FORM>
</BODY>
</HTML>
```

However, if you leave the first choice blank or specify "no selection" and the dog owners responding to your survey make no selection in this drop-down list, as shown in Figure 2-4, your results will be a bit closer to reality.

FIGURE 2-4

Having "no selection" as your default choice of dog will result in more accurate data from your survey.

FIGURE 2-4

```
<HTML>
<BODY>
<CENTER><H1>What's your dog?</H1></CENTER>
<FORM METHOD="POST" ACTION="mailto: yourname@your.email.address">
Please select the type of dog you fancy.<BR>
<SELECT NAME="Dog type" SIZE="1">
<OPTION>No Selection
<OPTION>Bluetick coonhound
<OPTION>Toy poodle
<OPTION>Australian shepherd
<OPTION>Blue heeler
<OPTION>Pembroke welsh corgi
</SELECT>
<P>
<INPUT TYPE="SUBMIT" VALUE="Submit">
<INPUT TYPE="RESET" VALUE="Reset">
</FORM>
</BODY>
</HTML>
```

This is just a minor point that should make your Web surveys more accurate.

How to Make Your Forms Work

This is the part you've probably been waiting for—how to get your form to send back the data.

Actually, getting a form to send data is the easy part. The main obstacle is finding someplace to send it. On the form side of things, you simply make the ACTION= attribute of the <FORM> tag a reference to the URL of a program that can handle the input and do something interesting with it.

Where to Send Your Form Data

You have several options for where to send data, depending on your resources. You need to shoot it to a Common Gateway Interface (CGI) program somewhere on the Web, but the destination doesn't need to be on the same Web server as the form. (CGI is discussed in detail in Chapter 10.) So if you can't run CGI programs at your site and your webmaster doesn't provide any kind of forms handling, you can find someone else, anywhere else, to do it for you. But let's take a step back and peek at all of your options. There are a couple of ways you can handle it:

- Use a forms handling service.

- Install a CGI program somebody else wrote.

- Create your own CGI program.

Using a Forms Handling Service

The simplest alternative is to find someone—whether your own Web provider or somebody out on the Internet—who can process your forms for you. You may have to pay a fee for each form processed, but it isn't likely to be very expensive. Once you get set up with the service, you simply point your ACTION= attribute to a URL provided to you by the service, and whatever data users enter into your forms and submit will be packaged into an e-mail message and sent to you.

You'll get one e-mail message each time somebody fills out a form, and it may look something like the one shown here:

```
To: <you@someplace.com>
From: "Bubba's Form Handlin' Service" <forms@bubba.com>
Subject: You gotta form

who bit=The mailman
location of bitee=On the front steps
where bit=butt
special instructions=Make him run a little first.
```

If you have more than one form going through a service, it's handy to have a way to easily sort through which response came from which form. The smart way to do this is to have a hidden field in each form with a name such as "Formname" and a value that tells you what it is. Some forms handlers will even have a specific field name they'll look for and put into the subject of the e-mail message for you. When you get your e-mail, you might want to use a mail filter to automatically sort the messages for you. In fact, you might want to have an automatic filter, such as procmail or slocal on UNIX or Windows systems, that sorts your form responses and even runs scripts on them. The messages could be collated and entered into a database or used to build and update a Web page automatically.

Using a CGI Program Someone Else Wrote

Plenty of programs are available on the Web that you can download and install on your site to handle your forms. These will generally do the same thing as the forms processing service, but you may be able to tweak them a little bit, and more important, you don't have to pay to use them. Chapter 10 provides a sample, minimal form mailer CGI script that you can type up and use on nearly any UNIX system. Similar scripts are available for Windows.

There are a couple of possible gotchas here: your Web server has to be configured to let you use CGI programs, and some providers won't let their users run them. If either of these situations is true for you, you're pretty much stuck with using a service somewhere else, as discussed earlier in this chapter.

A third gotcha is that getting a CGI program to work isn't always a snap—there are a few tricks, especially on UNIX systems. Chapter 10 goes into detail on what these tricks are, so if you get a program to handle your forms, check out the information in that chapter.

Create Your Own CGI Program

If you or somebody working with you on your Web site (or somebody you can talk into working with you on your site) knows even a little bit of programming, you can write your own CGI programs to handle forms. That way, you aren't limited to mailing your form data to yourself. In fact, you can use forms and CGI programs to do all kinds of nifty things, like give the latest information on some topic, such as the local temperature.

More important for receiving forms data, a custom CGI program that knows what kind of data to expect from the form can check it for errors before committing it. For instance, a CGI program to handle the Sassy's Worldwide Dogbite Service form might make sure users included their attorneys' information; if not, the program could print an HTML response that insists they have an attorney before Sassy will arrange their biting. It could also check their payment method, even automatically contacting a credit service to make sure the credit card number is a good one.

After sanity-checking the user's data, a CGI program can generate a custom "thank you" screen, maybe even giving information specific to their request. The dogbite program would look at the "location of bitee" field and figure out which dog handles that area. The response the user gets after submitting the form might be, "Thank you for your order. Your biting will be handled by

Rusty, a *Yorkshire terrier,* who is scheduled to bite the mailman at 3:45 PM on Tuesday. If you have any questions or complaints about our service, please mail sassy@dogbite.com." Of course, a user might want to weigh carefully sending a complaint to a company that specializes in dog bites.

For information on how to write CGI programs, check out Chapter 10.

3.

TABLES

Tables may seem like simply a way to arrange text into columns or perhaps to add a caption to an illustration, but creative Web developers have figured out ways to get a lot of mileage out of such a seemingly simple feature. With a bit of imagination, the <TABLE> tag can be a powerful formatting tool. If you keep in mind that tables don't have to consist of little boxes of text and numbers with lines drawn around them, you can do some cool things with the <TABLE> tag. For example, you don't need to display the outline of a table (the boxes or lines) at all. If you don't let the lines of a table show, you can use the <TABLE> tag to place text and graphics precisely, almost anywhere on a page—something that you could only do with "duct tape" workarounds before.

In this chapter, we'll start with the basics of creating tables, and then we'll take a look at a couple of ways to add pizzazz to a table with alignment and color.

The Basics of Tables

Before you can run, you have to learn to walk, so let's go over a quick explanation of the basic <TABLE> tags and attributes before we get to the fancy stuff. Although planning and creating tables can be tedious, the basic table tags and attributes are simple.

The <TABLE></TABLE> Tags

To create a table, you start with the <TABLE> tag and end with the </TABLE> tag. When you use the <TABLE></TABLE> tags, be aware that any table-specific formatting you add will have no effect if the entire text area you want to appear as a table is not defined at the beginning and end as being a table. Also remember, as is the case with many other tags, that <TABLE> has an automatic line break before the table and one after it.

The <TR></TR> Tags

The <TR></TR> (which stand for Table Row) tags surround data in each row within a table. Every row or line in a table needs to have a set of <TR></TR> tags. If a table has two sets of <TR></TR> tags, it will have two rows, as shown in Figure 3-1. If it has eight sets of <TR></TR> tags, the table will have eight rows. All text, other tags, and attributes that you want in a row need to be surrounded by the <TR></TR> tags.

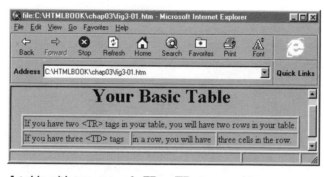

FIGURE 3-1

A table with two sets of <TR></TR> tags and two rows.

FIGURE 3-1

```
<HTML>
<BODY>
<H1 ALIGN=CENTER>Your Basic Table</H1>
<CENTER>
<TABLE BORDER>
  <TR>
    <TD COLSPAN=3>If you have two &lt;TR&gt; tags
    in your table, you will have
    two rows in your table.</TD>
  </TR>
  <TR>
    <TD>If you have three &lt;TD&gt;  tags</TD>
    <TD>in a row, you will have</TD>
    <TD>three cells in the row.</TD>
  </TR>
</TABLE>
</CENTER>
</BODY>
</HTML>
```

The <TD></TD> Tags

TIP

MICROSOFT INTERNET
EXPLORER LETS YOU SPEC-
IFY A DIFFERENT BACK-
GROUND COLOR FOR
EACH CELL IN
A TABLE.

Within a table row, you generally have items of data within cells of the table. The item of data (text or image) in each cell must be surrounded by a pair of <TD></TD> tags. The number of <TD></TD> tags in a row defines how many cells wide that row will be. A row with five <TD></TD> tags will be five cells wide.

You don't need to have the same number of cells in each row. For example, you can have one row with five <TD></TD> tags and five cells and another row with three <TD></TD> tags and three cells, as shown in Figure 3-2.

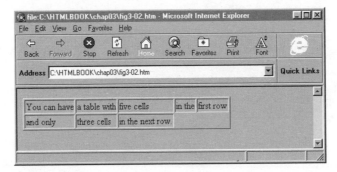

FIGURE 3-2

You can have a different number of cells in each row of a table.

FIGURE 3-2

```
<HTML>
<BODY>
<TABLE BORDER>
  <TR>
     <TD>You can have</TD>
     <TD>a table with</TD>
     <TD>five cells</TD>
     <TD>in the</TD>
     <TD>first row</TD>
  </TR>
  <TR>
     <TD>and only</TD>
```

```
        <TD>three cells</TD>
        <TD>in the next row.</TD>
    </TR>
</TABLE>
</BODY>
</HTML>
```

The <TH></TH> Tags

You can use table headers to give bold titles to columns and rows, as shown in Figure 3-3. <TH>
</TH> (Table Header) tags are similar to <TD></TD> tags except that the text inside <TH></TH>
tags is automatically bold and is centered by default. You can override the default and align the
text to the left or right. You can accomplish the same effect by using <TD></TD> tags, coupled
with the <B> tag and the ALIGN=CENTER attribute, but because some browsers aren't fond of
the <B> tag within tables, headers may be the best choice when you want a cell to have bold text
(Figure 3-3). You will notice that the code for Figure 3-3 uses the COLSPAN= and ROWSPAN=
attributes, which will be discussed next.

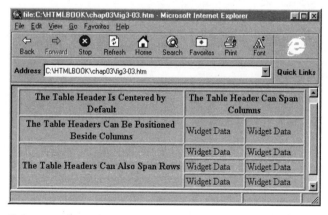

FIGURE 3-3   *Column and row headers can serve as titles in a table.*

FIGURE 3-3

```
<HTML>
<BODY>
<TABLE BORDER>
```

(continued)

FIGURE 3-3 continued

```
<TR>
  <TH>The Table Header Is Centered by Default</TH>
  <TH COLSPAN=2>The Table Header Can Span Columns</TH>
</TR>
<TR>
  <TH>The Table Headers Can Be Positioned Beside Columns</TH>
  <TD>Widget Data</TD>
  <TD>Widget Data</TD>
</TR>
<TR>
  <TH ROWSPAN=3>The Table Headers Can Also Span Rows</TH>
  <TD>Widget Data</TD>
  <TD>Widget Data</TD>
</TR>
<TR>
  <TD>Widget Data</TD>
  <TD>Widget Data</TD>
</TR>
<TR>
  <TD>Widget Data</TD>
  <TD>Widget Data</TD>
</TR>
</TABLE>
</BODY>
</HTML>
```

The NOWRAP Attribute

Normally, all text inside a table cell wordwraps (continues) to the next line if it is too long to fit in the cell on one line. However, when you use the NOWRAP attribute to modify <TH></TH> or <TD></TD> tags, the width of the cell expands to fit whatever text is inside it. This can be handy when used judiciously. For instance, if your company's corporate style guide insists that the company's name always appear on one line and never be broken between two lines, you can use the NOWRAP attribute to ensure compliance.

The COLSPAN= Attribute

You can also modify the <TD></TD> and <TH></TH> tags with the COLSPAN= (Column Span) attribute. If you want a cell to be wider than the cells above it or below it, you can use COLSPAN= to force the cell to stretch across any number of regular cells, as shown in Figure 3-4.

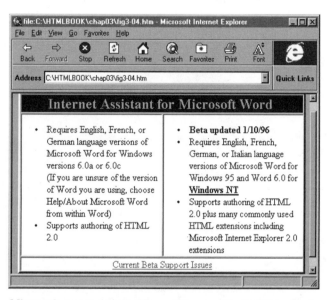

FIGURE 3-4

Microsoft created the table on this page for its Web site by using COLSPAN= to center and spread text across multiple columns.

FIGURE 3-4

```
<HTML>
<BODY>
<CENTER>
<TABLE BORDER=3>
  <TR>
    <TD BGCOLOR=NAVY COLSPAN=2>
    <H2>
    <CENTER>
    <FONT SIZE=5 COLOR=#C0C0C0>Internet Assistant for Microsoft Word</FONT>
    </CENTER>
```

(continued)

FIGURE 3-4 *continued*

```
          </H2>
         </TD>
      </TR>
      <TR>
        <TD BGCOLOR=WHITE WIDTH="300" VALIGN="TOP">
        <UL>
          <LI>Requires English, French, or German language versions of
Microsoft Word for Windows versions 6.0a or 6.0c<BR>
(If you are unsure of the version of Word you are using, choose Help/About
Microsoft Word from within Word)
          <LI>Supports authoring of HTML 2.0
        </UL>
        </TD>
        <TD BGCOLOR=WHITE WIDTH="300" VALIGN="TOP">
        <UL>
         <LI><B>Beta updated 1/10/96</B>
         <LI>Requires English, French, German, or Italian language versions of
Microsoft Word for Windows 95 and Word 6.0 for <U><B>Windows NT</B>
</U>
         <LI>Supports authoring of HTML 2.0 plus many commonly used HTML
extensions, including Microsoft Internet Explorer 2.0 extensions
        </UL>
        </TD>
      </TR>
      <TR>
        <TD BGCOLOR=WHITE COLSPAN=2><CENTER><A HREF="">Current Beta Support
Issues</A></CENTER>
        </TD>
      </TR>
    </TABLE>
    </CENTER>
    </BODY>
    </HTML>
```

The ROWSPAN= Attribute

The ROWSPAN= attribute, when used within the <TD></TD> and <TH></TH> tags, works much like the COLSPAN= attribute except that it sets how many rows a cell will span. If you set a cell to span more than one row, you must have rows below it to expand across. You cannot force a cell to hang below the rest of the table.

The WIDTH= Attribute

TIP

TO PROVIDE A SMALL BUT COMFORTABLE MARGIN BESIDE A TABLE, CENTER THE TABLE AND GIVE IT A WIDTH OF 90 PERCENT.

The WIDTH= attribute has two uses. You can use it inside the <TABLE> tag to specify the width of the whole table, or you can use it inside the <TR></TR> or <TH></TH> tags to specify the width of a particular cell or group of cells.

You can designate the width either in pixels or in percentages. When you use it with the <TABLE> tag, for example, WIDTH=250 will make the table 250 pixels wide, no matter how wide the page appears on a monitor. If you set WIDTH=50% in the <TABLE> tag, the table will be half the page size no matter how wide the page is displayed on a screen. So keep in mind that if a reader has the browser window sized to only a small window, your table may look a bit odd if you are using the percentage setting. If you use the pixel value and the table defined is too large to fit in the size of the browser, scroll bars will appear on the bottom of the browser's window so that the reader can move over to the left or the right and see the other parts of the table. Both types of settings can be useful depending on what you are trying to accomplish, as shown in Figure 3-5.

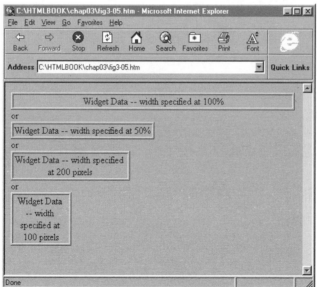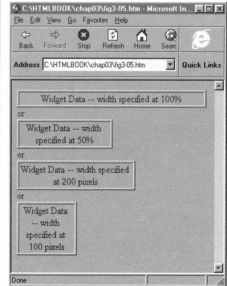

FIGURE 3-5 *You can use the WIDTH= attribute to make a table fill a specified percentage of the screen or to make a table a specified number of pixels wide.*

FIGURE 3-5

```
<HTML>
<BODY>
<TABLE BORDER WIDTH=100%>
  <TR>
    <TD ALIGN=CENTER>Widget Data--width specified at 100%</TD>
  </TR>
</TABLE>
or<BR>
<TABLE BORDER WIDTH=50%>
  <TR>
    <TD ALIGN=CENTER>Widget Data--width specified at 50%</TD>
  </TR>
</TABLE>
or<BR>
<TABLE BORDER WIDTH=200>
  <TR>
    <TD ALIGN=CENTER>Widget Data--width specified at 200 pixels</TD>
  </TR>
</TABLE>
or<BR>
<TABLE BORDER WIDTH=100>
  <TR>
    <TD ALIGN=CENTER>Widget Data--width specified at 100 pixels</TD>
  </TR>
</TABLE>
</BODY>
</HTML>
```

TIP

To keep track of what you're doing while working on positioning a large table, use **BORDER=2** so that you can see each cell. When the table looks the way you want it to look, you can remove the border.

CAUTION

Some browsers do not like the use of the percent sign (%) to specify size. Setting the unit of measurement to **RELATIVE** by using the **UNIT=** attribute will solve this for most browsers. The **UNIT=** attribute must be used within the <TABLE> tag.

The UNIT= Attribute

The UNIT= attribute of the <TABLE> tag determines the unit of measurement that will be used in specifying the size of the table as a whole and the size of individual columns. There are three choices for UNIT=:

- UNIT=EN This is the default setting and sets unit spacing to one en space. An en space is a typographical measure usually equal to the amount of space a typical letter "n" takes up. As a result, the actual space taken up by an en space depends on the size of the font. An en space in a large font is larger than in a small font. It is usually equal to half the font size. For instance, if you are using a 12-point font, an en space will be 6 points wide. Likewise, in an 8-point font an en space will be 4 points wide.

- UNIT=RELATIVE This is used to set the relative width of columns as a percentage of the total width of the table. This should be used, when possible, in place of setting widths to percentage values. (It accomplishes the same thing, but more browsers are likely to support it.) When using RELATIVE units, the numbers entered are treated as percentages of the column width.

- UNIT=PIXELS When you need to know exactly how wide your columns will be on the screen, the pixel is the best unit of measurement to specify. For example, <TABLE UNIT=PIXELS WIDTH=340> makes a table 340 pixels wide.

The COLSPEC= Attribute

The COLSPEC= attribute, used with the UNIT= attribute, defines how much space will be in each column of a table and how the data in each column will be aligned. It is used only within the <TABLE> tag.

COLSPEC= works by listing each individual column and specifying the alignment and size of each column. There are five possible alignments for a column or a cell: L for left, C for center, R for right, J for justified, and D for decimal. If a table has five columns, you can specify a different width and alignment for each column like this:

```
<TABLE UNIT=PIXELS COLSPEC="L10 C15 R20 J25 D30">
```

This sets up a table with the first column 10 pixels wide flush left, the second column 15 pixels wide centered, the third column 20 pixels wide flush right, the fourth column 25 pixels wide justified, and the fifth column 30 pixels wide aligned for decimals.

The DP= Attribute

The DP= (Decimal Point) attribute is used to define which character will be used as a decimal placeholder. DP="." (the default) sets a period as the decimal character. DP="," sets a comma as the placeholder.

CAUTION

BECAUSE SOME MONITORS CAN BE ADJUSTED TO DIFFERENT RESOLUTIONS, SETTING TABLE AND COLUMN WIDTHS IN PIXELS MAY MAKE TABLES APPEAR SMALLER ON MONITORS SET TO A HIGHER RESOLUTION. FOR INSTANCE, A TABLE THAT IS 680 PIXELS WIDE WILL FILL THE SCREEN ON A MONITOR SET FOR 640x480 RESOLUTION. IF THE SAME TABLE IS VIEWED ON A MONITOR WITH THE RESOLUTION SET TO 1024x768, IT WILL TAKE UP ONLY SLIGHTLY MORE THAN HALF THE WIDTH OF THE SCREEN.

Blank Cells

If you don't put any data in a cell, the cell will have no borders and will appear to be part of the cell to its left. If you want a cell that has borders but that appears to have no content, you must put something in it that won't be displayed. You can use a blank line, a <BR>, or a   to force a blank cell to have borders. You can also create whole columns that are blank by specifying the width for the column in pixels or relative units and simply entering no data in the cells. This can be a useful tool for spacing and positioning text and graphics on a page.

Many Web page developers use blank GIF images to position other images and text. To accomplish the same results but with faster loading and displaying of the page, use tables with non-breaking spaces ( ) in empty cells and the WIDTH= attribute.

The CELLPADDING= Attribute

The CELLPADDING= attribute defines the amount of space between the cell contents and the cell wall, setting margins inside a cell, as shown in Figure 3-6.

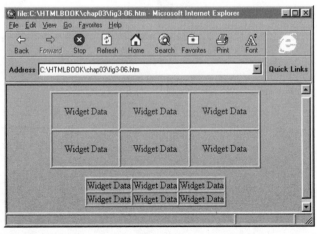

CAUTION

THE USE OF <P> AND
 INSIDE TABLES IS POORLY SUPPORTED BY SOME BROWSERS. ALTHOUGH YOU'RE USUALLY SAFE IN PLACING THESE TAGS INSIDE <TD></TD> TAGS, PLACING THEM OUTSIDE THESE TAGS CAN RESULT IN THE EXTRA SPACE BEING PLACED IN UNUSUAL AND UNINTENDED PLACES.

FIGURE 3-6

The CELLPADDING= attribute is used for setting margins inside cells.

FIGURE 3-6

```
<HTML>
<BODY>
<CENTER>
<TABLE BORDER CELLPADDING=20>
  <TR>
    <TD>Widget Data</TD>
    <TD>Widget Data</TD>
    <TD>Widget Data</TD>
  </TR>
  <TR>
    <TD>Widget Data</TD>
    <TD>Widget Data</TD>
    <TD>Widget Data</TD>
  </TR>
</TABLE>
<BR>
<TABLE BORDER CELLPADDING=0>
  <TR>
    <TD>Widget Data</TD>
    <TD>Widget Data</TD>
    <TD>Widget Data</TD>
  </TR>
  <TR>
    <TD>Widget Data</TD>
    <TD>Widget Data</TD>
    <TD>Widget Data</TD>
  </TR>
</TABLE>
</CENTER>
</BODY>
</HTML>
```

> **TIP**
>
> WHEN YOU PUT **<CENTER></CENTER>** AROUND A TABLE, YOU CENTER ONLY THE TABLE ITSELF. YOU CENTER THE CONTENTS OF THE TABLE SEPARATELY.

The ALIGN= and VALIGN= Attributes

You can modify the <TR>, <TD>, and <TH> tags by using the ALIGN= and VALIGN= attributes. ALIGN= specifies the horizontal alignment of text and graphics either flush left, flush right, or centered within a cell, as shown in Figure 3-7 on the following page. Horizontal Alignment can be set in several different ways:

ALIGN=BLEEDLEFT	This forces the cell contents to the extreme left side of a cell.
ALIGN=LEFT	This puts the cell contents flush left with the text margin of the cell set by CELLPADDING=.
ALIGN=CENTER	This centers the cell contents.
ALIGN=RIGHT	This forces the cell contents flush right with the text margin of the cell set by CELLPADDING=.

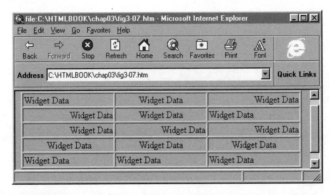

FIGURE 3-7

*The **ALIGN=** attribute specifies the horizontal alignment of text and graphics.*

FIGURE 3-7

```
<HTML>
<BODY>
<TABLE BORDER WIDTH=100%>
  <TR>
    <TD ALIGN=LEFT>Widget Data</TD>
    <TD ALIGN=CENTER>Widget Data</TD>
    <TD ALIGN=RIGHT>Widget Data</TD>
  </TR>
  <TR>
    <TD ALIGN=RIGHT>Widget Data</TD>
    <TD ALIGN=CENTER>Widget Data</TD>
    <TD ALIGN=LEFT>Widget Data</TD>
  </TR>
  <TR>
    <TD ALIGN=RIGHT>Widget Data</TD>
```

```
          <TD ALIGN=RIGHT>Widget Data</TD>
          <TD ALIGN=RIGHT>Widget Data</TD>
       </TR>
       <TR>
          <TD ALIGN=CENTER>Widget Data</TD>
          <TD ALIGN=CENTER>Widget Data</TD>
          <TD ALIGN=CENTER>Widget Data</TD>
       </TR>
       <TR>
          <TD ALIGN=LEFT>Widget Data</TD>
          <TD ALIGN=LEFT>Widget Data</TD>
          <TD ALIGN=LEFT>Widget Data</TD>
       </TR>
     </TABLE>
     </BODY>
     </HTML>
```

TIP

IF YOUR TABLE LOOKS MESSY AND YOU'RE NOT SURE WHY, TRY ADDING **VALIGN=TOP** TO ALL THE CELLS.

The VALIGN= attribute controls the vertical alignment of text or graphics within a cell, as shown in Figure 3-8. Vertical alignment can be set in several different ways:

VALIGN=TOP	This forces the cell contents to align with the top of the cell.
VALIGN=MIDDLE	This forces the cell contents to be centered vertically.
VALIGN=BOTTOM	This forces the cell contents to align with the bottom of the cell.

FIGURE 3-8

```
     <HTML>
     <BODY>
     <CENTER>
     <TABLE BORDER WIDTH=90%>
       <TR>
         <TD WIDTH=100>VALIGN= lets you place text and graphics in each cell of a row:
     </TD>
         <TD VALIGN=TOP>at the top,</TD>
         <TD VALIGN=MIDDLE>in the middle,</TD>
         <TD VALIGN=BOTTOM>at the bottom.</TD>
       </TR>
       <TR VALIGN=TOP>
         <TD>You can use VALIGN= to set the alignment for an entire row:</TD>
```

(continued)

FIGURE 3-8   *continued*

```
          <TD>at the top,</TD>
          <TD>at the top,</TD>
          <TD>at the top.</TD>
        </TR>
        <TR VALIGN=middle>
          <TD>You can use VALIGN= to set the alignment for an entire row:</TD>
          <TD>in the middle,</TD>
          <TD>in the middle,</TD>
          <TD>in the middle.</TD>
        </TR>
        <TR VALIGN=bottom>
          <TD>You can use VALIGN= to set the alignment for an entire row:</TD>
          <TD>at the bottom,</TD>
          <TD>at the bottom,</TD>
          <TD>at the bottom.</TD>
        </TR>
      </TABLE>
    </CENTER>
  </BODY>
</HTML>
```

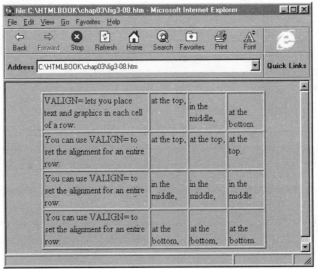

FIGURE 3-8

*The **VALIGN=** attribute controls the vertical alignment of text or graphics within a cell.*

The <CAPTION> Tag

The <CAPTION> tag lets you give your tables titles. Captions are by default centered either above (<CAPTION ALIGN=TOP>) or below (<CAPTION ALIGN=BOTTOM>) a table, as shown in Figure 3-9.

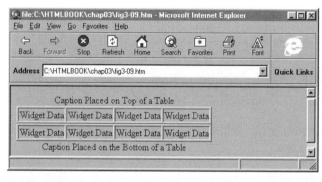

FIGURE 3-9 **Table captions can be positioned at the top or bottom of a table.**

FIGURE 3-9

```
<HTML>
<BODY>
<TABLE BORDER>
   <CAPTION ALIGN=TOP>Caption Placed on Top of a Table</CAPTION>
   <TR>
     <TD>Widget Data</TD>
     <TD>Widget Data</TD>
     <TD>Widget Data</TD>
     <TD>Widget Data</TD>
   </TR>
</TABLE>
<TABLE BORDER>
   <CAPTION ALIGN=BOTTOM>Caption Placed on the Bottom of a Table</CAPTION>
   <TR>
     <TD>Widget Data</TD>
     <TD>Widget Data</TD>
     <TD>Widget Data</TD>
     <TD>Widget Data</TD>
   </TR>
```

(continued)

FIGURE 3-9 *continued*

```
</TABLE>
</BODY>
</HTML>
```

You can place any text and images you like in a caption. The text will wordwrap to fit the width of the table. You can use the <CAPTION> tag to add a title to a graphic. Simply specify a table with no border, as shown in Figure 3-10.

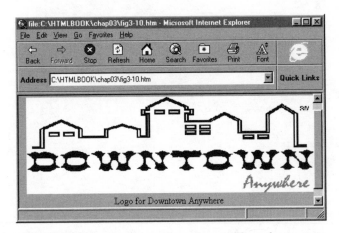

FIGURE 3-10

The CAPTION tag can be used to place a title under or over a graphic.

FIGURE 3-10

```
<HTML>
<BODY>
<TABLE>
  <CAPTION ALIGN=BOTTOM>Logo for Downtown Anywhere</CAPTION>
  <TR>
    <TD>
    <IMG ALIGN=BOTTOM SRC="dasolid.gif">
    </TD>
  </TR>
</TABLE>
</BODY>
</HTML>
```

The BORDER= Attribute

Using borders (or not using them) creatively can add unusual effects to your pages. Experiment with fat and very fat borders to discover some interesting uses for the BORDER= attribute. As we discussed earlier, tables can be used without borders as a device to place text or graphics precisely on a page.

Inside the <TABLE> tag, you can specify how the borders, or lines around your cells and table, will appear. If you don't specify a border, there will be no lines in your table, but the space for the lines will still be there. You can use <TABLE BORDER=0> and get the same effect. Sometimes you'll want to fatten up a border to make it stand out more. You can use really extreme borders to draw attention to a figure or text. When you build nested tables, each table can have a different border thickness so that each one stands out from the others, as shown in Figure 3-11.

FIGURE 3-11

A combination of thick and thin borders can be nested together to create unusual effects.

FIGURE 3-11

```
<HTML>
<BODY>
<TABLE BORDER=8  BORDERCOLOR=BLACK WIDTH=90% CELLPADDING=0 CELLSPACING=10>
  <TR>
    <TD ALIGN=CENTER><H1>NCT Web Magazine Business Pages</H1>
      <TABLE WIDTH="100%" BORDER CELLSPACING=1>
        <TR>
```

(continued)

FIGURE 3-11   continued

```
                              <TD ALIGN=CENTER COLSPAN=4><H3>Sassy's Worldwide Dogbite Service, Inc.
    </H3></TD>
          </TR>
          <TR>
            <TD ALIGN=CENTER>Widget Computer Systems, Inc.</TD>
            <TD ALIGN=CENTER>Crash &amp; Burn Software</TD>
            <TD ALIGN=CENTER>Don't Think Twice Memory Products</TD>
            <TD ALIGN=CENTER>Void Where Prohibited Public Relations, Inc.
    </TD>
          </TR>
        </TABLE>
      </TD>
    </TR>
  </TABLE>
</BODY>
</HTML>
```

The CELLSPACING= Attribute

The CELLSPACING= attribute defines in pixels the amount of space between cells. With no CELLSPACING= attribute set, there is by default a spacing of two pixels. You can use CELLSPACING= without borders to place text and graphics exactly where you want them. You can put a blank space in a cell if you need to leave an empty space. Figure 3-12 shows examples of using the CELLSPACING= attribute.

FIGURE 3-12

```
<HTML>
<BODY>
<CENTER>
<TABLE BORDER CELLSPACING=20>
  <TR>
    <TD>Widget Data</TD>
    <TD>Widget Data</TD>
    <TD>Widget Data</TD>
```

```
      </TR>
      <TR>
        <TD>Widget Data</TD>
        <TD>Widget Data</TD>
        <TD>Widget Data</TD>
      </TR>
</TABLE>

<TABLE CELLSPACING=20>
   <TR>
      <TD>Widget Data</TD>
      <TD>Widget Data</TD>
      <TD>Widget Data</TD>
   </TR>
   <TR>
      <TD>Widget Data</TD>
      <TD>Widget Data</TD>
      <TD>Widget Data</TD>
   </TR>
</TABLE>

<TABLE CELLSPACING=0>
   <TR>
      <TD>Widget Data</TD>
      <TD>Widget Data</TD>
      <TD>Widget Data</TD>
   </TR>
   <TR>
      <TD>Widget Data</TD>
      <TD></td>
      <TD>Widget Data</TD>
   </TR>
</TABLE>
</CENTER>
</BODY>
</HTML>
```

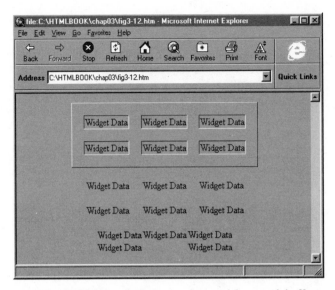

FIGURE 3-12

The **CELLSPACING=** *attribute can be used for special effects and for precision placement of text and graphics.*

The CELLSPACING= attribute can be used to create some interesting effects, such as fat picture frames around text and graphics, as shown in Figure 3-13.

FIGURE 3-13

```
<HTML>
<BODY>
<CENTER>
<TABLE BORDER=8 CELLSPACING=10>
  <CAPTION ALIGN=BOTTOM>George Washington</CAPTION>
  <TR>
    <TD>
      <TABLE BORDER=20>
        <TR>
          <TD><IMG SRC="gwash2.gif"></TD>
        </TR>
      </TABLE>
```

```
        </TD>
      </TR>
   </TABLE>
 </CENTER>
 </BODY>
 </HTML>
```

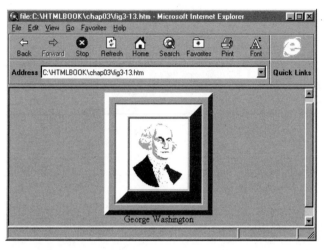

FIGURE 3-13 *You can use the **CELLSPACING**= attribute to add a frame around a picture.*

Creative Use of Tables

A <TABLE> tag can be used much like a drop-shadow box in a print layout. The <TABLE> tag can be used to draw boxes with thick or thin borders around text and graphics to make them stand out on a page, as shown in Figure 3-14 on the following page.

FIGURE 3-14

You can use a plain table with a thick border to make a special element stand out on the page. You don't need to use <TABLE> tags to make only traditional, organized tables of numbers and text.

FIGURE 3-14

```
<HTML>
<BODY>
<CENTER>
<TABLE CELLPADDING=10 CELLSPACING=0 BORDER=16>
  <TR>
    <TD ALIGN=CENTER>
    <H1>Special Sale</H1>
    <H3>This Week Only!</H3>
    <TABLE BORDER WIDTH=100%>
      <TR>
        <TD ALIGN=CENTER><I>Buy 10 Widgets, Get 1 FREE!</I></TD>
      </TR>
    </TABLE>
    </TD>
  </TR>
</TABLE>
</CENTER>
</BODY>
</HTML>
```

Setting Text in Columns

Keep in mind that most computer screens are too small to lend themselves well to reading text in columns as you often see in a magazine or on a newspaper page. Print publishers often break text into narrow columns so that the eye can move easily from line to line without losing its place on the page, as you can see in Figure 3-15. If lines of text are too long, the eye loses track of which line it should be moving to next as the reader moves down the page.

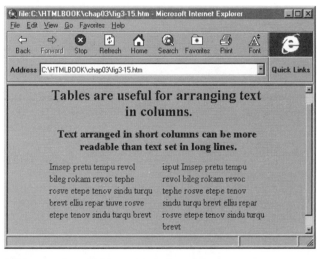

FIGURE 3-15

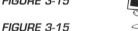

Tables can be used to set type in columns.

FIGURE 3-15

```
<HTML>
<BODY>
<CENTER>
<TABLE BORDER=0 WIDTH=80% CELLPADDING=6>
  <TR>
    <TD ALIGN=CENTER COLSPAN=2>
    <H2>Tables are useful for arranging text in columns.</H2>
     <H3>Text arranged in short columns can be more readable than text set
     in long lines.</H3>
    </TD>
  </TR>
```

(continued)

FIGURE 3-15 *continued*

```
            <TR>
             <TD WIDTH=50% VALIGN=TOP>
             Imsep pretu tempu revol bileg rokam revoc tephe rosve etepe tenov sindu
       turqu brevt elliu repar tiuve rosve etepe tenov sindu turqu brevt
             </TD>
             <TD VALIGN=TOP>
             isput Imsep pretu tempu revol bileg rokam revoc tephe rosve etepe tenov
       sindu turqu brevt elliu repar rosve etepe tenov sindu turqu brevt
             </TD>
            </TR>
          </TABLE>
          </CENTER>
          </BODY>
          </HTML>
```

On Web pages, however, care must be taken not to make the page so wide that the reader needs to use scroll bars to move from side to side. When a Web page is too wide to fit on the monitor, most browsers automatically add horizontal scroll bars on the bottom of the screen. Unless there is a particular design or content reason for having Web pages that are wider than a typical screen (640x480), you should avoid doing so. Setting text in columns simply because it can be done might result in awkward and hard-to-read pages.

Columns can eliminate the need for scrolling, as shown in Figure 3-16.

FIGURE 3-16

```
       <HTML>
       <BODY>
       <TABLE WIDTH=100% CELLPADDING=10 CELLSPACING=2>
         <TR ALIGN=LEFT BGCOLOR="#000099">
           <TD><FONT FACE="ARIAL" COLOR=WHITE SIZE=2>Control</FONT></TD>
           <TD><FONT FACE="ARIAL" COLOR=WHITE SIZE=2>Explanation</FONT></TD>
           <TD><FONT FACE="ARIAL" COLOR=WHITE SIZE=2>Example</FONT></TD>
           <TD><FONT FACE="ARIAL" COLOR=WHITE SIZE=2>Support</FONT></TD>
         </TR>
         <TR>
           <TD ALIGN=LEFT BGCOLOR="#EEEEEE" VALIGN=TOP>
           <FONT FACE="ARIAL" SIZE=2>Checkbox</FONT></TD>
           <TD ALIGN=LEFT BGCOLOR="#EEEEEE" VALIGN=TOP>
           <FONT FACE="ARIAL" SIZE=2>Used for simple Boolean attributes or
           for attributes that can take multiple values at the same time.
```

```
        It is represented by a number of check box fields, each of which
        has the same name. Each selected check box generates a separate
        name/value pair in the submitted data, even if this results in
        duplicate names. The default value for checkboxes is &quot;on&quot;
</FONT></TD>
    <TD ALIGN=LEFT BGCOLOR="#EEEEEE" VALIGN=TOP>
    <FONT FACE="COURIER NEW" SIZE=2>&lt;INPUT TYPE=&quot;CHECKBOX&quot;
    NAME=&quot;Control1&quot; VALUE=&quot;FALSE&quot;&gt;</FONT></TD>
    <TD ALIGN=LEFT BGCOLOR="#EEEEEE" VALIGN=TOP>
    <FONT FACE="ARIAL" SIZE=2>HTML2</FONT></TD>
  </TR>
</TABLE>
</BODY>
</HTML>
```

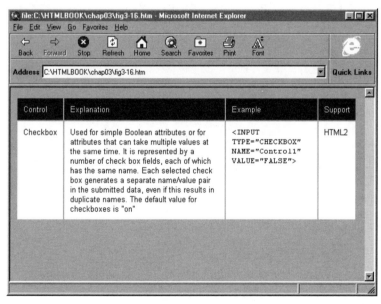

FIGURE 3-16   *The use of columns allows more information to be presented on one screen. This arrangement eliminates the need for scrolling down the page to read everything. Using table headers and specifying typefaces improve readability and design interest.*

Columns of text can be useful for presenting a large amount of information efficiently. Rather than have row after row of text scroll down a screen, you can arrange data in narrow columns side by side so that more information is presented to the reader all at once, in one screen.

 NOTE: HTML authors need to keep pushing the envelope and yet respect the current hardware and software standards. It's a bit of a tightrope. HTML is not sacred, but you should try to understand the motivation behind restrictions on HTML and the need for standardization (especially since the behavior of nonstandard code can be completely unpredictable across browsers). At the same time, if you're not flexible, chances are your pages won't be as widely appreciated as you might like. You need to be both responsible and responsive. The market doesn't have to dictate your every move, but you need to listen. Change is the only constant in this field, and that's what makes it so much fun.

Using Tables for Positioning

One nice feature of the <TABLE> tag is that no border will be displayed unless you request it. This allows you to use the <TABLE> tag to position text and graphics in interesting ways on a page without seeming to be using a table. The <TABLE> tag is currently the single most powerful formatting tool available in HTML. Web page designers now have almost the same freedom to use "white space" in graphic design as do print-page designers. More than any other feature, tables will influence the move away from hierarchical text layout on Web pages. An example of a creative use of invisible borders to create white space is shown in Figure 3-17.

FIGURE 3-17

```
<HTML>
<BODY>
<CENTER>
<TABLE>
  <TR>
    <TD VALIGN=TOP ALIGN=LEFT><IMG SRC="corner1.gif"></TD>
    <td>&#32;</td>
    <TD VALIGN=TOP ALIGN=RIGHT><IMG SRC="corner4.gif"></TD>
  </TR>
  <TR>
    <TD VALIGN=MIDDLE>&#32;</TD>
    <TD ALIGN=CENTER><H1>WIDGET SALE!</H1></TD>
    <TD>&#32;</TD>
```

```
    </TR>
    <TR>
      <TD VALIGN=BOTTOM ALIGN=LEFT><IMG SRC="corner2.gif"></TD>
      <TD ALIGN=CENTER>Using a table with no borders,<BR>
      you can place graphics and text with precision.</TD>
      <TD VALIGN=BOTTOM ALIGN=LEFT><IMG SRC="corner3.gif"></TD>
    </TR>
  </TABLE>
  </CENTER>
  </BODY>
  </HTML>
```

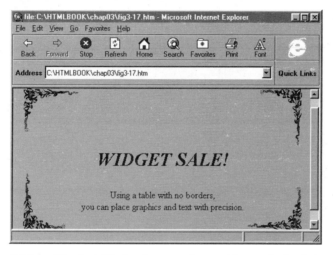

FIGURE 3-17 **Tables without visible borders can be used to precisely place text and graphics on the page.**

The use of the <TABLE> tag is limited only by your imagination. If a browser supports tables at all, it will usually correctly display the more interesting things that can be done with them.

Putting Color in Your Tables

Tables are a cool addition to HTML, but it takes color to really make a document sizzle. Leading browsers, such as Microsoft Internet Explorer and Netscape Navigator, let you display a bit of color. There are several ways to add color to your tables, and they tend to be browser-specific. Once again, as HTML evolves, one can only hope that each one of the wonderful new features will be implemented in all of the most popular browsers.

Color Borders with Netscape Navigator

Not only can you put a fancy fat border around a table, you can also specify a color for that border that is different from the rest of the text and the background. Create a plain gray GIF (or any GIF you would like to have for a background) and assign it in the <BODY> tag as the background for your page. Then set a color for your background in addition to the background GIF. So you end up with a <BODY> tag that looks something like this:

```
<BODY BACKGROUND= "coolbg.gif" BGCOLOR="#FF0000">
```

What you have done is create a double background—the first background is the GIF and the second background is the color you specified. As a result, the color will show though any table borders or horizontal rules (<HR>) on the page. If your background is a common gray GIF or a decorative GIF, the colored table borders and lines will stand out beautifully. As long as the GIF is not too complicated, this trick should result in only slightly slower page loading times.

The BGCOLOR= Attribute (Microsoft Internet Explorer)

Microsoft Internet Explorer allows you to specify color backgrounds for every cell in a table individually, as shown in Figure 3-18. You can add a BGCOLOR= attribute to any <TD> tag and specify a different color for each cell in a table.

FIGURE 3-18

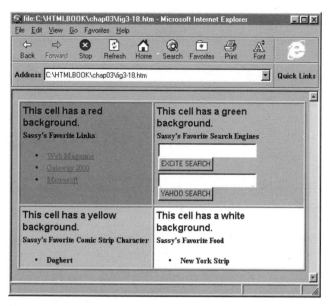

FIGURE 3-18

You can specify a different color for every cell in a table by
adding the **BGCOLOR=** attribute.

```
<HTML>
<BODY>
<CENTER>
<TABLE BORDER=1 CELLPADDING=4 CELLSPACING=2>
  <TR>
    <TD VALIGN=TOP ALIGN=LEFT BGCOLOR="RED" WIDTH=320>
    <FONT SIZE=3 FACE="ARIAL"><B>This cell has a red background.</B>
</FONT><BR>
    <FONT SIZE=2><B>Sassy's Favorite Links</B></FONT>
    <UL>
      <LI><FONT SIZE=2><A HREF="http://nctweb.com/nct">Web Magazine</A>
</FONT>
      <LI><FONT SIZE=2><A HREF="http://www.gw2k.com">Gateway 2000</A>
</FONT>
      <LI><FONT SIZE=2><A HREF="http://www.microsoft.com">Microsoft</A>
</FONT>
    </UL>
```

(continued)

FIGURE 3-18 *continued*

```
      </TD>
      <TD VALIGN=TOP ALIGN=LEFT BGCOLOR="GREEN" WIDTH=320>
      <FONT SIZE=3 FACE="ARIAL"><B>This cell has a green background.</B>
</FONT><BR>
      <FONT SIZE=2><B>Sassy's Favorite Search Engines</B></FONT>
      <TABLE BORDER=0 CELLPADDING=1 CELLSPACING=2>
        <TR>
          <TD><FONT SIZE=2>
          <FORM ACTION="http://www.excite.com/search.gw" METHOD=POST>
          <INPUT NAME="SEARCH" SIZE=30>
          <INPUT TYPE=SUBMIT  VALUE="EXCITE SEARCH">
          </FORM>
          </FONT>
          </TD>
        </TR>
        <TR>
          <TD><FONT SIZE=2>
          <FORM METHOD=GET ACTION="http://search.yahoo.com/bin/searchm">
          <INPUT SIZE=30 NAME=P>
          <INPUT TYPE="SUBMIT" VALUE="YAHOO SEARCH">
          <INPUT TYPE=HIDDEN NAME=R VALUE=MSN>
          </FORM>
          </FONT>
          </TD>
        </TR>
      </TABLE>
      </TD>
    </TR>
    <TR>
      <TD VALIGN=TOP ALIGN=LEFT BGCOLOR="YELLOW" WIDTH=320>
      <FONT SIZE=3 FACE="ARIAL"><B>This cell has a yellow background.</B>
</FONT><BR>
      <FONT SIZE=2><B>Sassy's Favorite Comic Strip Character</B></FONT>
      <UL>
        <LI><FONT SIZE=2><B>Dogbert</B></FONT>
      </UL>
      </TD>
      <TD VALIGN=TOP ALIGN=LEFT BGCOLOR="WHITE" WIDTH=320>
      <FONT SIZE=3 FACE="ARIAL"><B>This cell has a white background.</B>
```

```
</FONT><BR>
  <FONT SIZE=2><B>Sassy's Favorite Food</B></FONT>
  <UL>
    <LI><FONT SIZE=2><B>New York Strip</B></FONT>
  </UL>
  </TD>
 </TR>
</TABLE>
</CENTER>
</BODY>
</HTML>
```

The BORDERCOLOR= Attribute
(Microsoft Internet Explorer)

Microsoft Internet Explorer also allows you to specify the color of the lines around a table or around a particular cell in a table. All you have to do is add the BORDERCOLOR=*ColorCode* attribute to the <TABLE> or <TD> tag. Of course, when your target browser is Microsoft Internet Explorer, you can use color names, as shown in Figure 3-19.

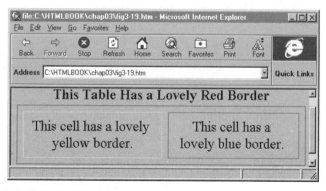

FIGURE 3-19

The BORDERCOLOR= attribute allows you to specify the border color of any cell in a table.

FIGURE 3-19

```
<HTML>
<BODY>
<TABLE BORDER CELLPADDING=10 CELLSPACING=10 BORDERCOLOR=RED>
  <CAPTION><H2>This Table Has a Lovely Red Border</H2></CAPTION>
  <TR ALIGN=CENTER>
    <TD BORDERCOLOR=YELLOW><FONT SIZE=5>
     This cell has a lovely yellow border.</FONT></TD>
    <TD BORDERCOLOR=BLUE><FONT SIZE=5>
     This cell has a lovely blue border.</FONT></TD>
  </TR>
</TABLE>
</BODY>
</HTML>
```

The BORDERCOLORDARK= and BORDERCOLORLIGHT= Attributes (Microsoft Internet Explorer)

Table borders show a slightly beveled, or 3-D, edge that normally shows up in two shades of gray. Using the BORDERCOLORLIGHT= and BORDERCOLORDARK= attributes, you can assign particular colors to each of the two 3-D edges of a table or to any cell within a table. I like to make my tables stand out a bit by using BORDERCOLORDARK=black to add a nice, clear definition to a border, as shown in Figure 3-20.

FIGURE 3-20

```
<HTML>
<BODY>
<TABLE BORDER BORDERCOLORDARK=BLACK BORDERCOLORLIGHT=RED CELLPADDING=10
CELLSPACING=10>
  <CAPTION><H2>This Table Has a Lovely Black and Red Border</H2></CAPTION>
  <TR>
    <TD BORDERCOLORLIGHT=YELLOW BORDERCOLORDARK=BLUE>
    <FONT SIZE=4>This cell has a lovely blue and yellow 3-D border.</FONT>
    </TD>
    <TD BORDERCOLORLIGHT=BLUE BORDERCOLORDARK=YELLOW>
    <FONT SIZE=4>This cell has a lovely yellow and blue 3-D border.</FONT>
    </TD>
```

```
      </TR>
    </TABLE>
  </BODY>
</HTML>
```

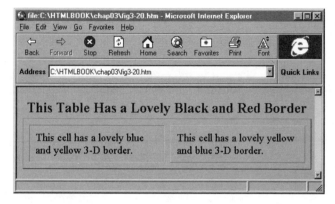

FIGURE 3-20

You can specify particular colors for each edge of a "3-D" table or cell border.

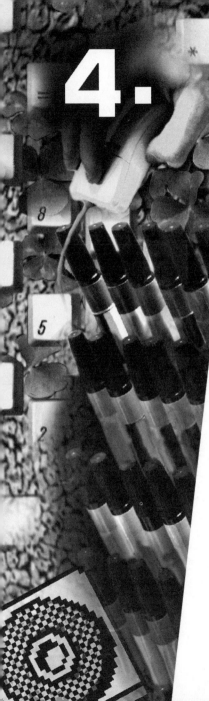

GRAPHICS

Although many people feel HTML is strictly about text and text formatting, even these HTML purists would agree that graphics are what really spice up a Web site. Of course, graphics do slow things down, and you need to be careful to keep your graphics file sizes as small as possible. Since most computer screens cannot display resolutions higher than 72 pixels per inch, there is usually little point in using graphics of higher resolution. But you don't need to confine yourself to preparing pages that will be viewed only by users with 9600 bps modems. If you aim your creative efforts at the lowest common denominator, your pages will seem pale and uninteresting to most viewers.

In this chapter, we'll discuss a few graphics tricks and techniques that not only will make your pages look better than average but will ensure that they load quickly.

Bounding Boxes and ALT= Attributes

To reduce the time it takes a browser to load a page containing graphics, it's wise to define the size of your images in the HTML code. If a browser knows the size of a graphic when it begins to load a page, it can immediately define the position of the graphic and then load the text on the page around the graphic, which takes longer to load. If you specify the size of a graphic, the browser saves room for it by drawing a bounding box where you call for an image. A visitor to your page can begin reading the text on a page while waiting for the rest of the graphic to load. This approach is considered a small courtesy to viewers.

How to Specify How Big a Graphic Will Be

Setting aside room for a graphic is easy to do if you have a graphics handling program such as Photoshop, HiJaak Pro, or LView Pro. First, open your graphic in the graphics handling program and check to see the size of the image in pixels. Add the width and height of the image to the image tag like this:

```
<IMG SRC="/gifsdir/logored.gif" WIDTH=413 HEIGHT=356>
```

CAUTION

IF YOU SPECIFY A WIDTH AND/
OR HEIGHT MEASUREMENT THAT
IS A DIFFERENT SIZE THAN THE
ACTUAL SIZE OF THE GRAPHIC,
THE BROWSER WILL CRAM OR
STRETCH YOUR IMAGE TO FIT
THE BOX YOU TOLD IT TO
DRAW. THIS CAN BE USED
TO DO ON-THE-FLY SCALING,
BUT IT CAN CAUSE THE
JAGGIES—STAIR-STEPPED
DIAGONAL LINES AND
CURVES INSTEAD OF
STRAIGHT, OR SMOOTH,
LINES. USE CARE WHEN
YOU SUPPLY GRAPHICS
DIMENSIONS.

If you don't specify the graphic size, a browser loading your page will begin loading each image as it comes to it and then continue loading text after the image is completely loaded. This takes a little while. But if you specify the size, many leading browsers will be able to insert a bounding box of the proper size. As soon as it sees you have been clever enough to state the size of the image, the browser will pop in a bounding box of the proper size and begin pouring the graphic into it. If there are other images on the page or if there is text, the browser can go ahead and work on other parts of the page while filling up the bounding box.

Although sophisticated, print-based graphic designers may find the state of graphics on the Web to be primitive, it probably won't remain that way for long. Great minds are being brought to bear on making the Web graphically sophisticated and, as bandwidth and modem speeds increase, it's bound to happen.

The ALT= Attribute

The ALT= attribute of the IMG tag allows readers with text-only browsers (or readers running their browsers with graphics turned off) to have a description of what the graphic is or its purpose. Microsoft's Internet Explorer also displays the text of the ALT= attribute in the bounding box while the image is loading. Netscape Navigator will display the text if the Auto Load Images option is turned off.

For example, if the image is a magnifying glass and the ALT= text is "Search this site," the readers will know that they can click on that bounding box to search the site without having to wait for the image to load before knowing what clicking the image would do, as shown in Figure 4-1. This is how the <IMG> tag would look with the ALT= attribute:

```
<IMG SRC="search.gif" HEIGHT=50 WIDTH=100 ALT="Search this site">
```

FIGURE 4-1

```
<HTML>
<BODY>
<IMG SRC="nothing.gif" ALT="Welcome to our example Web site" width=500
height=50><BR>
<IMG SRC="nothing.gif" ALT="Search this site" width=100 height=50>
<IMG SRC="nothing.gif" ALT="Downloads" width=100 height=50>
<IMG SRC="nothing.gif" ALT="Frequently asked questions" WIDTH=100 HEIGHT=50>
```

(continued)

FIGURE 4-1   *continued*

```
<IMG SRC="nothing.gif" ALT="Technical help" WIDTH=100 HEIGHT=50>
<IMG SRC="nothing.gif" ALT="Other sites of interest" WIDTH=100 HEIGHT=50><BR>
This is an example of how the ALT attribute of the IMG tag will look in
Microsoft's Internet Explorer while the images are loading or if the
graphics are turned off in the Options.
</BODY>
</HTML>
```

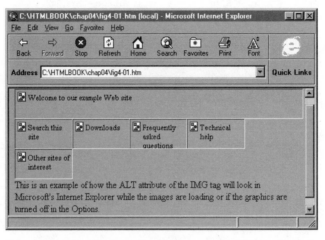

FIGURE 4-1   *Images that have not yet loaded have their ALT= attribute text displayed in place of the image.*

With a little imagination and a few specialized tools, you can already make graphics on your Web site something to be proud of. A few interesting Web personalities have taken the available tools and pushed them to the limits, creating sites that not only are graphically stimulating but use graphic design to inform and delight, which is exactly what good graphic design is all about.

Some will argue that a few Web designers have gone too far, clogging up bandwidth with the indiscriminate use of graphics with obscure purposes. Surely they are right. There will always be those, in any field, who go too far, just as there are those who lag behind. Learn from those pushing the limits, and incorporate the ideas that can make your Web site more attractive and effective.

Let's start with a few simple ideas that will make your site look better.

Transparent Images

You've no doubt seen graphics on the Web that seem to float over the background they appear on. If your browser has the background set to common gray, white, or chartreuse, the background color shows through the design of the graphic image. These graphics were created as transparent images. The difference between a regular image and a transparent image is shown in Figure 4-2. Even though most browsers have a gray default background color, it's not always safe to assume that all those who view your pages will have chosen gray for the background. I usually keep my browser set to a light gray background, but some people set theirs to light blue and even yellow.

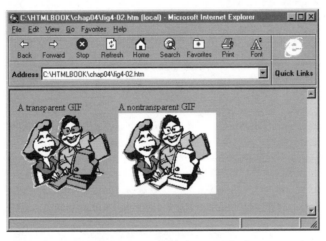

FIGURE 4-2

The image on the left is a regular image. The image on the right is a transparent image. As you can see, the transparent version will look better in almost all situations.

Fortunately, converting your graphics to have a transparent background is quite simple.

What a browser calls the background of a bitmap is simply the color that appears to be the prominent background color. When you "make a background transparent," you are making one color in the image transparent, no matter whether that color is the background or another part of the image. So, for example, if you have an image with a gray background and the image contains an airplane that is gray, when the image is made transparent (the gray being designated as the transparent color), the airplane will also become transparent along with the background.

Graphics File Formats— Bitmaps and Vectors

Computer-generated graphics generally come in one of two flavors: bitmaps or vector graphics. At this time, the Web supports only bitmapped images. (Macintosh users know bitmapped graphics as raster graphics.)

Bitmapped images are usually created in a paint program such as Windows Paintbrush or CorelPHOTO-PAINT. Scanner output is usually in some form of bitmapped image. Bitmapped images are defined by a computer dot by dot (actually pixel by pixel). The overall area of a graphic is defined, and the color of each dot, or pixel, is described one by one—including the color of the background area. So, by definition, bitmapped images have solid backgrounds. File formats usually associated with bitmapped images include BMP, PCX, and TIF.

Draw and CAD programs create graphic images in vector format. Computers create vector graphics by defining the coordinates of the lines that make up the graphic. A vector graphic is a series of instructions telling the computer to draw lines of a specified thickness from point A to point B. A background does not have to be defined. Vector graphics are usually associated with file formats such as WMF, DXF, and CDR. Unfortunately, because Web browsers work only with bitmapped images, you have to convert vector graphics to a bitmapped format before you can use them on the Web. Even though vector graphics don't necessarily start out with a solid background, they will have a solid background after you convert them, and you may well want to get rid of it. This isn't as bad as it seems. Backgrounds are easy to manipulate. GIF and JPEG are the graphic file formats most browsers recognize, and GIF is the only format that supports transparent backgrounds.

How to Create a Transparent Graphic

If you have decided you have a graphic that needs to be transparent, you need to do a couple of things to get it ready for conversion. If the background isn't solid—say it has some stray textures—you should open it up in a paint or an image-editing program and clean it up. Otherwise, any stray speck of color will remain visible after the background is converted to transparent. A few minutes in Adobe Photoshop or even Windows Paintbrush is usually all it will take for you to clean things up. While you're doing this, find out the Red-Green-Blue (RGB) value of the color you are going to use for your background. The RGB value for a color will vary from program to program. Some browsers display the RGB values in the status bar while the mouse pointer is over the image, and others display the values during various modes of editing. Consult your graphics-handling program's documentation or online help to determine how to do this. You may need this information later. These values will look like 207 207 207 (this is a common browser gray), which stands for the amount of each hue in the color. Each color is made up of various amounts of red, green, and blue. These amounts of hue are designated by a value between 0 and 255.

While you're in your paint program, you need to convert any file format your graphic happens to be in to a GIF file. With HiJaak, Photoshop, and similar programs, the conversion to GIF is simply a matter of opening your original graphic file and saving or exporting it to a GIF file format.

GIF files come in two flavors: 87a and 89a. The Graphics Gods have further deemed that only 89a GIFs can be made transparent, and most graphics programs do only 87a. Fortunately, the conversion from 87a to 89a is a snap. To convert the image to 89a, simply open and then save the image in a program that supports the 89a format.

Next you need to make sure the background color isn't used anywhere else in the graphic. Transparency conversion programs search the whole graphic for all the pixels of the color you select to be transparent and whack them out. Remember that the browser's background color will show through anywhere the color you select once was. For instance, suppose you have a graphic of a person's head on a white background and the graphic shows the whites of the person's eyes. If you make this graphic transparent and view it on a gray background, not only will the background around the head be gray but the eyes will also be gray. Likewise, any other piece of the graphic that used to be white before conversion will be gray. This could be awkward, as shown in Figure 4-2. If you have enough forethought to make the eyes blue, they will appear blue when viewed on any color background.

A few browsers don't support transparent GIF images; they simply display the original colors of the image. To maintain the quality of your graphics when viewed with these browsers, it's a good idea to use light gray as the background color prior to conversion. Since, as previously mentioned, most browsers use light gray as the default background color, you have a better chance of your graphics looking good if they start out with a gray background.

Now that you have cleaned up your graphic, you're ready to convert. There are several popular programs available to use for conversion. Some have a graphical interface and some utilize the command line. LView Pro is so easy to use that I never bothered with command line tools or other

TIP

LView Pro is shareware. To get a copy, you can contact the program's author at: mmedia@world.std.com. Leonardo Haddad Loureiro 1501 East Hallandale Beach Boulevard, #254 Hallandale, FL 33009 USA. You can also find numerous places to download LView Pro on the Internet, such as: http://nctweb.com/NCT

conversion tools after the first time I used it. Basically, you just open a graphic file in LView Pro, indicate the existing background color, and save it, and you're done.

Using LView Pro

See the tip on page 91 to find out where you can get a copy. After you download it, unzip it, register it, and get it set up, all you have to do is open your graphic file in LView Pro. LView Pro will let you open BMP, PCX, GIF, TIF, and a few other file formats. You can even open multiple files and convert all of them at the same time.

After you open your graphic in LView Pro, select Options Background Color and pick the color you want to make transparent. LView Pro conveniently displays a selection of every color in the graphic. If it's not immediately obvious which color to choose, LView Pro tells you the RGB value of the color you've clicked on so that you can be sure you are matching the RGB values of your background. If you remember the values of the background color, this will be no problem.

Now all you have to do is save the file. When you choose File Save or File Save As, LView Pro asks you whether you would like to save the file as a GIF89a. This is the flavor of GIF you need to make the graphic transparent. So save the file as a GIF89a.

You're done. Your graphic is now transparent. When you check out your work in your browser, be sure you flush the browser's cache before loading your converted graphic so that you don't just load the old, nontransparent image that had been stored in memory while you were busy converting.

LView Pro can do a lot more than this. It can make your images "interlaced" (our next topic) at the same time it's making the backgrounds transparent.

Interlaced Images

You've probably seen graphics that appeared on your browser's screen slowly, as if a series of veils were being opened one by one in front of the image. A rough, blurry image appeared first, and in successive stages the image became sharper and sharper as more of the pixels were downloaded onto your screen. These are interlaced images.

Although interlaced images appear to load faster than regular images, my timing tests show that they don't actually load any faster. They do *seem* to load faster. So what's the point? Apparent

TIP

YOU PROBABLY KNOW YOU CAN COPY THE HTML USED TO CREATE A PAGE YOU ADMIRE ON THE WEB BY USING THE SAVE AS COMMAND FROM YOUR BROWSER WHILE YOU ARE VIEWING A PAGE. THIS SAVES A TEXT COPY OF THE HTML CODE NEEDED TO CREATE THE PAGE YOU ARE SEEING SO THAT YOU CAN USE IT ON YOUR OWN COMPUTER. YOU CAN ALSO COPY AND PASTE PIECES FROM PAGES YOU ARE VIEWING BY CHOOSING THE VIEW SOURCE COMMAND IN INTERNET EXPLORER (OR THE EQUIVALENT COMMAND IN ANOTHER BROWSER). AFTER YOU COPY THE CODE YOU WANT, YOU CAN USE THE HTML CODE TO RE-CREATE SOME OF THE THINGS YOU'VE SEEN ON THE WEB.

speed vs. perceived speed. If we can't get images to load faster, at least we can cause them to *seem* to load faster. Compare the loading of an interlaced GIF with a regular GIF, as shown in Figure 4-3.

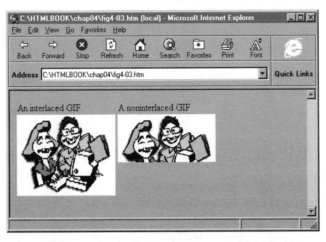

FIGURE 4-3 *The interlaced GIF, at left, is recognizable sooner than the noninterlaced GIF, at right. Even though the GIF at left is still a bit fuzzy, you can get a good idea of what the picture is all about. The GIF at right is only partially loaded, and you'll have to wait a bit longer to figure out what the picture is all about.*

The regular GIF begins loading from the top down, and in most cases, it needs to be mostly loaded before it is recognizable. Interlaced GIFs load a blurry image of the entire graphic almost immediately. With an interlaced GIF, those viewing the image can usually figure out what the image is supposed to be sooner than with a noninterlaced GIF. They can then make up their minds whether to hang around to see the image in all its glory or surf on. For this reason, I almost always save my GIFs as interlaced.

Aside from the fact that interlaced GIFs simply look cool, there is another advantage to using them—since they are so easy to create, there's not much point in skipping them.

Several image-editing programs are available that offer the ability to save GIFs and JPEGs in interlaced formats. With most of these programs, you need to do little more than open the file in the program and save the file again immediately with the interlacing option. It's very easy, clean, and neat.

How to Create an Interlaced Graphic

Using LView Pro, converting a regular GIF to an interlaced GIF is simply a matter of opening the GIF file and saving it again by opening the Options menu and choosing the Save GIFs Interlaced option. You don't have to save the file as an 89a GIF. In fact, if you want to save an image as interlaced without a transparent background, you may need to save it in 87a format to avoid the transparency effect.

That's all there is to it. If you keep the Save GIFs Interlaced option checked (that is, you don't choose it a second time and turn the option off), every time you save a GIF with LView Pro it will automatically become interlaced with no more effort on your part. Since I haven't found any reason not to use interlaced GIFs, I keep this option checked and save all my GIF images as interlaced.

Image Maps

Graphical image maps, or mouse-sensitive images, can give your site a free-form graphic menu that readers can use to navigate your back alleys and main Web thoroughfares. An image map is simply a graphic with so-called hot spots that provide links to URLs of other pages or sites. The image map works like this: When the user clicks on an image that is defined as being a mapped image by the ISMAP attribute of the IMG tag, the coordinates of the location of the click are sent to the Web server. The Web server then checks the map file for a hot spot that contains the coordinates of the user's mouse click. If the server finds a match, the URL defined in the map file is then invoked, sending the user's browser to a new location.

A graphical way to display information is almost always superior to plain text. "A picture is worth a thousand words" is as true on the Web as it is in the print world. Although a list of text links works well, an interesting graphic with the same choices can entice your readers deeper into your pages.

Eye-catching graphics do more than just catch the eye. They say something more than mere words can say. Advertising agencies are well aware that pictures project an image of a product or a company much better than words. You can combine your Web site menus and project an image at the same time with image maps.

Depending on your target browser, you may need access to your Web server's cgi-bin directory. You might need to ask the system administrator for your Web server for permission to put files

TIP

If you right-click on an image on a page (using MS Explorer or Netscape Navigator), you are offered a nifty menu that gives you the choice of snarfing the graphic you clicked on and saving it to some subdirectory on your hard drive. However, be sure you have permission to use the graphic. Don't assume you can use it just because it's on the Web. Shame on you if you make improper use of graphics.

there. Still, image maps are quite easy to set up. At first they may look hard to create, but several programs are available that make creating them as easy as tracing your proposed hot spots with your mouse and assigning URLs to them.

Client-Side vs. Server-Side Image Maps

There are two kinds of image maps: server-side image maps and the newer client-side image maps. Server-side image maps use the server to hunt for the URL assigned to a hot area and deliver the page to the browser. Client-side image maps build the hot spot information into the HTML on the page so that the browser can figure out which areas are hot and then can ask the server to send the page.

Client-side image maps have several advantages. For one, pages with client-side image maps are portable between servers. The server doesn't have any extra work to do (like looking up all the information about the image map hot spots), so there is less server load. If you use server-side image maps, you need to place a script with all the image map details on the server in the cgi-bin directory. For security reasons, many service providers are not keen on letting people muck around on their servers, adding scripts to the cgi-bin directory. If you are renting or otherwise using space on someone else's server, you may have to beg or wheedle your way into getting your image map scripts where they need to be to make the map work.

The drawback to client-side image maps is that currently only browsers that support HTML 3.0 (such as Netscape Navigator 2.0, Microsoft Internet Explorer, and Spry's Enhanced Mosaic 2.0) can process client-side image maps. Anyone using another browser will find a nonclickable graphic on your page. You must choose from among three options: using client-side image maps, which may alienate those people who are not quick to change to the latest, coolest browsers; sticking with server-side image maps that almost everyone can use; or using both kinds of image map on the same page. The last choice may be the best, since it will leave you in good shape for the HTML 3.0 future and still provide for older browsers.

How to Create an Image Map

There are two steps to mapping an image map. You must first define the areas on an image that you want to be hot spots, and then you must link them to the URLs you want them to point to. You define the hot spots by listing the coordinates (in pixels) of the areas you want hot. You can

TIP

WHEN YOU DESIGN THE GRAPHIC YOU'RE GOING TO USE, DRAW YOUR HOT AREAS SO THAT THEY AREN'T TOO SMALL, THEY AREN'T TOO HARD TO FIND, THEY DON'T OVERLAP, AND THEY AREN'T TOO CLOSE TOGETHER. THE POINTING FINGER THAT BROWSERS USE AS THE MOUSE POINTER WHEN IT'S ON A HOT SPOT IS NOT A VERY ACCURATE POINTING TOOL. SO SPACE OUT YOUR HOT AREAS AND MAKE THEM FAIRLY LARGE, HALF AN INCH WIDE AT LEAST.

TIP

You can set up your image maps so that any area outside a hot spot is also a hot spot, linking someone who happens to click outside where you really want them to click to a default URL. The default URL might simply point to the current page. That way, readers can keep trying until they get the pointer in the right place, on the hot spot. This can be very hard for some people to do.

figure all this out by hand, plotting the corner coordinates of your hot spots, but it's far easier to use a program such as MapEdit or MapThis! to create an image map.

Where to get it: http://www.ecaetc.ohio-state.edu/tc/mt/

MapThis! will create both server-side image maps and client-side image maps, and it's free. It is a 32-bit program, but it works with Windows 3.1 or Windows 3.11 when running Win32s (which you can also download from the MapThis! site.)

Drawing the image map is easy. You simply open up the image file in MapThis!, choose the shape you want for the hot spots, and then point, click, and drag with your mouse to trace the shape. The program automatically creates a file that describes the boundaries of the hot spot. You then assign a URL to the hot spot. You can draw rectangle, polygon, and circle hot spots anywhere on an image and link URLs to them. You can even overlap hot spots, although this could create problems. It is important to be sure you leave a little bit of space between hot spots so that readers can be sure they are pointing to the correct link. Most browsers handle overlapped hot spots by making the first area that is defined as a hot spot the hot spot for any area that overlaps it.

The hot spots are defined by coordinates that set the corners of rectangles and polygons or the center point and radius of circles. Here's how a simple image map and its .MAP file look:

```
rect /subdir/subdir/webpage.html          21,168 97,202
rect /subdir/subdir/otherwebpage.html     148,169 357,205
rect /subdir/otherdir/webpage.html        410,169 567,202
```

When you finish creating your image, you can save your file in NCSA or CERN format for a server-side image map or CSIM format for a client-side image map. The rest of the work is done for you by MapThis! The server-side map file is created, or the client-side map file is installed in the HTML file that you have chosen. If you have chosen to create a client-side image map, MapThis! will create only the data for the <MAP> tags. You will have to create the image tag with the USEMAP attribute on your own and place it after the </MAP> tag. Just remember to use the # symbol before the map name in the USEMAP attribute, as follows:

```
<IMG SRC="mymap.gif" USEMAP="#sitemap">
```

The HTML Tag

When you have your image all mapped out and your URLs assigned to the hot areas, you have to place the image in your HTML page. That's done in different ways, depending on whether you are going with client-side or server-side maps.

Server-Side Image Maps

The older, established way of creating image maps (that is, under HTML 2.0) requires that you use the ISMAP attribute in your image tag. Your image tag refers to the image that you are using for your map, and you put it between the beginning and ending tags of the link to the map file. You would enter something like this in your HTML file:

```
<A HREF="path/to/somemap.map"><IMG SRC="path/to/somemap.gif" ISMAP></A>
```

The ISMAP attribute tells your browser that the graphic is an image map. When a section of the image is clicked on, the attribute sends a message to the server that includes the coordinates of the pointer location when the mouse was clicked. If you have ever passed your pointer over an image map, you may have noticed in the status bar at the bottom of your Web browser something like this:

```
http://www.somewhere.com/something/somemap.map?300,20
```

The numbers after the question mark are the coordinates of the pointer's position. You will see these coordinates only with server-side image maps. Client-side image maps display the URL or link associated with that area of the map.

Some server software needs to be told to run a special program to process a map. This means that the URL in your browser's status bar might look like this:

```
http://www.somewhere.com/cgi-bin/imagemap/something/somemap.map?300,20
```

In this case, the server uses a program called image map in the cgi-bin directory to process the image map. To make sure your maps work, you will have to contact your system administrator to find out exactly what your server needs in order to process image maps. Depending on your server software, your entries in your HTML file for image maps will look something like one of these:

```
<A HREF="somemap.map"><IMG SRC="somemap.gif" ISMAP></A>
```

or

```
<A HREF="/cgi-bin/imagemap/somemap.map"><IMG SRC="somemap.gif" ISMAP></A>
```

The first example is for server software that doesn't require an image map program. The second example is for server software that needs an image map program to process image maps.

Client-Side Image Maps

Unlike server-side image maps, client-side image maps work independently of server software and remain consistent in format, even if you move your files to another server. Client-side image maps require only two things: a browser that supports HTML 3.0 and the map data written into the HTML file. The correct format for entering the data into the HTML file for this kind of map is as follows:

```
<MAP NAME="clientside.map">
<AREA SHAPE="rectangle, circle, or polygon" COORDS="x,y,..."
HREF="link">
</MAP>
<IMG SRC="somemap.gif" USEMAP="#clientside.map>
```

Note that if the SHAPE= attribute is omitted, SHAPE="RECT" is assumed. The COORDS= attribute gives the coordinates of the shape, using pixels as the units. The USEMAP= attribute in the <IMG> tag functions like a jump-to link. If the map is preceded by only the # symbol, USEMAP= assumes that the map is in the same file as the <IMG> tag.

Don't let the coordinates scare you off. With the software available today (such as MapThis!), you only have to place circles, squares, or polygons over the parts of images that you want to be hot spots linked to URLs, and the software will automatically generate the coordinates.

Combining Client-Side and Server-Side Image Maps

To be conservative, you may want to make your image maps work as both client-side and server-side image maps.

After you have created both your server-side and client-side image maps, combining the two in your HTML file is easy. You simply put the same entry into your HTML file that you would with a server-side image map, but you also include the USEMAP= attribute in your image tag, like this:

```
<A HREF="somemap.map"><IMG SRC="somemap.gif" ISMAP USEMAP="#clientside.map"></A>
```

The USEMAP= attribute has a higher precedence than the ISMAP tag and will be recognized by browsers that support client-side image maps. If a browser doesn't support client-side image maps, the USEMAP= attribute will be ignored.

Small Teaser Images, or Thumbnails

It's hard to avoid the temptation to use spectacular, high-resolution graphics. Many subjects need to be illustrated with images that are just, well, huge. There is a way to use them without choking the computers of visitors to your site and causing your visitors to flee your site after waiting 10 minutes for one particularly cool image to load.

In the main body of your text, where you would like the huge, fancy, cool image to be, place a very small copy of the image and link it to the full-sized, glorious, high-resolution creation. Visitors who are really interested can choose to have a look, and casual surfers can browse right by without slowing down. This technique is particularly well suited for book covers, box shots, and product flyers that not all readers will want to peruse in detail. Write the code like this:

```
<AHREF="/fullsizeimage.gif"><IMGSRC="/thumbnailimage.gif></A>
```

BACKGROUNDS

No longer do Web page backgrounds need to be gray. HTML 3.0 allows graphics backgrounds, and browser-specific extensions to HTML allow color backgrounds. Some HTML traditionalists might complain that colorful, graphical backgrounds overload the sometimes limited resources of the Web and interfere with the intended purpose of HTML—the organized presentation of text. But it's clear that background colors and graphics are here to stay. In fact, it's becoming harder and harder to find Web pages in standard HTML gray anymore.

Microsoft Internet Explorer, Netscape Navigator, and other leading browsers now support both color backgrounds and graphics backgrounds in the GIF and JPEG graphics file formats. They also support customized colors for foreground text, already explored links, and as yet unexplored links.

Specifying unique backgrounds is easy to do, but there are a few things to keep in mind.

- Carefully choosing the color for text on a page can be important if you plan on specifying a background color or graphic that might obscure text. A dark background can make it difficult to read the default, black, text.

- Complicated graphics used for backgrounds not only can slow page loading but also can be distracting. While you're striving for interesting and attractive pages, it is important not to get carried away with backgrounds just because using them is cool.

- Viewers using black-and-white monitors may see your fancy background color as a dark gray smear that completely obscures all text and graphics on a page. While I don't spend too much time worrying about people using black-and-white monitors, I do try to keep readability in mind and keep my backgrounds conservative.

Background Basics

You can add color, a tiled background GIF, or a watermark to a page by including the specific attribute in the <BODY> tag.

Creating Color Backgrounds
with the BGCOLOR= Attribute

To change the background color of your page, you include the BGCOLOR= attribute in the <BODY>
tag and specify RGB (red, green, blue) values:

```
<BODY BGCOLOR="RRGGBB">
```

Place the opening <BODY> tag directly under the <TITLE> tag, and place the closing </BODY>
tag at the end of the document. The *"RRGGBB"* stands for the hexadecimal values for red, green,
and blue that combine to form the desired color. If you're optimizing your page for Netscape
Navigator 2.0 or Microsoft Internet Explorer, you can use simple color names such as "red,"
"black," and "yellow" instead of hexadecimal values. For example, the tag for a blue background
optimized for these browsers looks like this:

```
<BODY BGCOLOR="BLUE">
```

Any background you set will apply only to one page, the page enclosed in the <BODY></BODY> tags.

The HTML code to make the background of a page that is optimized for Netscape Navigator 2.0
or Microsoft Internet Explorer a lovely light yellow would look like this:

```
<HTML>
<HEAD>
<TITLE>Sample Page Demonstrating a Colored Background</TITLE>
<BODY BGCOLOR=YELLOW>
<H1> Sample Page Demonstrating a Colored Background</H1><P>
This page has a lovely yellow background instead of the default, ugly, gray that
most browsers select for you. We should all rejoice that we can now easily
manipulate background colors.
</P>
</BODY>
</HTML>
```

This simply changes the background color. The text and link colors remain the default black and blue.

Using a Graphic for a Background with the BACKGROUND= Attribute

To insert a GIF or JPEG file as a background, insert the filename and pathname of the graphic file after the BACKGROUND= attribute in the <BODY> tag, as follows:

```
<BODY BACKGROUND="wackygif.gif">
```

The graphic will automatically be tiled (repeated in the same size) to fill the entire page.

It's important to select a graphic that is not too complicated, not only to keep the file size small and consequently the loading time quick but also to keep text from being obscured. Using a busy graphic as a background may seem like fun at first, but your readers will not appreciate having to strain to read your text. Aesthetics, of course, should also be a factor in selecting graphics for backgrounds. Overuse of complicated graphics for backgrounds can grow old in a hurry. Gentle textures can make pleasant, eye-catching backgrounds. Consider the following example shown in Figure 5-1:

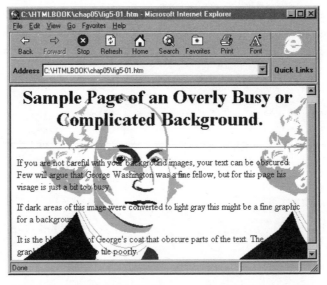

FIGURE 5-1 *A busy background graphic, however nice it looks by itself, may obscure text in some areas of a page.*

FIGURE 5-1

```
<HTML>
<BODY BACKGROUND="gwash.gif">
<H1 ALIGN=CENTER>Sample Page of an Overly Busy or Complicated Background.
</H1><HR>
If you are not careful with your background images, your text can be
obscured. Few will argue that George Washington was a fine fellow, but for
this page his visage is just a bit too busy.<P>
If dark areas of this image were converted to light gray this might be a
fine graphic for a background.<P>
It is the black areas of George's coat that obscure parts of the text. The
size of the graphic also causes it to tile poorly.
</BODY>
</HTML>
```

Even adjusting text colors may not compensate for overdone and garish background images. Conservative, black-and-white or light-colored textures add interest without overwhelming textual content, as shown in Figure 5-2.

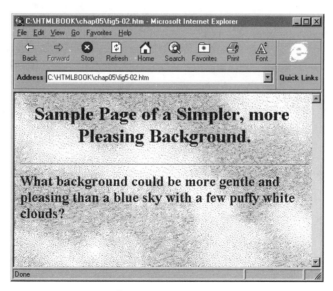

FIGURE 5-2

A simple, conservative background can add interest to a page without overwhelming the text.

FIGURE 5-2

```
<HTML>
<BODY BACKGROUND="clouds.gif">
<H1 ALIGN=CENTER>Sample Page of a Simpler, more Pleasing Background.
</H1><HR>
<H2>What background could be more gentle and pleasing than a blue sky with
a few puffy white clouds?</H2>
</BODY>
</HTML>
```

As with background colors, you can't set a graphic background for more than one page. Also, you can't use more than one background on the same page.

Creating a Watermark with the BGPROPERTIES=FIXED Attribute (Microsoft Internet Explorer)

If your page is optimized for Microsoft Internet Explorer, you can add a graphic watermark—an image that appears behind the text, much as a regular background graphic does, but that doesn't scroll with the page. A watermark image tiles automatically, like a regular background graphic. To add a watermark, you use the BGPROPERTIES=FIXED attribute in the <BODY> tag. Figure 5-3 shows how you can place an image of George Washington behind text on a page. If you size the watermark graphic to approximately fill a browser screen or to tile neatly, you can create interesting effects on an otherwise dull page. With watermarks, you can get away with a bit more complicated and busy background graphics because the text will scroll past the graphic. When the text reaches a clear area on the screen, it can be read unobscured.

FIGURE 5-3

```
<HTML>
<BODY BACKGROUND="gwash.gif" BGPROPERTIES=FIXED>
<H1>Using a Fixed Watermark</H1>
With Microsoft Internet Explorer, you can set a background image so it's
fixed in one place behind any text or graphics that appear on the page.<P>
The background image remains in place as the page elements scroll. A good
use of the BGPROPERTIES=FIXED attribute is to place your company's logo as
a watermark (in a delicate shade of some noncomplicated color).<P>
Since the text moves and the background doesn't, the dark areas in George
Washington's coat do not present the same text-obscuring problem as they
```

```
would if the graphic were a regular (scrolling) background. As the text
scrolls up and down the page, it will eventually be in a clear, readable
area.
</BODY>
</HTML>
```

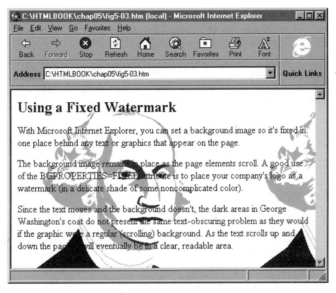

FIGURE 5-3   *The text on a page scrolls over a watermark, which is fixed
in place by the BGPROPERTIES=FIXED attribute.*

Sizing and Tiling a Background Image

Any graphic included with a Web page adds to the time required for a browser to load the page.
Even a small graphic will increase loading time. To minimize the download time, it's a good idea to
keep your background images small and uncomplicated. Since most browsers will take any graphic
used for a background, cache it, and tile it to fill the entire page, you can usually get away with
using a small graphic. Usually the smaller the graphic, the smaller the file size. If your graphic is
too small, however, the browser will spend more time tiling it than you will save by using a small

graphic file. A background graphic that is 1 pixel by 1 pixel will take much longer to tile than a background graphic 50 pixels by 50 pixels will take to load. Use your graphics editing software to size your images.

If your background graphic has a pattern that must be displayed in a particular size, be sure to save it at its proper size before you make it available to your HTML code. Otherwise, the results may not be what you intended, as shown in Figure 5-4 and Figure 5-5. Browsers can tile background graphics only in their original sizes.

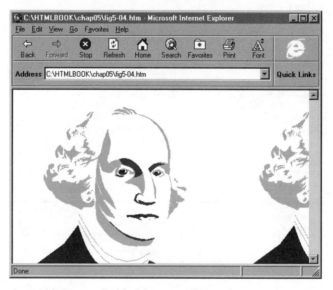

FIGURE 5-4 *A graphic image tiled in its proper size.*

A fairly plain textured graphic can be quite effective, even if it's very small. A carefully selected background will not appear to be tiled at all.

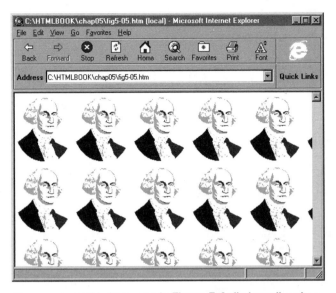

FIGURE 5-5

The same graphic image as in Figure 5-4 tiled smaller than its proper size.

Combining a Graphics Background and a Color Background

You can specify *both* a graphics background *and* a color background on the same page. Simply add both BGCOLOR= and BACKGROUND= attributes to your <BODY> tag. When you combine a graphic and a color, the background color will show through horizontal rules created with <HR> and through table borders. You can use this characteristic of combination backgrounds to give the appearance of a color border on a table. To do this, use a graphic that is simply a solid standard gray contrasting with the BGCOLOR= attribute. Your readers will puzzle over how you managed to make your table borders a different color. This is also a good technique for getting table borders to stand out distinctly against a light background image.

```
<BODY BACKGROUND="somegif.gif" BGCOLOR="#rrggbb">
<TABLE BORDER=6 CELLPADDING=6>
<TR>
<TD>
This is a Web page with a GIF background and a table that has colored borders.
</TD>
</TR>
</TABLE>
</BODY>
```

Adding a Gradient Background

Long a staple of graphics designers who work in print, gradient fills can make interesting backgrounds in HTML pages. (A gradient fill is an area of a page that gradually goes from one color or shade to another.)

To create a gradient fill, use CorelDRAW or another graphics program to draw a narrow rectangle about the width of a regular page and about a quarter-inch high. Using the Gradient Fill tool in CorelDRAW or a similar command in another program, fill the rectangle with a color or colors that blend into one another. Make sure the rectangle has no border. To end up with a smooth blend, choose a setting that provides for a generous number of stages in the blend; 256 colors or shades of gray will look much better than 16. Export the file as a GIF. I find I usually need to open the file in HiJaak from Inset Systems or Adobe Photoshop and trim off a sliver all the way around the rectangle. If you don't do this, a thin seam will appear between each instance of the fill once the graphic is tiled.

The most efficient height seems to be about 12 pixels, although you can get away with fatter or narrower bands. Light colors usually work best. The gradient fill should run from side to side rather than vertically. Save this graphic as a GIF or JPEG file, and specify that file in the <BODY BACKGROUND=*"filename"*> tag. Microsoft Internet Explorer and Netscape Navigator will tile the graphic to make an attractive gradient fill behind your page. Gray-scale gradient fills look good as a Web page background, as shown in Figure 5-6.

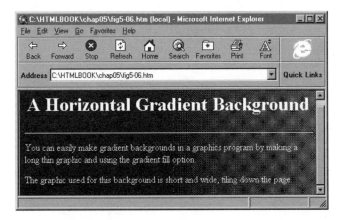

FIGURE 5-6

A page with a horizontal gradient fill.

You can do the same thing with a vertical gradient fill, as shown in Figure 5-7. Simply turn the graphic on its side in the originating program. Be sure the graphic is long enough to reach from the top of the page all the way to the bottom. If it isn't, Netscape Navigator will retile the graphic before the end of the page.

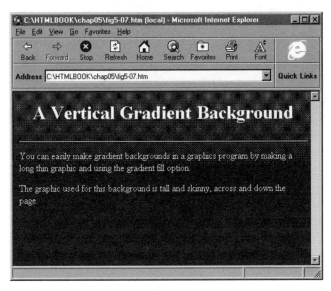

FIGURE 5-7

A page with a vertical gradient fill.

CAUTION

BE SURE TO GET PERMISSION TO USE COPYRIGHTED IMAGES. DON'T ASSUME THAT A GRAPHIC IS FREE TO USE JUST BECAUSE IT'S ON THE WEB.

Where to Get Graphics to Use as Backgrounds

Dozens of Web sites offer libraries of background graphics you can use freely. You can find hundreds, perhaps thousands, of shareware and free graphics, and most draw and paint programs come with libraries of graphics suitable for backgrounds. If you have a scanner (even a black-and-white scanner will do for Web work) and a little bit of imagination, you can create your own background graphics by scanning leaves, cloth, or anything else that can be scanned. CorelDRAW and other graphics programs have some fascinating tools for creating textures, blends, and fractals that you can use for backgrounds.

Setting Text Colors

If you have designated an interesting background color for your page, you may need to change the color of the text to keep it readable. If you set your background to a dark blue, for instance, regular black text may not show up well. In that case, you may want to specify white or light yellow text. You may want to use bright-colored text on a regular gray background just to grab a reader's attention. Attributes available in Microsoft Internet Explorer and Netscape Navigator now allow you to specify more than one color of text on the same page. See Chapter 1 for details on specifying text colors.

You can, however, specify the default colors for all the text on a page in the <BODY> tag. There are four different types of text that can appear in a typical Web document: regular body text, text indicating a link, text indicating a link that has already been followed, and text indicating a link that is active or is being looked for. As the default, regular text appears black, linked text appears blue, links already followed appear purple, and active links appear red. Tags are available to designate the color (in RGB) of each type of text.

Add the TEXT= attribute to the <BODY> tag to indicate a color (in RGB) for the main body text of a page.

```
<BODY TEXT="RRGGBB">
```

The LINK=, VLINK=, and ALINK= attributes can all be set in the <BODY> tag. It is not necessary to specify a TEXT= attribute in order to specify the LINK=, VLINK=, and ALINK= attributes.

```
<BODY LINK="#RRGGBB" ALINK="#RRGGBB" VLINK="#RRGGBB">
```

If you're not careful, you can create some horrible-looking and unreadable pages with these particular tools. Be sure you take the time to experiment with these features and check the readability of the colors you set before committing pages with unusual text colors to your Web site. Realize that simply changing the background color can make some types of text exceptionally difficult to read. Be sure to check the readability of links, active links, and visited links, even if you have only changed the background color. You may need to designate specific colors for text types other than regular text.

Browser-Specific Issues with Backgrounds

If a visitor to your page has the images option in the browser turned off, any background images you specify will not be loaded. To keep things clean and neat, if you did not specify a background color and, for whatever reason, the specified background graphic does not load, none of the text color attributes will be applied. Otherwise, you could end up with text the same color as your background and the appearance of a blank Web page.

Many browsers do not support backgrounds at all. I haven't run into any that can't read a page at all if it has a background attribute set, but that certainly doesn't mean there aren't any.

Video settings definitely can cause problems with backgrounds. If a computer is using a video setting of fewer than 256 colors, background colors other than the basic 16 colors may show up as murky, dithered blends making text unreadable and the entire page rather, well, unattractive. A pukey mess is the way one viewer described such pages. It is a bit much to ask people to change video drivers just to view your pages (although some Web sites actually do recommend that a 256-color video driver be used), so it may be wise to stick to the basic 16 colors supported by generic video drivers if you want the widest possible audience to be able to view your page. However, it is also a bit much to ask Web page designers to stick to a mere 16 colors; so, although it may be wise to stick to 16 colors, I don't expect many creative types to pay any attention to this admonition.

Keep in mind that many computers are set to use the plain vanilla Windows VGA driver, and it does not handle background colors well.

Also keep in mind that black-and-white monitors will display most background colors as black— for the whole page. Many workstation users are stuck with powerful UNIX machines with over-size 20-inch monitors that are black-and-white, so some visitors to your site might have black-and-white monitors. That doesn't mean you shouldn't use color, but if you do, you should advise visitors that you are.

6.

MULTIMEDIA
by Charlie Morris

Adding multimedia to your Web site is easy enough. The problem is the limited bandwidth available to most Web surfers. The bandwidth bottleneck dictates that you must use multimedia elements sparingly and configure them carefully to squeeze every last ounce of performance out of the tools that are now available. Real-time audio and video tools that use "streaming" techniques currently allow playback of an audio or video file while the file is still downloading, rather than requiring that you download and then play the file. Another new multimedia tool for the Web is Virtual Reality Modeling Language (VRML), which a Web site developer can use to create three-dimensional worlds through which a user can navigate. Within the next few years, new products and increased bandwidth at a reasonable cost will eventually make the Web a multimedia paradise. But until then, a good working knowledge of multimedia elements, such as audio and video, will be needed to get the most out of today's tools.

Audio

Using audio in a Web page is theoretically as simple as specifying a URL that points to a sound file, just as you would link to any other kind of file. As we shall see, however, audio files can be huge, and different formats abound. A complete primer on digital audio is beyond the scope of this book, but this section will discuss the basic parameters of digital recording and how the parameters affect sound quality and file size. We'll also look at some common audio file formats.

Sampling, Sampling Rates, and Frequency Response

Sound is energy that travels as a wave. With traditional sound recording systems, sound is represented by an electronic signal that theoretically duplicates the waveform of the original sound, producing an analog recording. To be processed by a computer, an analog signal must be converted to a digital (numeric) signal, as shown in Figure 6-1. This is done with a gadget called an analog-digital (A/D) converter. An A/D converter, which is incorporated into a Mac or a PC sound card, takes periodic measurements of the sound—called samples—and assigns each one a number. Each sample is like a digital snapshot of sound at a particular moment in time. The recording and playback processes are shown in Figure 6-2 on the following page.

The two most basic parameters of digital recording are the number of bits assigned to each sample (resolution) and the speed at which these samples are taken (sampling rate). Higher resolutions and sampling rates mean that a larger range of values are available to represent the sound: hence better quality at the cost of larger file sizes. The resolution determines the dynamic range of the audio signal, and the sampling rate determines the frequency response.

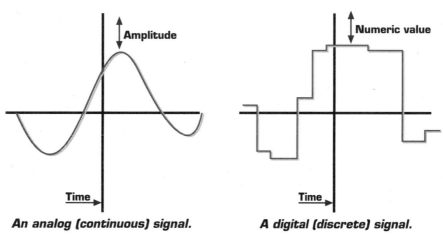

An analog (continuous) signal.   **A digital (discrete) signal.**

FIGURE 6-1   *An analog (continuous) signal and a digital (discrete) signal.*

The dynamic range of an audio device is the difference between the softest and loudest sounds that can be reproduced and is expressed in decibels (dB). The dynamic range of a digitized signal is limited by the number of bits per sample, typically either 8 or 16. An 8-bit sample has a 48-dB dynamic range, and a 16-bit sample has a 96-dB dynamic range, equal to that of a CD.

Recording

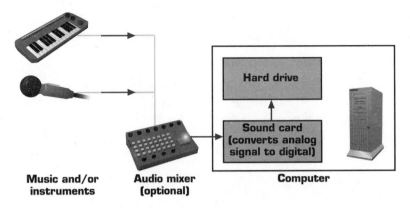

Music and/or instruments   Audio mixer (optional)   Computer

Playback

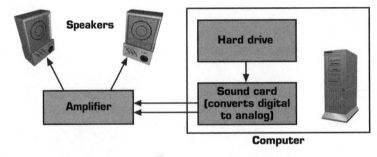

Computer

FIGURE 6-2 *Recording and playback on a basic computer audio setup.*

The human ear can hear frequencies from around 20 vibrations per second to around 20,000 vibrations per second (hertz, abbreviated Hz). Although it varies according to individual and environmental factors, this 20-Hz through 20-KHz range is widely used as a rule of thumb. In sound reproduction, frequency response—the difference between the highest and lowest sounds that can be reproduced—is one of the most critical criteria of quality. A cheap cassette deck produces muffled-sounding recordings because it lacks the frequency response to capture the high end of the audible range. Recordings made on professional analog and digital formats, however, sparkle with highs that almost make the music sound live.

Since most of the energy of the human voice is concentrated around 1 KHz, it is not necessary to have a full 20-20 frequency response (20-Hz–20-KHz) to reproduce speech intelligibly. Indeed, a very limited frequency response may be adequate for speech, as the little speakers made for telephone handsets demonstrate. For musical purposes, however, frequency response should be at least 10 KHz, and for high-quality audio the 20-20 mark must be equaled or exceeded.

Note that although the sampling rate, like frequency, is often expressed in hertz, the more technically correct term is "samples per second." The higher the sampling rate, the better the frequency response. As a practical matter, to capture the full audible spectrum, sound must be sampled at a little over double the highest audible frequency (20 KHz), which is why high-quality digital recording is done with sample rates in the 40s or above.

Since digital audio must be played back at the same sample rate at which it was recorded, it is desirable to standardize this parameter. While the normal audio world has pretty much established a standard of 44.1-KHz 16-bit sound, the quest for smaller file sizes and the number of different hardware platforms have given the computer sound scene a raft of rates and a flurry of formats. Telephony, pro audio, Mac, and PC have all established their own sampling rates. Other than those based on the CD and Mac sampling rates and the 8-KHz U-LAW rate, most of these will seldom be encountered in the computer world, but you never know. The most common audio sampling rates are shown in the following table.

Audio Sampling Rates

SAMPLES PER SECOND	DESCRIPTION
8000	Originally a telephone standard, used for U-LAW (pronounced mu-law—the u stands for the Greek letter mu), encoding.
11,025	A quarter of the CD sampling rate.
11,127	Half the Mac sampling rate.
18,900	A CD-ROM/XA standard. (XA allows the simultaneous display of pictures and playing of audio.)
22,050	Half the CD sampling rate.
22,255	The Mac sampling rate.
32,000	Used by digital radio, the Japanese HDTV format, and some DAT (Digital Audio Tape) recorders.
37,800	A CD-ROM/XA standard.

(continued)

SAMPLES PER SECOND	DESCRIPTION
44,056	Used by some professional audio/video equipment.
44,100	The CD and DAT standard.
48,000	Used by some DAT recorders and a few high-end sound cards.
88,200	Used by some DAT recorders.
96,000	Used by some DAT recorders.

Another parameter to be considered is the number of channels—mono (one channel) or stereo (two channels). A stereophonic signal is actually two signals, perfectly synchronized but slightly different. This creates a more lifelike reproduction by providing a slightly different signal to each ear. Incidentally, the term "stereo equipment" is usually used for home audio systems, which shows how universal stereo processing is in the audio world. In the multimedia world, however, stereo processing gets less respect. The fact that it doubles file sizes means that it is usually the first thing sacrificed to bandwidth. Unless a sound was originally recorded in stereo and is played back in stereo from a pair of decent speakers, the stereo processing is pointless. There is no reason to use it on a voice recording or other nonmusical sound except as a special effect.

These three configurations are becoming fairly standard:

- 8-KHz 8-bit U-LAW mono

- 22.05-KHz 8-bit mono or stereo

- 44.1-KHz 16-bit mono or stereo

Approximate file sizes range from 2.5 kilobytes (KB) per second of audio for 8-KHz U-LAW files to 160 KB per second for 44.1-KHz stereo. A 30-second clip of top-quality sound can eat up 5 megabytes (MB), or about 50 minutes with a 14.4-bps modem and 25 minutes with a 28.8-bps modem. So with the limited bandwidth of the Web, it should be apparent that audio file sizes must be managed with care. To make the most of the bandwidth available, consider using 8-KB U-LAW files for voice and other nonmusical sounds and 22-KB mono for music. Use 44.1-KHz stereo only if you are offering something worth waiting for. Label audio links with the file size, and consider giving your users a choice of high-quality or low-quality versions of each file. Most important, study up on the new technologies for audio transfer that are becoming available. Fight a rearguard action while waiting for the bandwidth cavalry.

TIP

The limited bandwidth of the Web requires a minimalist approach to multimedia. But sometimes simple sound or pictures can be very effective. Where a full-color video clip would be impractical, a black-and-white "slide show" may get the point across just as well.

Audio File Formats

Different computer platforms have come and gone, leaving a litter of file formats in their wake. At the moment, .AIFF (audio interchange file format) is the most popular in the Mac world, and .WAV rules the PC roost. (But look out—here comes RealAudio [.RA].) Although you may encounter many formats in the chaotic world of the Web, you can convert between different file formats and different sample rates using one of a number of programs. One of the most popular is Sound Exchange, or SOX, a shareware program written by Lance Norskog that is billed as "the Swiss Army knife of sound tools." You can obtain it at http://www.spies.com/Sox/.

Some formats support different ways to encode the data and different settings for parameters, such as resolution, sampling rate, and number of channels. Such self-describing formats usually have a header that specifies these values. In other formats, the encoding and parameters are fixed. Some formats allow for some form of compression.

The following sound file formats are the most common.

- The .AIFF format is the standard Mac format (extension .AIF or .AIFF). It allows a variable sampling rate, resolution, and number of channels. .AIFC is a version that allows for compression.

- The .AU and .SND formats are used by NeXT and Sun workstations. They allow a variable sampling rate, resolution, and number of channels. The extension .SND, however, can also refer to another format, a headerless 8-bit mono format for the Mac or the PC, with a variable sampling rate.

- The .VOC format is used by the Soundblaster family of sound cards. It is an 8-bit mono format.

- The .WAV format is the Microsoft Windows sound file format. It allows a variable sampling rate, resolution, and number of channels.

- The HCOM format is an 8-bit mono format for the Mac.

- The .MOD or .NST format is interesting. Originated on the Amiga, it is a bit like a cross between a sound file and a MIDI file. A .MOD file contains a bank of samples and sequencing information to play the samples.

- The .UL format is the standard U-LAW format, an 8-bit mono format with an 8-KHz sampling rate.

- The .RA format is Progressive Networks' RealAudio format.

TIP

SIMPLER MUSIC TENDS TO TRANSLATE BETTER TO LOW-BANDWIDTH SITUATIONS. IF YOUR BACKGROUND SCORE IS A FULL BAND WITH GUITARS AND VOCALS, BY THE TIME YOU CUT IT DOWN TO 22K MONO AND SQUIRT IT THROUGH SOME SURFER'S PEE WEE COMPUTER SPEAKERS, IT'S GOING TO SOUND STEPPED ON. A VERY SIMPLE ARRANGEMENT, SUCH AS A SOLO FLUTE, COULD STILL SOUND ALL RIGHT. ALWAYS LOOK FOR THE MOST BANDWIDTH-EFFECTIVE SOLUTION.

- MIDI (Musical Instrument Digital Interface) is not an audio file format, but a code that tells a receiving device (sound card) what notes to play. It cannot be used to record voice or other sounds, only to trigger sounds already stored on a sound card or another audio device. MIDI files are much smaller than audio data files, and the standard MIDI format (.MID) will play music on most sound cards.

Streaming Audio

Faced with the size of audio files and the meager bandwidth of the Web, folks are putting a lot of effort into finding new ways to transfer sound over the net. One promising new technology involves "streaming," shown in Figure 6-3, which enables a file to play as it is downloading. The data streams directly to the user's sound card but is not copied to the hard drive.

The first of these systems was RealAudio, created by Progressive Networks. It consists of three applications: the player, the studio, and the server. To receive RealAudio sounds, you must have the player, which will work with almost any browser. The studio allows you to create your own RealAudio clips. The server works on almost any Web server that supports configurable MIME (Multipurpose Internet Mail Extension) types. Incorporating RealAudio files into an HTML document involves using a metafile. (A metafile is a temporary file used to redirect other files.) The metafile sends the location of the compressed RealAudio (.RA) file to the player, which then requests the file from the RealAudio server. The file is sent to the player, is buffered, and is played. On the user end, the RealAudio player pops up and plays the clip at a transfer rate of about 1 KB per second. The client can choose between 16-bit and 8-bit sound and between an 8-KHz and 11-KHz sampling rate. The RealAudio applications can be downloaded at http://www.realaudio.com.

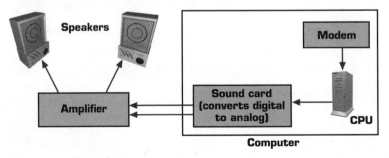

FIGURE 6-3   Playback using the "streaming" technology.

Two new real-time audio systems, IWave and TrueSpeech, are now available. From the user's standpoint, they work like RealAudio. They each use a player, which the user downloads and sets up to work with any browser. IWave and TrueSpeech use both streaming techniques and proprietary compression algorithms.

Internet Wave, or IWave, is from VocalTec. VocalTec also makes an application named Internet Phone, which allows two-way conversation over the Internet and requires a full-duplex sound card. The IWave system uses compressed .WAV and .AU files and supports several sampling rates. The CBS radio network is currently using IWave to present interviews and other news, and there are even Internet "radio stations" cropping up that use IWave to broadcast (after a fashion) both speech and music programs. You'll find IWave at http://www.vocaltec.com.

TrueSpeech is made by DSP Group. To use TrueSpeech on a Web page, you must use 16-bit, 8-KHz sound files, and you must convert them from PCM (Pulse Code Modulation) .WAV files to a special TrueSpeech .WAV format. Windows 95 and Windows NT Sound System both support the TrueSpeech .WAV format. If you use another operating system, you can download a converter. You'll find TrueSpeech at http://www.dspg.com.

Video

TIP

SOME WEB SITES ARE DESIGNED TO DAZZLE, WHILE OTHERS ARE INTENDED SIMPLY TO LET PEOPLE ACCESS INFORMATION QUICKLY. HOW MUCH MULTIMEDIA TO INDULGE IN DEPENDS ON THE TARGET AUDIENCE FOR A PARTICULAR SITE. ALWAYS USE MULTIMEDIA ELEMENTS WHERE THEY WILL DO THE MOST GOOD.

As greedy for processing resources as audio is, video is even hungrier. Although several flavors of digital audio recording have been around for a while, the art of creating visual images digitally is still comparatively new. Several professional-level digital videotape systems (D1, D2, and so forth) are now available, and material shot on motion picture film can be digitized with a gadget called a telecine transfer unit, although this sort of thing goes on only at the very top end of the industry. A consumer digital video standard was introduced in October 1995, and Sony and Panasonic are now shipping digital camcorders, but it will likely be a while before digital video is as pervasive as digital audio. Therefore, it is usually safe to assume that "desktop video" is a digitization of something originally recorded on analog video tape. Although it is possible to reproduce high-quality video on a computer if one has access to very expensive professional gear, for most of us the bandwidth constraints of desktop video dictate serious quality compromises. Audio can, of course, be recorded directly to disk, and a very high standard of quality can be achieved at moderate cost. It is only the limited bandwidth of the Web that necessitates space-saving reductions in audio quality. With desktop video, on the other hand, even with powerful hardware, one cannot expect optimal quality. The additional constraints of the Internet mean that Web video is pretty rough indeed. The quest for quality video over the Web, however, is well under way, and new approaches to the problem are cropping up every day.

The video recording and playback processes are shown in Figure 6-4.

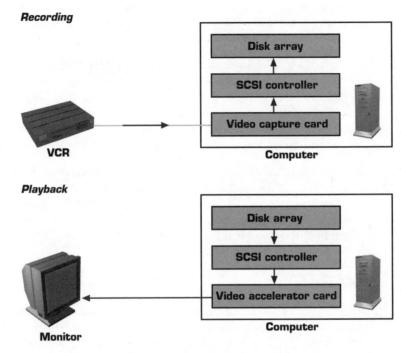

Recording

Disk array

SCSI controller

Video capture card

VCR

Computer

Playback

Disk array

SCSI controller

Video accelerator card

Monitor

Computer

FIGURE 6-4

Video recording and playback on a basic computer video setup.

Computer Video Formats

The most popular computer video file format is QuickTime, originally for the Mac but now also available as QuickTime for Windows. AVI is the original Windows video format. Both allow for the incorporation of many different graphic and audio file types into a finished "movie."

Playing video in real time requires a high sustained data transfer rate at all points in the signal path. A signal that approximates S-VHS quality (30 frames per second, 60 fields, millions of colors, with a 4:1 compression ratio) sucks up 5 MB or more per second of video. To sustain a data transfer rate of 5 MB per second (Mbps) requires something on the order of a disk array with a fast and wide SCSI connection, and a video card with hardware compression. For the average Jane and Joe, there is no point in sitting through a week-long download to obtain video files of this quality because they won't run on the average user's system anyway. A system with a 486/66 processor with 16 MB of RAM *might* be able to handle around 500 KB per second (Kbps). As with audio, there are several parameters that you can adjust to reduce file size, each of which affects different aspects of signal quality. These parameters include the number of frames per second, number of colors, screen size, and compression.

NTSC (National Television Standards Committee) Video is shot at 30 frames per second (actually, to be precise, 29.97 fps), with two interlaced fields per frame. Since it's almost impossible to achieve this frame rate without hardware compression, which not everyone has, desktop video usually happens at a lower frame rate. The trade-off is jerkier motion. The movie textbooks say that at around 18 fps, the illusion of continuous motion is lost. Video for CD-ROMs, however, is usually presented at 15 fps, and some applications, such as teleconferencing, use even lower frame rates.

Common Frame Rates

FRAME RATE	USE
30 frames per second (2 interlaced fields per frame)	NTSC video (American standard)
25 frames per second (2 interlaced fields per frame)	PAL video (European standard)
24 frames per second	Film
15 frames per second	Most CD-ROM video clips
1 frame per second	Used by the MBONE and by some teleconferencing systems

You need to select a frame rate with the playback platform in mind. Trying to play full-motion video on a system with inadequate data transfer speed can result in dropped frames and system crashes. The user can reduce throughput needs by using fewer colors or a smaller playback window.

Compression is a fact of life with desktop video. High-end video cards feature various forms of hardware compression, which is required for top performance. Many forms of software compression are available. The Apple QuickTime system includes several different software compression modes, or codecs, each of which has its pros and cons for different situations. Codecs are either "lossless," which means that they preserve all the data of the original signal, or "lossy," which means that they allow a certain amount of data to be lost. Compression ratios range from 4:1 to 50:1. Higher compression ratios reduce picture quality in different ways, depending on the type of compression used. Often the image becomes more pixellated, or grainy.

When considering which format to use (what point along the quality vs. file size continuum to shoot for), you must consider not only the download time but also the capabilities of the receiving machine. For a user to be able to play a 500-Kbps video file correctly, that 500-Kbps rate must be maintained at all points along the user's signal path, from hard drive to video card. As is the case with all large files, you should let your users know the size of the file before they begin downloading. If you plan to make relatively high-quality video files available, you might consider listing some minimum system requirements (such as continuous data throughput rates) so that unknowledgeable users don't spend hours downloading files that they can't play and clogging up your system as well.

The MBONE

Using current techniques, real-time video transmission across the Web is not very practical, to put it mildly. However, through a LAN with sufficient hardware, it is quite possible. The Multicast Backbone, or MBONE, is a virtual network that allows video images and audio to be multicast over the Internet. That is, data is sent over the Internet to many LANs (subnets), each of which then distributes the signal within its own network. The advantage of multicasting is that it is bandwidth efficient. The signal can reach more end users without using any more of the Internet bandwidth.

The MBONE uses IP multicast addressing, which is supported by Sun and Silicon Graphics workstations. The multicast packets are encapsulated into regular IP (Internet Protocol) packets so that they can be forwarded through Internet routers that do not support multicasting. To receive the multicast packets, a LAN must have an mrouter, which strips off this packet encapsulation. You also need plenty of bandwidth. The MBONE folks recommend at least a high-speed digital T1 line with 1.5 Mbps. They also point out that setting it up is "not for the faint of heart," as it is a complex and developing technology.

The current parameters of the MBONE are more like teleconferencing than MTV. Video is provided at 1 fps (128 Kbps), along with voice-quality audio (32 or 64 Kbps). The MBONE has been used to provide live broadcasts of many events, including spacewalks. Three applications available for use with the MBONE are UNIX packages named Net Video, Visual Audio Tool, and Whiteboard.

StreamWorks

StreamWorks, developed by Xing Technology Corporation, is a system for delivery of video and audio over any kind of network. It supports live multicasting, such as the MBONE and on-demand applications. NBC and Reuters, among others, are using StreamWorks to deliver live video broadcasts to commercial subscribers. Several Web radio stations use StreamWorks to deliver music, from country to classical. Some work with 14.4-bps modems, while others claim to be able to squirt 44.1-KHz stereo sound or live full-motion video at 112 Kbps (with an ISDN, or Integrated Services Digital Network, line). StreamWorks incorporates streaming techniques, MPEG compression, and multicast IP protocols. You can get the latest at http://www.xingtech.com/.

VRML

A group of developers is working on what could prove to be the wildest Web multimedia application of all. Virtual Reality Modeling Language is a way to create three-dimensional virtual worlds that can be viewed across the Web. VRML 1.0 was released in April 1995, and the group of developers is hard at work adding new functionality. Their ultimate goal is to create a complete cyberworld, à la the Matrix described in William Gibson's book *Neuromancer*. Objects in a three-dimensional world could incorporate all the goodies: text, images, audio, video, and JAVA-style applications.

VRML viewers available include WorldView from Intervista (http://www.webmaster.com/vrml/) and WebSpace from Silicon Graphics (http://webspace.sgi.com/). The best place to start boning up on VRML is at Wired's VRML Forum (http://vrml.wired.com/).

Some existing pages using VRML include Wax Web (http://bug.village.virginia.edu), Virtual SoMa (http://www.planet9.com), and Virtual Vegas (http://www.virtualvegas.com).

Three-dimensional content created with most applications, including animation and CAD packages, can be converted to VRML using the Open Inventor file format. Applications designed specifically for creating VRML for the Web will soon be available. VRML could be used by a webmaster to create a unique cyberworld. The ultimate vision of creator Mark Pesce, however, is that there will be only one virtual world (just as there is only one Internet) and that individual users will place objects there. One of the basic objectives is to establish a connection between a set of spatial coordinates and a host address. Each object has a set of three values representing its location on the x, y, and z-axes of three-dimensional space. These three values are its address in cyberspace, which has no relation to the physical location of its host machine or its Internet address.

Chat services are jumping on the 3-D bandwagon. There are now various cyberworlds that support multiuser functionality. One of these is Worlds Chat, from Worlds, Inc. Worlds Chat lets you create a virtual character called an avatar, and your avatar can cruise around a space station and carry on conversations with other avatars. Worlds, Inc. is at http://www.worlds.net. Similar programs include WorldsAway (available on CompuServe), Virtual Places on America Online, Prospero's Global Chat (http://www.prospero.com), and the Internet Round Table Society's WebChat (http://www.irsociety.com).

TIP

GIVE PEOPLE A CHOICE. SOME SITES LET THE USER CHOOSE BETWEEN TEXT-ONLY AND FULL MULTIMEDIA VERSIONS. THOSE WITH SLOWER CONNECTIONS CAN CHOOSE THE "LIGHT" VERSION.

Three-dimensional rendering is a very processor-greedy application even without the bandwidth constraints of the Web, although a number of projects are under way to maximize the speed. For example, the complex polygons needed to render 3-D objects could be stored on a CD-ROM and made available at the user's end, which would streamline downloading. These CD-ROMs would have predefined shapes and images stored on them, and the Web page would reference the appropriate shape or image, instead of downloading the shape or image each time. Ultimately, of course, the VRMLers' goals (which include nothing less than a detailed rendering of the entire earth) depend once again on bandwidth. 3-D graphics also greatly benefit from special graphics rendering hardware on the client, which not everyone has. However, Creative Labs and others are now shipping low-cost 3-D graphics boards, so maybe it won't be too long before Web pages are replaced by Web buildings, cities, and worlds.

So Now What?

Multimedia is one of the most alluring areas on the Web, but it is also one in which a lot of work remains to be done. It may be that the Web will remain the stepchild of the multimedia scene until the knight of bandwidth shows up. But in the meantime, every day brings new developments. Wise webmasters who want to do a good job with multimedia not only must keep abreast of Web technology but should have a good working knowledge of graphic, audio, and video media in general.

Charlie Morris has written many articles about computers and music. A graduate of Eckerd College, he lives in Florida, where he works on audio and multimedia projects in his own recording studio.

ANIMATIONS
by Nick Bicanic

In your Web browsing, you've probably seen some unusual effects on Web pages and taken a quick view of the source code, resulting in a comment like "Ahhhh, so that's how they made the title scroll."

However, every so often you've probably seen something really amazing—like an inline animation—and the source HTML told you absolutely nothing about how to duplicate the feat on your own Web page. You've probably encountered the dreaded cgi-bin, which is a special directory that is designated by the server software to allow the execution of CGI scripts only from specified directories, making the system more secure. Inline animations play immediately as opposed to downloaded animations, which result from a link to an MPEG of an animation.

The aim of this chapter is not only to teach you how to include animations in your Web pages but also to inspire you to experiment further with this idea. To start, there are a few items you need:

- Netscape Navigator 1.1 or later
- Access to a Web server (to modify pages and add scripts)
- Some knowledge of the UNIX operating system and PERL, a programming language used in UNIX

Chances are, if you've gotten this far in this book, you already possess at least the first two. Knowledge of UNIX and PERL is helpful, perhaps even essential, for a complete understanding of this chapter, but don't let the lack of that knowledge stop you. You might be surprised at how much you'll pick up just by following along with the examples. If you want to learn more about UNIX and PERL, pick up a copy of *Programming PERL* (O'Reilly and Associates).

The teaching part of this chapter is divided into three main sections.

- How Inline Animations Work
- A Five-Minute Guide
- An Advanced Guide

Feel free to skip to the second section, "A Five-Minute Guide," to start. You don't need to read the first section, "How Inline Animations Work," to get an animation going, but it's helpful to understand what's happening behind the scenes, so even if you skip ahead now, you'll probably be back to read it later.

 NOTE: You'll find examples of inline animations at
http://bakmes.colorado.edu/~bicanic/altindex.html,
http://www.batmanforever.com/, and
http://www. enterprise.net/iw/testpage.html.

An imaginative use of inline animations is shown in Figures 7-1 through 7-3 and can be seen on line at http://bakmes.colorado.edu/bicanic/testcat.html.

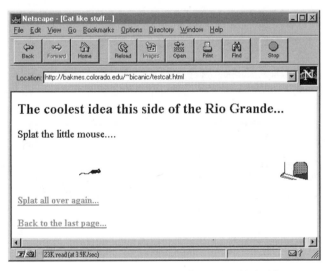

FIGURE 7-1   *A clever use of inline animations—Splat the Little Mouse— lets you try to splat the mouse as it scampers across the screen. The mouse is a server-push image map with links to the "splatted" and "missed" pages. If you click on the mouse before it gets to the mouse hole, you are taken to the "splatted" page, shown in Figure 7-3.*

FIGURE 7-2 If you score a near miss on the mouse, you get another try before it reaches the safety of the mouse hole.

FIGURE 7-3 If you "splat" the mouse, you see the consequences.

How Inline Animations Work

When you include a line in your HTML code something like the following, a browser will simply request this file from the appropriate server and try to display what is sent to it.

```
<IMG SRC="oggydoo.gif">
```

However, the server knows that it's supposed to send out files with .GIF extensions as binary data of the .GIF format. So it tells the browser what it's about to do by sending a header with the appropriate MIME type, which in this case looks like the following:

```
Content-Type: image/gif
```

Because an animation is merely a series of pictures that change quickly, you might assume that all you must do is get the server to send down a number of GIFs one after another. Although this is true, the trick is to get the browser to display each new GIF one after another instead of the old one repeatedly—in other words, you want the browser to animate the GIFs.

The easiest way to visualize this is to think about the GIFs appearing on top of one another. Fortunately, Netscape developed an experimental content type (type of data) that can be used for this very purpose. It looks like this:

```
Content-Type: multipart/x-mixed-replace
```

If the browser receives a header like this, it knows it must update whatever data it is sent next when it is told to do so. How does the browser know when one bit of data (in this case, one image) ends and another begins? How does it know when it must replace the old stuff with the new stuff? The boundary line, that's how. The full version of the line in our example should be:

```
Content-type: multipart/x-mixed-replace;boundary=sometext
```

Every time the browser receives the boundary line from the server, it knows that the next bit of data begins to overwrite the old bit of data. This is all there is to it.

Well, OK, there is a little more to it, but the script you will learn to use in the next two sections punches out the *multipart/x-mixed-replace* portion of the header in our example and then keeps sending GIFs, one after the other, with boundaries in between.

You set up a working animation as outlined in the following section.

TIP

SHOCKWAVE AND GIF89 OFFER ALTERNATIVE ROUTES TO WEB ANIMATION. SHOCK-WAVE FILES CAN BE QUITE LARGE AND SLOW TO DOWNLOAD. CURRENTLY GIF89 IS NOT SUPPORTED BY ALL MAINSTREAM BROWSERS.

A Five-Minute Guide

To create a simple inline animation, use the following steps. (This is where a knowledge of PERL is useful.)

You can write the script in any plain-text editor that does not insert special formatting characters, such as Microsoft Windows Notepad.

1. Enter this script:

```
#! /usr/bin/perl
#
# Nick Bicanic © 1995
# nick@never.com
#
$|=1;
print "HTTP/1.0 200 Okay\n";
print "Content-Type: multipart/x-mixed-replace;boundary=sometext\n";

print "\n--sometext\n";

open(imagelist,@ARGV[0]) || die "Cannot open @ARGV[0]: $!";
while (<imagelist>) {
        chop $_;
        print "Content-Type: image/gif\n";
        print "\n";
        open (sendgif, $_);
        print (<sendgif>);
        close sendgif;
        print "\n--sometext\n";
}
close(imagelist);
```

(You can download this script from http://bakmers.colorado.edu/~bicanic/nphmyanim.txt. Don't forget to rename it.)

2. After transferring the script to the cgi-bin directory on the server, make the script executable by entering the following from the command line in a Telnet session:

```
chmod 755 nph-animations.cgi
```

3. Make a simple series of GIFs. It could be any series, but for the sake of this example, we'll assume you drew a few pictures of a ball bouncing and you named them ball1.gif, ball2.gif, ball3.gif, and ball4.gif.

4. Save these images in the directory in which you saved the script.

5. Create a text file that lists the images in the order you want them to appear. For this example, create a text file named ball.txt that looks like this:

```
ball1.gif
ball2.gif
ball3.gif
ball4.gif
```

6. Save this text file in the directory in which the previous .GIF files and the script are saved.

7. Now all that remains is to put the animation into your page. For the sake of this example, create a simple page like this one:

```
<HTML>
<HEAD>
<TITLE>My first animation</TITLE>
</HEAD>
<BODY>
<H1>This ball is bouncing</H1>
<IMG SRC="nph-animations.cgi?ball.txt">
<H2>I am so proud of me...</H2>
</BODY>
</HTML>
```

When viewed, the page will show your bouncing ball animation. If it doesn't work the first time, check the rest of the chapter for common problems and their solutions.

An Advanced Guide

Before you read this section, I strongly recommend that you read both of the preceding sections. In any case, I'll talk you through the script presented here so that you know what is going on and where. With a little bit of luck and a little knowledge of PERL, you'll be writing your own scripts in no time. The first line looks like this:

```
#! /usr/bin/perl
```

If you're familiar with PERL, you know this line. This is the path of the PERL interpreter on your system. Forgetting to include this line is one of the common errors when trying to run this script and is one of many errors that are covered in greater detail later in this chapter. Now here are the next lines:

```
$!=1
print "HTTP/1.0 200 Okay\n"
print "Content-type: multipart/x-mixed-replace;boundary=sometext\n"
print "\n--sometext\n"
```

These lines are crucial. The first line unbuffers STDOUT (standard output file descriptor) and allows the output of the program to be sent directly to the browser with no delay. This approach makes for a smoother animation.

The next three lines are related to the nph (Non-Parsed Header) naming of a file. When you save a file as nph-something, the server knows that it's supposed to send the file as a non-parsed header file—meaning that it is up to the program to send all the relevant headers—in this case, the *multi-part/x-mixed-replace* header, which, as we already know, tells the browser to expect to replace a series of incoming items, one after another. The first line of the nph-naming process is this:

```
open (imagelist,@ARGV[0]) !! die "Cannot open @ARGV[0]:$!"
```

This line opens the file designated by the @ARGV[0] variable, which in PERL means the first argument to the script. That is why you reference the script in Web pages with this line:

```
nph-animations.cgi?ball.txt
```

In this case, the script will open the file ball.txt and extract information from it.

The rest of the script looks like this:

```
while(<imagelist>){
chop $_
print "Content-Type: image/gif\n"
print "\n"
```

```
open (sendgif,$_)
print (<sendgif>)
close sendgif
print "\n--sometext\n"
}
close (imagelist)
```

This loop takes each line from the argument file and prints out the contents to STDOUT. In plain English, it takes each GIF in turn and sends it to the browser.

That's all there is to it.

Problems

I hate to rain on your parade, especially when you are riding high on the euphoria of doing something new on the Web, but there are a few problems that you may encounter. Almost all have straightforward solutions.

The symptoms of the problems are obvious. You have followed the instructions set out in this chapter to the letter, but you don't see a little animation on the Web page. What you are likely to see is a broken image icon (the icon with the X in it).

Before trying to fix the problem, you need to determine what the problem actually is. There are two main ways of debugging this process:

- Run the program from the UNIX shell.

- Try to view the image directly in the browser.

It is more instructive to attempt to run the script from the shell simply because if it doesn't work perfectly there, it will not be coaxed into working when you try to access it from the Web.

So change to the directory where the script is saved, and type the following:

```
nph-animations.cgi ball.txt
```

This is an attempt to do the same thing that you tried to do in the demo HTML page except that the output is being directed to the screen instead of to the browser.

If you get an error immediately, it is highly likely that you have made one of two mistakes:

- You forgot to make the script executable.
- You are using the wrong PERL path.

To correct the first mistake, type the following:

```
chmod 755 nph-animations.cgi
```

For more information on what *chmod* does, use the *man chmod* command.

If you are using the wrong PERL path, the system cannot find the PERL interpreter at the location you are pointing to in the first line of the script. To find out where the PERL executable is on your system, do this:

```
which perl
```

Adjust the first line of the script accordingly. More often than not, PERL will be in one of these two paths:

```
/usr/bin/perl
/usr/local/bin/perl
```

If you do not get an error, the output you should expect is as follows:

```
HTTP/1.0 200 Okay
Content-type: multipart/x-mixed-replace;boundary=sometext
--sometext
Content-Type: image/gif
```

This will be followed by lots of binhex data (that is, a GIF image). Binhex is a format for representing a binary file using only printable characters (plain text) so that the characters can be stored on most computers and sent through most electronic mail systems.

After the first set of image data, the GIF headers repeat until the script reaches the end of the animation. If you are debugging a very long animation, there is little value in waiting for the entire process to finish. You are only trying to establish that the script is running properly.

If there is no problem at this stage, relax. The likelihood is that anything wrong can be fixed very easily.

The next step is working out why the animation was not seen from the Web. However, remember to try the animation from the Web every time you make a change. There's no point in fixing something if it "ain't broke" anymore.

 NOTE: All examples with URLs assume that the server you are using is www.dweeb.com and that all the standard NCSA defaults apply.

First, try to access only the script directly—that is, attempt to open the URL.

```
http://www.dweeb.com/~john/nph-animations.cgi
```

If the text of the script appears in the browser window, you have probably solved your problem already. Your server is not treating the file as a script. It has not been told to. The simplest way around this is to add the following line to your server's srm.conf file:

```
AddType application/x-httpd-cgi .cgi
```

When you restart the server, it will treat any file with a .cgi extension as a script. However, a lot of people do not run their own servers and will not have the ability to do this. Be sure you kill the current server process and then restart it. Otherwise, the configuration won't be picked up.

Alternative Solutions

Some alternative solutions to the common problems are as follows:

- Beg your Webmaster to change the files as described earlier in this chapter.
- Ask your Webmaster to include the script in the server's global cgi-bin.
- Ask your Webmaster to set up a cgi-bin in your home directory.

The first of these alternatives is the preferred one since it allows you to keep the path information as trivial as it was in the examples.

More Alternatives

A lot of people have accounts with Internet Service Providers who are nervous about letting just anyone put scripts in the cgi-bin because of the potential security risk. Let's go through a workaround for this situation too.

Even if you have access to a cgi-bin (either the global one or your personal one), you cannot just put all the files in there. Instead, you must give the script full information about where the text file is. Suppose you used a global cgi-bin that was in this directory:

```
/usr/local/bin/httpd/cgi-bin
```

This means that the full path of the script (by "full path" I mean exactly that—the full path on the host machine's directory structure) would be as follows:

```
/usr/local/bin/httpd/cgi-bin/nph-animations.cgi
```

Now let's suppose that the full path to the text file is as follows:

```
/usr/people/john/public_html/ball.txt
```

To call this script from the Web, you would merely need to use this command:

```
http://www.dweeb.com/cgi-bin/nph-animations.cgi?/usr/people/john/public_html/
ball.txt
```

Note that in this case (assuming the GIFs were in the same place as the text file) the file ball.txt would look like this:

```
/usr/ people/john/public_html/ball1.gif
/usr/ people/john/public_html/ball2.gif
/usr/ people/john/public_html/ball3.gif
/usr/ people/john/public_html/ball4.gif
```

You can also try to view the image directly. Just type the full URL path, which will look something like this:

```
http://www.dweeb.com/~john/nph-animations.cgi?ball.txt
```

You can often glean useful information from the browser itself in this way. For example, the demo HTML file will just show a broken image icon, but an animation viewed in this way would tell you the file was not found, and you would find out that you were pointing the browser to the wrong place.

By now, you are happily looking at a short animation and wondering how you ever got along without one. Hopefully, you are already concocting ways to make this even better. If not, read on, and you should find some inspiration.

Extra Tricks

Let's start with a few simple animation tricks.

The animation you have created is fundamentally part of an HTML <IMG> tag. It's dynamically updated, but it's essentially only an image. This means that anything that you can do to an ordinary image you can do to the animation. For example, you could make the animation a link. Going back to the previous example, the line with the <IMG> tag in it becomes the following:

```
<A HREF="otherfile.html"><IMG SRC="nph-animations.cgi?ball.txt"></A>
```

That was painless.

A similar change can make any animation a dynamic image map and change the size of the image. To change the size of an image, you specify the height and the width of the image as follows:

```
<IMG SRC="nph-animations.cgi?ball.txt" HEIGHT=200 WIDTH=400>
```

Although it may be tempting to double the size of the animation to save on download time, remember that some browsers cannot render big images quickly. Some experimentation is necessary with this technique to get the size vs. speed balance right.

So much for HTML-based tricks. The next few tricks involve changes to the script. The changes are not very complicated, but they are changes nonetheless.

Sometimes you might want to keep an animation going in a loop. This is easily accomplished.

Likewise, to introduce a delay between successive animation frames, just include the following line at the end of the loop:

```
select (undef,undef,undef,x);
```

where *x* is the delay in seconds.

If a browser other than Netscape Navigator comes across a Web page with an animation like the one you have just made, it will see only a broken image icon. It would be nice if you could find out which browser a person is using and behave accordingly. Well, you can, and it is a trivial matter of adding a few lines of code to the script.

The following version of the example script includes lines for looping the animation and for accommodating non-Netscape browsers:

```
# Nick Bicanic 1995
# nick@never.com
#
$single="nonnetscape.gif"
$|=1;
print "HTTP/1.0 200 Okay\n";
if ($browser =~ /^Mozilla/i){
        print "Content-Type: multipart/x-mixed-replace;boundary=sometext\n";
        print "\n--sometext\n";

for (;;) {
        open(imagelist,@ARGV[0]) || die "Cannot open @ARGV[0]: $!";
        while (<imagelist>) {
                chop $_;
                print "Content-Type: image/gif\n";
                print "\n";
                open (sendgif, $_);
                    print (<sendgif>);
                close sendgif;
                print "\n--sometext\n";
        }
         close(imagelist);
        select (undef,undef,undef,x);
      }

else {
        print "Content-Type: image/gif\n";
                print "\n";
                open (sendgif, $single);
                print (<sendgif>);
                close sendgif;
        end;
}
```

Line to accommodate non-Netscape browsers — `$single="nonnetscape.gif"`

Line to accommodate non-Netscape browsers — `if ($browser =~ /^Mozilla/i){`

Line to begin loop — `for (;;) {`

Line to end loop — `}`

Line to add time delay between loops — `select (undef,undef,undef,x);`

Beginning of lines to accommodate non-Netscape browsers — `}`

End of lines to accommodate non-Netscape browsers — `}`

TIP

THE MOUSE ANIMATION
DESCRIBED IN THIS CHAPTER
IS MADE UP OF NUMEROUS
LONG, NARROW TRANS-
PARENT GRAPHICS,
WITH THE MOUSE
IN A DIFFERENT
POSITION IN
EACH ONE.

Make the Animation a Link

To close this chapter, let's look at an interesting example of what you can do with this technique if you experiment a bit. Let's use the animation of the mouse running across the screen that you saw at the beginning of this chapter.

Specifically, let's look at how to make the animation interactive—when the user clicks on the mouse, the mouse "splats," but when the user misses it, the mouse keeps on running. You point the link of the animation to a script. (For the sake of this example, let's call it nph-cool.cgi.) This script (for the moment, don't worry about what it looks like) needs to know two things to determine whether the mouse was killed or not:

- The xy-coordinates of the user's click

- Where the mouse was at the time of the click

The first criterion can be easily satisfied by adding the ISMAP attribute to the <IMG> tag of the mouse animation (that is, an animated image map, like the one we mentioned earlier).

Remember that you still have not made any modifications to the animation script. You need to make only one small one—you must record the current frame number of the animation in a file so that at the very instant the user clicks somewhere, the xy-coordinates of the click are sent to nph-cool.cgi, and nph-cool.cgi can pick out the current frame number from the file. This is known as *keeping state*.

That's it. You can then set up simple criteria that determine whether the mouse lives or dies. If it dies, you can have nph-cool.cgi spit back the appropriate GIF showing the death. If it lives, you can have nph-cool.cgi restart the animation from the appropriate point. And there you have it— an interactive real-time animation on the Web.

Nick Bicanic graduated from Cambridge University with an honors degree in chemistry in July 1994. Since then, he has spent most of his time playing and working on line, with time out for watching 3-D animations on his SGI.

8. ACROBAT

A couple of years ago, just before the Web explosion, I was invited to an editors' luncheon at Comdex that was in reality a dog-and-pony show presented by John Warnock of Adobe. At a typical event like this, a vendor lures the trade press to a conference room in an upscale hotel with promises of free food and drink. Once the guests are inside and well fed, the vendor figuratively inserts funnels in the journalists' ears and pours in an hour or so worth of hype about the latest new software tool or widget. Being as susceptible as the next person to being wined and dined, I assented to Adobe's offer of food, wine, funnel, and hype. To my surprise, the new technology Mr. Warnock described—Acrobat—was actually quite interesting and promised to open up some neat possibilities for publishing.

Adobe got its money's worth from me out of that luncheon. Since then, I've written and sold at least seven articles about Acrobat. It's a neat tool—it's easy to use, it's simple, and it fills a real need. I was quite impressed at the time, and I remain impressed.

Will Acrobat and the Web help bring the vision of the paperless office closer to reality? As different operating systems and computer types proliferate, the problems of file incompatibility seem to grow larger, causing even more paper to flow. (Paper, after all, is the one nearly universal medium.) Although software vendors frequently promise compatibility, we the everyday users know differently. If you create a document in WordPerfect, save it as an ASCII file, and bring it into AmiPro, all your formatting will be gone. If you create a document in WordPerfect for Windows and bring it into WordPerfect for MS-DOS, you will have lost some formatting. How about reading those files on a Mac or a UNIX system? All your beautiful fonts, columns, and tabs are going to be trashed. Adobe's Acrobat goes a long way toward fixing these problems, making seamless file transfers across multiple computing platforms a real possibility.

What Acrobat Does

Basically, Acrobat lets you create a document with fancy fonts, colors, and graphics on a Mac, PC, or UNIX computer using any software that can print to a printer and save the document in a file that can be viewed in all its glory by any of these computers. Although not designed specifically with the Web in mind, Acrobat, with its sophisticated hyperlinking and searching capabilities, lends itself remarkably well to the Web environment and partially solves the problem of the design limitations that are currently a part of HTML.

How Acrobat Works

Using an Acrobat document on your Web site involves basically two steps:

1. Create a PDF (Acrobat format) file of the document you want to have appear lifelike.

2. Put a link in your Web page that points to it.

As I said, Acrobat is easy to use. To help you understand what's involved, let me add some detail to each of these two steps.

1. Create a PDF (Acrobat format) file of the document you want to have appear lifelike. For example, let's take a few pages from a magazine and link them together for the Web.

   - Install Acrobat Exchange on your PC, Mac, or UNIX computer.

   - Open up a fancy magazine layout that you've created in PageMaker, and print a few pages, each to a separate PDF file. For Web use, each page of a document should be a separate file that you link to the other pages with URLs, just as you do with any other HTML files.

   - Select PDF Writer as your printer instead of an actual printer.

   - Print the files.

   - The file will print to the disk or directory you tell it to. As an example, let's print three or four pages of the magazine layout to PDF files.

   - Put those files in the subdirectories in which you usually keep your HTML files for your Web site.

   - You now have PDF documents.

2. Create a link in an HTML page (for example, your home page) that points to the new PDF files. Adobe offers free use of a nifty little icon that can be used as the link that tips readers

off to the existence of the Acrobat files. Modern browsers should automatically launch the free Acrobat reader program when a reader selects one of these links. You can go through these PDF pages, adding URLs back and forth all over the place between the PDF pages or back to other pages on your Web site or anywhere on the Web, just as you do with any other URLs.

Printing to a PDF file is as easy as printing to your laser printer. Viewing the files with Reader or Microsoft Exchange is as simple as clicking on the program icon to start the viewer and clicking on the file name after browsing to find it. It always amazes me how nice the files look and how easily and quickly I can zoom in to read a page or move from page to page. Adding links between PDF pages is actually easier than adding links to regular HTML pages.

Although PDF files are usually larger than HTML files with similar content, you minimize file sizes in a variety of ways. There are several options for selecting levels and types of compression. Generally, the more compression, the less detail in the final file. You can, of course, be careful with use of color in your designs (to try to reduce the file size), but if you're going to do that, why bother with PDF at all? Actually, PDF should be used when the layout and the design of pages are of paramount importance or when you want to present documents already created with regular graphics design tools. If your organization is struggling with the idea of translating foreign language documents into Web documents, perhaps PDF could be an answer. Japanese and other double-bit languages can be nicely displayed using PDF files, but French can be too.

Annual reports are possible candidates for PDF treatment. You can take an annual report and add hyperlinks throughout it. You can spice it up and make it more useful in other ways as well. Acrobat lets you sprinkle little "sticky" notes throughout the report. Yellow is the default color, but you can make the notes different colors. Used conservatively, these sticky notes are a fine way to annotate documents.

Acrobat also has sophisticated search abilities. This search ability makes browsing a database of hundreds of PDF documents quite practical. You can index thick engineering reports and search them later—time-consuming tasks that normally a company simply can't afford to perform.

Adding Acrobat PDF files to your Web site is a great way to include fancy designs that you've created in a page-layout program. Acrobat is one more design tool that will compete in the emerging arena of Web design software.

You can download Adobe Acrobat software at http://www.adobe.com/Acrobat.

JAVA AND HOTJAVA
by Jack Ricard

In the final week of May 1995, Sun Microsystems released two essentially free products that may alter the very architecture of the Internet and specifically the World Wide Web in coming months: Java and HotJava.

Java is a new object-oriented programming language closely resembling C++ in both form and capabilities. It is designed to use a network (more specifically, the World Wide Web), and it looks like the most architecture-neutral method of developing new functions for the World Wide Web. It is optimized for creation of distributed executable applications.

HotJava is a World Wide Web browser that can execute "applets," programs written in Java and included, like images, in HTML pages. It is essentially a free browser that demonstrates the capabilities of Java.

Currently, alpha versions of the HotJava browser, the Java language, and more documentation than you can possibly read are already available, at no charge, for SPARC-based Solaris machines, and for Microsoft Windows 95/Windows NT. They are available from the Sun Java World Wide Web page at http://java.sun.com. Actually, the source for the Solaris version of the language is also available for download.

Sun describes Java as a simple, object-oriented, distributed, interpreted, robust, secure, architecture-neutral, portable, high-performance, multithreaded, and dynamic language. This amazing list might seem like just another collection of buzzwords, but Sun has actually defined what each means in some useful ways.

Simple

Sun wanted to build a system that could be programmed easily but that wouldn't require programmers to learn an entirely new, unfamiliar system. So they designed Java to look and act a lot like C++, which they felt was the most familiar object-oriented programming language. As a result, Java has "automatic garbage collection" (clearing of objects from memory when they are no longer needed), freeing the programmer from dealing with memory allocation issues. Sun also simply deleted some of the more troublesome virtues of C++ such as operator overloading and multiple inheritance.

Object-Oriented

Everything in software these days is object-oriented, but very few people have a clue what "object-oriented" means. It generally means reusable software modules written as general "devices" that perform certain operations on data. More generally, the software views data itself as an object with a certain interface to access it usefully. Once you write code to access the data through this interface, the code module becomes reusable on any similar data with a similar interface.

Distributed

Java has an extensive library of routines for coping easily with TCP/IP protocols such as HTTP and FTP. Java applications can open and access objects across the net via URLs with the same ease that programmers are accustomed to when they access a local file system.

Robust

"Robust" is a term frequently used to describe software that doesn't break easily. Sun has attempted to make Java robust by providing a large degree of compile-time error checking beyond what happens with C and C++ compilers. Most notably, Java has true arrays rather than pointers and pointer arithmetic, which is one of the leading causes of overwriting memory and corrupting data in C. Freeing the programmer from memory corruption concerns should lead to fewer errors.

Secure

Java is intended to be used in networked and distributed environments. To that end, a lot of emphasis has been placed on security. Java enables the construction of virus-free, tamper-free systems. The authentication techniques are based on public-key encryption. There is a strong interplay between "robust" and "secure." For example, the changes to the semantics of pointers make it impossible for applications to forge access to data structures or to access private data in objects that they have access to. This closes the door on most activities of viruses.

Architecture Neutral

One of the most important aspects of Java is that it is theoretically architecture neutral. Java was designed to support applications on networks. In general, networks are composed of a variety of systems with a variety of CPU and operating system architectures. To enable a Java application to execute anywhere on the network, the compiler generates an architecture-neutral object file format—a kind of pseudocode they call bytecode. This compiled code is executable on many processors, given the presence of the Java run-time system for that platform.

This is useful not only for networks but also for single-system software distribution. In the present personal computer market, application writers have to produce versions of their application that are compatible with the IBM PC and with the Apple Macintosh. With the PC market (through Windows NT) diversifying into many CPU architectures, and Apple moving off the Motorola 68000 microprocessor toward the PowerPC chip, the production of software that runs on all platforms becomes almost impossible. With Java, the same version of the application runs on all platforms.

The Java compiler does this by generating bytecode instructions, which have nothing to do with a particular computer architecture. Rather, they are designed to be both easy to interpret on any machine and easy to translate into native machine code on the fly. So the bytecode is distributed, and then it is interpreted and run by the Java run time, which is machine specific. Sun has even alluded to future bytecode compilers that can convert the bytecode object files to true executables with performance similar to C++.

Portable

Being architecture neutral is a big part of being portable, but there's more to it than that. Unlike C and C++, Java has no "implementation-dependent" aspects in its specification. The sizes of the primitive data types are specified, as is the behavior of arithmetic on them. For example, *int* always means a signed two's compliment 32-bit integer, and *float* always means a 32-bit IEEE 754 floating-point number. Making these choices is feasible in this day and age because the most widely used CPUs share these characteristics.

The libraries that are a part of the system define portable interfaces. For example, Java has an abstract Windows class and has implementations of it for UNIX and the Macintosh too. The Java system itself is quite portable. The new compiler is written in Java, and the run-time version is written in ANSI C, with a clean portability boundary. The portability boundary is essentially POSIX.

Interpreted

The Java interpreter can execute Java bytecodes directly on any machine to which the interpreter has been ported. The pseudocode generated by the compiler is transmitted over the network, and the actual interpreter specific to that machine runs the program. This again is the source of the architecture-neutral aspect of Java.

High-Performance

While the performance of interpreted bytecodes is usually more than adequate, there are situations in which higher performance is required. The bytecodes can be translated on the fly (at run time) into machine code for the particular CPU the application is running on. For those accustomed to the normal design of a compiler and dynamic loader, this is somewhat like putting the final machine code generator in the dynamic loader.

The bytecode format was designed with generating machine codes in mind, so the actual process of generating machine code is generally simple. Reasonably good code is produced: it does automatic register allocation, and the compiler does some optimization when it produces the bytecodes.

Using interpreted code, Sun gets some 300,000 method calls per second on a Sun Microsystems SPARCStation 10. The performance of bytecodes converted to machine code is almost indistinguishable from native C or C++.

Multithreaded

Many things go on at the same time in the world around us—the same is true in a networked world. Multithreading is a way of building applications that handle multiple tasks and appear to do so simultaneously. Unfortunately, writing programs that deal with many things happening at once can be much more difficult than writing in the conventional single-threaded C and C++ style.

Java has a sophisticated set of synchronization primitives that are based on the widely used "monitor and condition variable" paradigm that was introduced by C.A.R. Hoare. Much of the style of this integration came from Xerox's Cedar/Mesa system. By integrating these concepts into the language, Java becomes much easier to use and more robust.

Multithreading also means better interactive responsiveness and real-time behavior. This is limited, however, by the underlying platform: stand-alone Java run-time environments have good real-time behavior. Running on top of another system such as UNIX, Windows, the Macintosh, or Windows NT limits the real-time responsiveness to that of the underlying system.

Dynamic

In a number of ways, Java is a more dynamic language than C or C++. It was designed to adapt to an evolving environment. For example, one major problem with using C++ in a production environment is a side effect of the way that code is always implemented. If company A produces a class library (a library of plug-and-play components) and company B buys it and uses it in their product, and A changes its library and distributes a new release, B will almost certainly have to recompile and redistribute their own software. In an environment where the end user gets A's and B's software independently (for example, where A is an OS vendor and B is an application vendor), problems can result.

If A distributes an upgrade to its libraries, all of the software from B will break. It is possible to avoid this problem in C++, but it is extraordinarily difficult and it effectively means not using any of the language's object-oriented features directly.

By making these interconnections between modules later, Java completely avoids these problems and makes use of the object-oriented paradigm in a much more straightforward way. Libraries can freely add new methods and instance variables without any effect on their clients.

So How Does This Change the Web?

The World Wide Web is designed as a hypertext system for presenting documents. On line, we want to do many things, and not all of them really are documents, nor do they lend themselves to this document model.

Web browsers are instead focused on allowing you to view documents, and they are already somewhat extensible. You can add programs to a browser. These "helper" applications all work out of the browser. If the browser receives a file from the Web server with a certain filename convention—for example, an .MPG file—the browser can detect it and will recognize that it doesn't know how to present an .MPG file on screen. But you can associate an MPEG viewer with the .MPG filename extension. When the browser receives the file, it calls the MPEG viewer program and passes it the filename. This helper application then pops up on the screen and displays the movie received in the MPEG file format.

But because the Web is entirely focused on passing documents and viewing them, it can be awkward to present a file in an unusual format—for example, a Still Picture Bumbling Novice Group (SPBNG) standard—when no one has a viewer for SPBNG files. Imagine being able to present the file and the SPBNG viewer all in the same document and have the browser download the viewer, unpack it, install it, configure it for your system, and display the SPBNG file. This is essentially what Java does.

Sun has proposed an extension to HTML that is a new tag titled APP. All text between <APP> and </APP> would be the pseudocode for a software program or "application." The code would actually be the Java bytecode. I suppose in theory this could even be extended to handle other types of code, but for the moment, let's follow along with Java.

This all assumes that you as a developer or online service operator have the Java compiler to produce the bytecode. It further assumes that everyone has a browser with a Java run-time interpreter built into it. If those two things were true, you could write new servers using whatever language you like, such as Visual Basic. You could also write a client to access the server in Java.

Thereafter, anyone who accessed your Web page would receive the code between the APP tags, and the Java interpreter would immediately run it as a client. The client could then "talk" to your server over the Internet and do whatever you had designed it to do. That could be almost anything.

Let's say you operate a Web page and you want to display to anyone who contacts your system the current stock price of all stocks related to green beans. You simply write an "applet" in Java that creates a window on the screen, receives data from your server, and scrolls it across the window in ticker-tape fashion.

Or let's say you want to run a real-time chat server, but you don't want to run an IRC site, you don't want users to access your BBS with Telnet, and you want your server to do something no one else does: randomly insert some expletive or rude comment after every fourth word typed by a user. You also want to display each character as it is typed, which none of the Web functions can do. You would simply write an applet in Java, include it on a page on your Web server so that anyone paying your $400 fee can access that page, receive the applet, and start into a journey of confusion and hard feelings.

The key is that no one has to have your client before they come to the party. They get it automatically as a side effect of accessing your Web page. When they leave, they can throw the client away. It will be there, and probably in an updated form, when they come back.

I thought this looked a bit wasteful when I first pictured it. But in a world in which graphic images often run 60 or 80 KB in size, and MPEG movies are measured in megabytes, it becomes trivial. With most of the networking in the interpreter, not the code, the programs will likely be very small.

We're not talking just about document viewers, although that could probably be done as well for our fictitious SPBNG files. Java essentially allows you to modify the protocol itself. It opens the door to an infinite number of server variations done as CGI scripts or some other technique because you can develop both the server and the client with the assurance that everyone who visits has the client in its latest release form. Essentially, this presents the possibility of an endlessly extensible World Wide Web with no consideration of the usual issues of deploying the client software to end users.

The protocols that Internet hosts use to communicate among themselves are key components of the net. For the World Wide Web, the hypertext transmission protocol (HTTP) is the most important of these communication protocols. In documents on the Web, a Uniform Resource Locator (URL) contains the name of a protocol—HTTP for example—that is used to find that document. Current Web browsers have the knowledge of HTTP built in. HotJava, rather than having built-in protocol handlers, uses the protocol name to link to the appropriate handler. This allows new protocols to be incorporated dynamically.

The dynamic incorporation of protocols has special significance for how business is done on the Internet. Many vendors are providing new Web browsers and servers with added capabilities such as billing and security. These capabilities most often take the form of new protocols. Each vendor tends to implement something unique—a new style of security, for example—and sells a server and a browser that speak this new protocol. If a user wants to access data on multiple servers, each having a proprietary new protocol, the user needs multiple browsers. Needing several browsers is clumsy and defeats the synergistic cooperation that makes the WWW work.

With HotJava as a base, vendors can produce and sell exactly the piece that is their added value to what exists and can integrate it smoothly with the products of other vendors. This seamless integration creates a final result that is convenient for the end user.

Protocol handlers are installed in a sequence similar to the way content handlers are installed. HotJava is given a reference to an object (a URL). If the handler for that protocol is already loaded, that handler is used. If it is not loaded, HotJava searches for it, first on the local system and then on the system that is the target of the URL.

Java has a number of minor features that I've found interesting. Most notable is that the *char* function does not use American Standard Code for Information Interchange (ASCII). ASCII has been the lingua franca for associating the alphabet with the numerics used by computers approximately forever, and a good deal of ASCII is so old that it refers to bells, line feeds, and other elements originally used on teletype machines. A total of 256 symbols can be represented in the 8-bit world of ASCII.

Java does not use ASCII. It uses Unicode. Unicode has been around for several years as a proposed 16-bit code that supports some 64,000 characters. Why do we need 64,000 characters? Well, if we want to represent 10,000 or so Chinese characters, it will help. Japanese, Cyrillic, Arabic, and other languages with a large number of characters also could be represented in more or less 64,000 characters. Unicode has an International Standards Organization (ISO) implementation. It just doesn't have much showing up in software.

Java's weak area is that you allow anyone in the universe to compile a program, put it on their Web site, and when you access the site your system automatically retrieves the program and runs it. To some users, this doesn't sound good. Sun insists that Java has tons of security features that make the writing of virus programs very nearly impossible. It doesn't have to be a virus to scare me a bit. The BBS community suffered from Trojan Horse programs more than it ever did viruses. If the program can erase CONFIG.SYS, it's a problem. And if it can't, the language has pretty limited utility.

There are a couple of interesting elements to Java. You can write programs that can't access the net at all, you can write programs to freely access the net, or you can write a program that accesses ONLY the site from which it was downloaded. You might conceivably write the next netwide killer application in Java. Or you might prefer that the program access ONLY your own site and be essentially useless for anyone else's. It's a Java thing.

The key elements to success for Java are, of course, the relatively universal availability of the Java interpreter. This received a big boost when Netscape Communications announced that they had agreed to license the Java technology from Sun and incorporate it in the next release of the Netscape Web browser. Netscape is already available for UNIX, Windows, Windows NT, and the Macintosh.

Sun is approaching the entire Web function with a remarkable spirit of generosity in many ways. Sun is allowing free downloads of the HotJava browser and Java compiler for Solaris and Windows NT, essentially as a product to demonstrate the use of Java. But they've also made source code for Java itself freely available. Sun retains all rights to the products, but they've been remarkably generous in allowing everyone to use them in an attempt to gain universal acceptance. We need universal acceptance of something, so we should wish them well. I've found that http://java.sun.com/documentation.html provides good information on Java.

Jack Ricard is Publisher and Editor-in-Chief of Boardwatch Magazine.

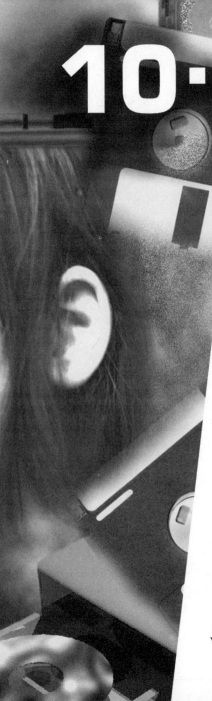

CGI PROGRAMS
by Kief Morris

The prospect of creating CGI programs might strike fear into the hearts of brave Web page designers, but CGI programs are just too useful to ignore. CGI not only lets you collect data from your forms, it can bring your Web site to life, making it truly interactive.

What CGI Programs Are

CGI (Common Gateway Interface) is a specification for programs that a user can run on the World Wide Web. Although many people think they're exotic, CGI programs aren't very different from other programs except that they are run on the server instead of on the user's computer. The big difference is that their input and output come from and go to Web browsers, but even that doesn't make them particularly special.

CGI is not a language; it's a standard for how a Web server interacts with your programs. Contrary to popular belief, you don't have to write CGI programs in PERL. PERL is popular with CGI programmers because it's well suited to the things CGI programs typically do, and the programs can easily be run on different types of systems.

In fact, you don't need to know how to write your own CGI programs to use one. All you need to know is how to use someone else's CGI program, and there are many available. You can find the CGI specification at http://hoohoo.ncsa.uiuc.edu/cgi/. You'll find pointers to CGI references and useful programs at http://www.stars.com/seminars/cgi.

How CGI Programs Work

Web users can start a CGI program the same way they view an HTML page—by clicking on a link that points to the program or by typing the URL in the browser. The URL might include extra information, or parameters, after the name of the program. The browser uses the CGI program's URL to contact the Web server where the program is installed, and the server runs it.

How to Install a CGI Program

There are three steps for setting up a CGI program to run at your site:

1. Make sure the program can run on your Web site.

2. Put it in the proper directory, with a .cgi extension if necessary.

3. Set the proper permissions on the program and associated files.

Make Sure the Program Can Run on Your Web Site

Programs come in two flavors—compiled binary programs and interpreted scripts. Compiled programs have to be compiled especially for the particular type of computer and operating system they'll run on. In the world of PCs and Macs, programs are commonly distributed already compiled, but programs intended to run on UNIX systems are usually distributed as source code, which you have to compile yourself.

If you need to compile a UNIX program, chances are the program comes with a Makefile. With a Makefile, you put all the files associated with the program in a directory and then type *make* at the system prompt. If the program doesn't compile successfully, you need to debug it (figure out how to make it work) or find someone who can. Programs written for UNIX sometimes will compile on Windows or Mac systems, but more often they require some modification.

Interpreted CGI scripts for UNIX are usually written in PERL, or sometimes as shell scripts. The bad news is that these programs require that the Web server have support for the PERL language installed. The good news is that almost every UNIX system, especially the ones set up as Web servers, will have it installed already. PERL and shell script interpreters are available for PCs and Macs. Mac and Windows systems have their own interpreted script languages—Hypercard and Visual Basic respectively—which you can use for CGI if the server software supports them.

Make Sure It's in the Proper Directory—the cgi-bin Directory

Web servers won't let Web users run just any program on their systems—that would be a major security hazard. So your system administrator configures the Web server to run only CGI programs that are located in certain directories, generally called the cgi-bin directory. Different system administrators have different policies about this—some allow each user with a Web page to have a personal cgi-bin directory as part of the base fee, others charge extra for the privilege, and some won't allow it at all.

If you don't have a cgi-bin directory set up already, contact your system administrator to find out whether you can get one. If you are your own system administrator, take a look in your Web server's documentation to figure out how to set it up. While you're talking to your system administrator or reading the documentation, find out whether your programs need to have a special extension, such as .cgi, to work.

Make Sure the CGI Programs and Permissions Are Set Correctly

Operating systems with security built in introduce a few extra things to worry about. These systems restrict which users on the system can run, read, or write to each file. You might test a CGI program by running it from the command line but find that it doesn't work when you run it from a browser. Most likely, the server software doesn't have permission to execute the program.

On UNIX systems, Web servers usually run as a user named "nobody." Because your CGI program is actually run by the server software, you need to make sure "nobody" can run the program. (Okay, this sounds odd, but it means you have to make sure that everybody can run it, that the file is world executable.) The command to do this is chmod 755 <filename>. If your system is Windows NT, check your server's documentation to find out the name of the user the Web server runs as, and then make sure your CGI program file can be executed by that user.

TIP

IF YOU'VE WRITTEN A SCRIPT AND YOU DON'T WANT OTHER USERS ON YOUR UNIX SYSTEM TO BE ABLE TO READ OR COPY IT, YOU CAN SET THE WORLD AND GROUP READ PERMISSIONS OFF BY USING THE COMMAND CHMOD 711 <FILENAME>.

How to Write a CGI Program

Many people who are starting out to write a CGI program think they'll need to learn a new programming language and its associated techniques. In fact, if you know how to program in a language supported by the system you want to run the CGI program on, you already know most of what you need to know.

The Server and Your CGI Program

How you write a CGI program is determined by the way your server feeds information to the program. Most servers follow a standard way of doing this, but some, especially Windows and Mac servers, might vary some of the details, so it's a good idea to check the CGI documentation for your server.

Servers pass information to CGI programs in one of two ways: they put the information in environment variables, or they send the information to your standard input so that you can read it with the same commands and function calls you use for reading keyboard input. On the following page is a list of the standard environment variables set by Web servers.

Standard Environment Variables

VARIABLE NAME	CONTENTS
SERVER_SOFTWARE	The name and version of the Web server software answering the request. Format: name/version.
SERVER_NAME	The server's host name, Domain Name Server (DNS) alias, or Internet Protocol (IP) address. This can be handy for scripts that need to call themselves again. (This type of script is called self referencing.)
GATEWAY_INTERFACE	The version of the CGI specification to which this server complies. This book covers version 1.1. Format: CGI/version.
SERVER_PROTOCOL	The name and revision of the information protocol this request came in with. Usually HTTP/1.0. Format: protocol/revision.
SERVER_PORT	The Web server port number to which the request was sent.
REQUEST_METHOD	The method by which the request was made, generally either GET or POST. This is handy for scripts that handle form data because it lets you figure out how to get the data.
PATH_INFO	The extra path information, as given by the client. In other words, scripts can be accessed by their virtual pathname, followed by extra information at the end of this path. The extra information is sent as PATH_INFO. For example, if a script named myscript were called as http://www.mysite.com/myscript/mypath/extrainfo.html, this field would contain mypath/extrainfo.html.
PATH_TRANSLATED	The path from PATH_INFO, translated to your local file system. In the previous example, extra information might be translated to /httpd/htdocs/mypath/extrainfo.html. This is often used for CGI programs that process a Web page and pass it on to the user.
SCRIPT_NAME	The path part of the URL that is used to access your CGI program. You can combine this with SERVER_NAME to figure out which URL you use to call your own program again—a self-referencing URL.
QUERY_STRING	The information that follows the ? in the URL that referenced this script, or form data passed using the GET method. This information will be in URL encoded format, so you'll have to decode it yourself. See the section titled "Decoding Your Data" later in this chapter for information on decoding.

TIP

NOTE THAT THE CGI PROGRAMS YOU USE DON'T HAVE TO BE LOCATED ON THE SAME SYSTEM AS YOUR HTML PAGES. IF YOU CAN'T USE CGI AT YOUR SITE BUT YOU KNOW SOMEONE WHO CAN SET THEM UP FOR YOU, YOU CAN HAVE LINKS IN YOUR HTML PAGES POINT TO THE CGI PROGRAMS WHEREVER THEY ARE ON THE WEB.

(continued)

VARIABLE NAME	CONTENTS
REMOTE_HOST	The name of the host where the browser making the request is running. If the server does not have this information, it will set REMOTE_ADDR and leave this variable unset.
REMOTE_ADDR	The IP address of the user's computer.
AUTH_TYPE	If the server supports user authentication and the script is protected, this is the protocol-specific authentication method used to validate the user.
REMOTE_USER	If the server supports user authentication and the script is protected, this is the user name by which the user has been authenticated.
REMOTE_IDENT	If the HTTP server supports RFC 931 identification, this variable will be set to the remote user name retrieved from the server. Most servers don't do this, so don't count on being able to use it.
CONTENT_TYPE	For queries that have attached information, such as HTTP POST and PUT, this is the MIME content type of the data. Format (usually): application/x-www-form-urlencoded.
CONTENT_LENGTH	The length of the content according to the client.

In addition to these standard variables, browsers might send to the server header lines that will be set as environment variables named HTTP_<header name>. Two common HTTP_ variables are given in the following table.

VARIABLE NAME	CONTENTS
HTTP_ACCEPT	The MIME types that the browser can handle, separated by commas. Format: type/subtype, type/subtype.
HTTP_USER_AGENT	The browser you're talking to. General format: software/version library/ version. For example, my copy of Netscape Navigator sets this to Mozilla/ 3.0b3(Win95;I).

How you read environment variables depends on the language and system you're using. The following is a PERL script that reads all the environment variables and shows them to the user. This script is handy for finding out what these fields look like with your particular server and browser.

```perl
#!/usr/local/bin/perl
# showenv.cgi - Show environment variables set by the server

print "Content-type: text/html\n\n";
print "<HTML><HEAD><TITLE>Environment Variables</TITLE></HEAD><BODY>";
print "<H2>Environment variables:</H2>";
print "<HR>\n";
foreach $evar( keys( %ENV ) ){
        print "<B>$evar:</B> $ENV{$evar}<BR>";
}
print "</BODY></HTML>\n";
```

Accepting and Decoding Form Data

If your script is called from a form that uses METHOD=GET in the <FORM> tag, the form data will be in the QUERY_STRING field. If it uses METHOD=POST, the data will be sent to your standard input. Because most systems have a limit on how long an environment variable's data can be, the GET method is generally a bad way to go because you may lose data. If you aren't sure which method will be used, it's a good idea to test the REQUEST_METHOD variable and act accordingly.

Accepting the data from standard input is pretty easy, but there's one trick. You might think you would receive an end-of-file (EOF) marker when the server has sent you all of the data, but you won't. If you write a program using the typical while($input_line = <STDIN>) loop, the program will hang when you call it with your browser. The trick is to check the amount of data you've read against the CONTENT_LENGTH variable so that you'll know when you're done. In C, you can actually use malloc() to create a buffer of exactly the right size and inhale the data with a single read() call.

TIP

THE "FORBIDDEN" MESSAGE ALMOST ALWAYS MEANS YOU HAVEN'T MADE THE CGI PROGRAM EXECUTABLE BY THE SERVER.

Decoding Your Data

Whether you get your data from a query string or from standard input, the data isn't ready to go yet. As you'll recall from form design, each of your input items has a NAME tag. When your CGI program receives the data, it is in a series of NAME=VALUE strings, each separated by an "&". The NAME is whatever name you gave to the field, and the VALUE is whatever the user entered in the field. So your first step is to break the data up into these pairs, with something like this:

```
@datafields = split( "/&/", $input_data );
```

(If you aren't a PERL programmer, you can probably see by this why PERL is so popular with CGI programmers! To do the same thing in another programming language normally takes much more code.)

The data probably isn't in a usable form yet. The data handed to you in the query string or standard input is in a format called URL-encoded, although the encoding is pretty simple. It is mainly used to escape certain characters that have special meanings in URLs.

You have two concerns in the decoding process. First, the spaces have turned into plus signs. Second, some characters are now in hexadecimal notation. The first concern is simple to handle—replace any plus sign you find with a space. (Actual plus signs will be encoded in hexadecimal.)

```
$data_field =~ s/\+/ /g;
```

The second concern is only a little trickier. Characters in hexadecimal notation are in the format %xx, where the x's are hexadecimal digits. Look for percent signs, take the next two characters, find the character that those two characters represent in ASCII, and replace the percent sign and the next two characters with the ASCII character.

```
$data_field =~ s/%(..)/pack("c", hex($1))/ge;
```

It might seem more efficient to do the URL decoding on all of the data before splitting it up, rather than splitting it first and then decoding each data field one at a time, but it's not a good idea. If the input includes an "&" character, it will have been encoded as "%26", and decoding it back to "&" before splitting the data fields will cause you to split it incorrectly. Replacing the pluses with spaces before the splitting, however, is safe and efficient.

Writing Output

After you have the data that the browser and server give you, you can use it in any way you like without concern that your program is CGI. When it comes time to generate your output, however (including error messages), you have a few considerations.

The Content Type

Anything you print to standard output goes to the browser. However, Web browsers expect to be told what they're getting before you send it to them so that they know how to display it. As a result, the first output in a CGI program must be "Content-type:" and then the MIME content type, followed by two newline characters. DON'T FORGET THIS! If you read newsgroups for CGI programmers, you'll quickly see that this is one of the most common mistakes new CGI programmers make. You must print the content type first, and then you must use two newline characters. Otherwise, your program won't work. The content type you'll almost always use is "text/html", so the line at the top of a PERL CGI program is this:

```
print "Content-type: text/html\n\n";
```

Some other useful content types include:

- text/plain—Non-HTML text

- image/gif—GIF file

- image/jpeg—JPEG file

- audio/x-wav—Windows WAV file

- audio/basic—Raw audio (.au) file

TIP

To send a user a file that is available on the Web (such as a graphic), send the line "Location:<URL>" where <URL> is the URL for the file.

As you may have guessed, this means you can send image or audio files to the user instead of text. To do this, simply print the appropriate content-type line, and then read the file and write its contents to standard output. Keep in mind that you can't send more than one file in the same program unless you use server push.

This technique can be used in clever ways. For example, people have implemented access counters to put an image tag in an HTML document that actually references a CGI program. The program increments the number of accesses stored in a file on disk and then returns a GIF that it builds on the fly to show the number of hits. Libraries exist for building GIFs.

Printing the Output

Normally you'll print text, although you'll probably want to dress it up with HTML code. You just print strings with the appropriate HTML, as we did with the code that prints environment variables.

Reading and Writing Files

If your CGI program needs to read other files, write other files, or both read and write other files on the system, you have a few extra considerations. It's common for a CGI programmer to write and test a CGI program that runs properly on the command line but that doesn't work properly when run from a browser. In avoiding this, you have to keep in mind that your CGI program is being run by the server software, and what that means.

First, you shouldn't assume that your program's working directory will be the directory in which it's located. You need to specify the full path of any file you access, rather than specifying just the name. For instance, if you want to write to a log file in the directory where your program is located, you shouldn't open myprog.log. Instead you should specify the whole path, such as /homes/myname/www-home/cgi-bin/myprog.log.

Another consideration is that on systems such as UNIX and Windows NT, the Web server may be running as a user who doesn't have permission to read or write the same files that you do. With the log file example, chances are that the file is owned by you, and only you have permission to write to it. For your CGI program to be able to write to it, you'll need to set the log file's permissions to let anyone write to it, although this obviously has its own dangers. The same factors have to be considered for files your program needs to read.

When the server runs your CGI program, it won't necessarily have the same environment you do when you run the program. The most likely example is the path. If your CGI program runs another program, it's a good idea to specify the full path to the program file rather than the name alone. Just because the program is in your path doesn't mean it will be in the server's.

TIP

DON'T LEAVE SOURCE CODE OR MAKEFILES IN YOUR CGI-BIN OR OTHER WEB-ACCESSIBLE DIRECTORY. BAD GUYS CAN GUESS THEIR NAMES AND DOWNLOAD THEM, LOOKING FOR SECURITY HOLES TO EXPLOIT.

Server Push

As I mentioned earlier in this chapter, CGI programs can send only one data file as output to the browser—an HTML file, a GIF, a sound file, or some other file. I lied. The truth is, you can send only one data file unless the browser you're talking to supports server push. If you want to be sure, check the HTTP_USER_AGENT field and use server push only if it shows Mozilla 1.1 or later.

The key to server push is the Content-type field. Netscape has proposed a new content type named "multipart/x-mixed-replace." The "x-" means it hasn't been accepted as an official standard yet, so other browsers don't necessarily support it. When you send Netscape Navigator a content type of multipart/x-mixed-replace, it knows that you're going to send multiple documents. As you send each new document, Netscape Navigator will clear the old one and show the new one.

There is no limit to how many documents you can send, or how long you must wait between sending them. The server push will stop only when your program stops, when the user clicks the Stop button, or when something unexpected happens to the connection. Keep in mind, however, that you're using up server resources. A server can serve only so many clients at one time. If your server push program is popular, it could tie up the server.

The syntax of what you send to the browser for a server-pushed set of documents looks like this:

```
------------------------
Content-type: multipart/x-mixed-replace; boundary=***unique-boundary***
***unique-boundary***
Content-type: text/html
Some text
***unique-boundary***
Content-type: text/html
some other text
***unique-boundary***
Content-type: text/html
yet more text
***unique-boundary***
------------------------
```

The boundary field signals the end of the data block you're sending. It can be pretty much any string that doesn't show up in any of the data you send. If it does, the browser will think it has reached the end of a block. When you send the browser a new Content-type, it will clear the previous data block from the user's viewer and start showing the next one.

This technique can be used to make animations or to continually update the user on information that changes from moment to moment.

Security Issues

TIP

WATCH OUT FOR BACK-UP FILES (FOR EXAMPLE, MYPROG.CGI~) THAT SOME EDITOR PROGRAMS LEAVE AROUND.

Since anybody with Web access can run your CGI program, you have to be careful not to open up any holes that will let malicious users or careless errors wreak havoc on your Web site. The main issue is that any data that users submit must be handled carefully before being used to run programs or access files. Clever users can pass to your script data that contains characters with special meaning to your system, thus directing the script to run only commands they want.

Even deciding to display a file passed in the PATH_INFO field can be dangerous. A clever user can add a few "../../" characters at the start of a path and start browsing your files unless you strip them out before opening the file. If you run programs, especially using a shell, and pass them user-supplied data as arguments, the user can slip in a semicolon and start running whatever commands they like on your system.

If you don't understand these and other situations, make sure you do before you write CGI programs and allow the world to run them.

Sample Form Data Mailer

The following sample program, f2mail.cgi, is a generic form data mailer. Install f2mail.cgi in your CGI directory, and set the action URL of any form to the URL of the program. When a user fills out the form and submits it, f2mail decodes the data and mails it to the email address given by the $mailto variable.

I find that having the data mailed to me, perhaps filtered and added to a database automatically, is easier than worrying about how to get a CGI program to write to a file on a UNIX system.

This program assumes it's being run on a UNIX system with sendmail. It should be easy to modify for other systems. The important thing is that it demonstrates how to retrieve and decode data, and how to print output to the user.

```perl
#!/usr/local/bin/perl
# f2mail.cgi--mail the data from a form to yourself.

# Who to mail the form data to, and the full path to the
# mail program to use. The full path is necessary to make
# sure the correct program is used, and for security.

$mailto = "you@email.address";
$mailprog = "/usr/lib/sendmail -i -t";

# The get_data function gets and decodes the form data -
# we'll see how it works later.

%datafields = &get_data;
```

```
# Start the mail program. This is a crucial security spot -
# if we were passing it data we had gotten from the user
# (for instance, if we were going to send the mail to them)
# we would have to be careful to check the $mailto variable
# for dangerous characters.

open ( SENDMAIL, "|$mailprog $mailto" ) ||
    &error_page( "Couldn't run mail program" );

# Print the header fields of the mail message.
# We could put other headers in if we wanted.

select( SENDMAIL );
print "To: $mailto\n";
print "Subject: f2Mail Form\n\n";

print "FORM DATA:\n";
print "***********************************\n";
foreach $field( keys( %datafields ) )
{
    print "$field:\t$datafields{$field}\n";
}
print "***********************************\r\n";
close( SENDMAIL );

# We have sent the mail message. We will now send an
# HTML page to the user, so they know we got their
# form. html_header is a handy function to start off
# an HTML page, and html_footer finishes it up.

select( STDOUT );
&html_header( "Form Submitted" );
print "<HR>\n";
print "<H2 ALIGN=\"CENTER\">Your form has been submitted. Thank you.</H2>\n";
&html_footer;

# ERROR_PAGE
# This function prints an error message for the browser user
```

(continued)

```
# to read. You pass it the error message to print in the
# body of the page.

sub error_page
{
    select( STDOUT );
    &html_header( "Forms2Mail Error" );
    print "<HR><H2 ALIGN=\"CENTER\">$_[0]</H2>\n";
    &html_footer;
}

# HTML_HEADER
# Start an HTML page. You pass it a string to use as the title.

sub html_header
{
    local( $title ) = $_[0];
    print( "Content-type: text/html\n\n" );
    print( "<HTML><HEAD><TITLE>$title</TITLE><HEAD>\n" );
    print( "<BODY>\n" );
    print( "<H1 ALIGN=\"CENTER\">$title</H1>\n" );
}

# HTML_FOOTER
# Finish an HTML page.

sub html_footer
{
    print( "<HR>\n" );
    print( "<H4 ALIGN=\"CENTER\">" );
    print( "<A HREF=\"mailto:$mailto\">$mailto</A></H4>" );
    print( "</BODY></HTML>\n" );
}

# GET_DATA
# Retrieves the data submitted to the CGI program, whether
# it's GET or PUSH. It returns an associative array of
# NAME, VALUE pairs.

sub get_data
```

```
{
  local ($index, $key, $val, $data, @data, %data);

  # Get the form data by whichever method it was passed.

  if ( $ENV{'REQUEST_METHOD'} eq "GET" ){
    $data = $ENV{'QUERY_STRING'};
  }
  elsif ($ENV{'REQUEST_METHOD'} eq "POST"){
    # We need to read exactly the amount of data that is
    # there, since we won't get an EOF.
    read(STDIN, $data, $ENV{'CONTENT_LENGTH'} );
  }

  # Convert pluses to spaces, and then split the fields.
  $index =~ s/\+/ /g;
  @data = split( /&/, $data);

  # Decode each field.
  foreach $index ( @data )
  {
    # Split into key and value.
    ($key, $val) = split(/=/, $index, 2);

    # Convert hex numbers to alphanumeric.
    $key =~ s/%(..)/pack("c",hex($1))/ge;
    $val =~ s/%(..)/pack("c",hex($1))/ge;

    # Associate key and value.
    $data{$key} .= "\0" if (defined($data{$key}));
    $data{$key} .= $val;
  }

  return %data;
}
```

Kief Morris is a system administrator, a webmaster, and a graduate student at the University of Tennessee's computer science department.

11· FRAMES

One of the most interesting and useful HTML features is frames. Frames, even more than tables, let you organize and present information on a Web page so that the information is more accessible and useful to your readers. Frames let you design a user interface and organize where your data appears on the browser's screen.

Because frames are fairly new, some users might find them unfamiliar and have trouble getting around in a site that uses a lot of frames.

No doubt some page designers have overused frames. As is the case with any new HTML technique, the tendency to overuse is hard to avoid. But the navigational benefits can outweigh the navigational weirdness if frames are used carefully and appropriately.

What Is a Frame?

In one sense, a *frame* is just what it sounds like it would be: the frame around a picture, a window, or a page. By adding a frame with the <FRAME> tag, the HTML page designer can block off an area of the browser screen to be separate from other parts of the screen. As a result, a person browsing the screen can scroll the frame separately from the rest of the page. In fact, a browser that recognizes frames can load a different page in each section, or *frame,* of the screen. For instance, you can set up a page so that an ad banner is fixed at the top of the screen while the rest of the page can scroll as usual. You can set up navigational buttons on the side of the screen that are fixed and don't move when a reader clicks on them so that part of the screen changes while the navigational bars remain the same, as shown in Figure 11-1.

One way to help readers who are unfamiliar with frames is to add navigational buttons or links horizontally *and* vertically. In Figure 11-1, the navigational features in the left frame help readers move around the entire Web site, and navigational features in the top frame help readers navigate around the frame itself. This means viewers don't have to use the right mouse button to go backward or forward in the frame. Viewers new to frames might find this feature a lifesaver.

FIGURE 11-1

You can use the <FRAME> tag to set up separate, independent areas of the browser screen. The navigational features in the top horizontal frame allow viewers to navigate within the main frame without having to right-click.

Note that I might be using the terms *screen, page,* and *window* in a slightly different way than you've heard those terms used before. Because frames are new, the terminology hasn't been standardized, so here's how I use those terms. I refer to the entire screen or the regular page area of a browser as the *screen*. A *frame* goes around a *window*. A *page* goes in a *window*. Until frames came along, *page* referred to everything that appeared on the browser screen. Thus a "home" page or any other kind of HTML page filled the whole browser viewing area, or screen. With frames, a browser screen can display several frames, with a different page in each frame or window. For that reason, I think we need to call an HTML document a *page* and the whole browser display area the *screen*.

When to Use Frames

Although anchoring a banner at the top of a screen and anchoring navigational tools at the bottom or side of a screen are the most obvious ways to use frames, that doesn't mean these are the only ways to use the unique advantages of frames. It just means that is the first thing most designers can think of to do with frames. I'm not saying that using a frame to keep your company's logo in constant view is a bad use of frames, nor is keeping navigational tools in constant sight. But every time you add a frame to the browser's screen, you cut into screen real estate that can be used to display data. The more frames you add, the smaller the useful area of the screen becomes and the more likely you are to confuse your readers who are new and unfamiliar to navigating a Web site that uses frames.

For example, you might consider keeping the company logo in a frame on only the first few levels of hub pages and using pages without frames for the bulk of your data.

Some uses of frames provide unique functionality for special situations. Consider the case of a highly technical document sprinkled with numerous arcane and esoteric terms that are defined in a hyperlinked glossary. A user might find that leaving the main document to look up a word is distracting and that returning to the same place in the document is difficult without some fancy mouse work. When I'm reading such an article, I hesitate to use a hyperlink to find a definition—even briefly—and tend to stumble along in ignorance, hoping the meaning of the unfamiliar term will become clear if I simply persevere and somehow read harder. Even when I'm reading a paper-based book, I hate to leave the main pages and look up something in the glossary at the back of the book. In those situations, why not add the glossary at the bottom of the page in a frame? When you click on a hyperlinked term in the main document, you won't lose your place—the definition will simply pop up in the frame at the bottom of the page. The same could be done for footnotes and other references, as in Figure 11-2.

Another, similar, use for frames is linking to more thorough explanations of technical details. Technical illustrations with links to more detailed drawings or text-based explanatory descriptions could be enhanced by using frames. You might also consider adding a frame to a static technical drawing of an object with a link to a ShockWave or Java application that shows the object rotating through a 360-degree view.

With a bit of imagination, layouts using the unique advantages of frames can add to the overall readability and usefulness of a document.

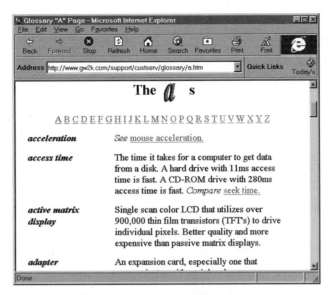

FIGURE 11-2

Frames are uniquely suited to providing links to reference materials from within technical documents.

How Frames Work

At first glance, frames might seem confusing and complicated, but I believe frames are easier to understand if you realize that frames behave much like cells in tables. You set up a screenful of frames almost exactly the way you would set up a table—the tags and attributes work much the same as they do with tables. However, while it is useful to think of an individual frame on a page as being similar to a cell in a table on that page, you need to realize that there is a big difference between a frame and a cell. The cell content is included in the page of HTML code that defines the layout of the table. The text or graphic that is inside each cell is actually entered on the same page of HTML code as a tag or an attribute that describes the layout of the table. A screenful of frames, on the other hand, is organized or defined in an HTML page called a *frameset*. The frame content is an individual HTML page that can exist anywhere—in another directory, on a local server, or on a distant server somewhere else on the net. The frameset defines only the way the screenful of frames is organized and says where the starting content of each frame is located. A URL is defined for each frame, describing where the content of that frame or cell is located. Most of the time, no individual frame content is actually on the frameset page. A frameset page is usually short, describing only the layout of the screenful of frames. Once you have a document loaded in a frame, you can click on links in that document to make other documents appear in the other frames you have set up in the frameset.

Creating a Simple Framed Page

Before we get into the details of setting up framed pages, let's set up a couple of simple pages with frames so that you can see what the basic tags and attributes do and what the anatomy of a framed page is all about.

Let's design a page with two frames. Let's set up a table of contents frame on the left and put titles and a page on the right containing the articles. Let's set it up so that when a user clicks on a link to an article on the table of contents side of the screen, that article will appear in the frame on the right side of the screen. This is a common, basic use of frames.

Laying Out the Frameset

First we have to lay out the overall page—where and what size each frame will be. Then we'll think about the content of each frame. The following is the code for a simple frameset using the <FRAMESET> tag. (Note that a frameset page does not have to have a <BODY> tag.)

```
<HTML>
<HEAD>
<TITLE>A Simple Frameset Page</TITLE>
</HEAD>
  <FRAMESET COLS="25%, 75%">
  <FRAME SRC="content.htm>
  <FRAME SRC="sassy1.htm" NAME="main">
  </FRAMESET>

<NOFRAMES>
You are looking at this page with a browser that doesn't support frames. We
suggest you upgrade if you would like to view these pages in all their glory.
</NOFRAMES>
</HTML>
```

That's all the code we need for the frameset page. (Notice the <NOFRAMES> tag part of the code. We'll get to that in a minute.) This is going to give us a screen divided into two windows. The window on the left will take up 25 percent of the screen and will contain a page named content.htm. The page on the right will take up 75 percent of the screen and will *start out* containing a page named sassy1.htm. We don't have either content.htm or sassy1.htm yet, so we'll see a page with two empty frames. We'll have to click through a couple of error messages before we can see the page because the browser will try to find the nonexistent pages. Notice that we named the right-hand page "main" by stating this:

```
<FRAME SRC="sassy1.htm" NAME="main">
```

This means the frame is going to be known as "main" and will contain the page sassy1.htm. Notice that because we aren't going to have any pages except content.htm in the left frame, we didn't need to bother to name it, as shown in Figure 11-3.

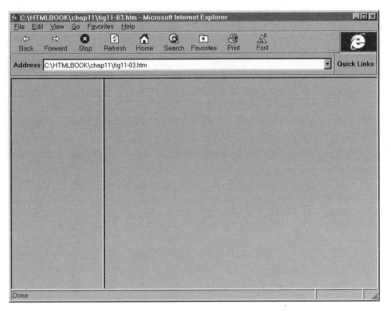

FIGURE 11-3   *The result of a simple <FRAMESET> tag with no content.*

FIGURE 11-3

```
<FRAMESET COLS="25%, 75%">
  <FRAME SRC="">
  <FRAME SRC="">
</FRAMESET>
</HTML>
```

Preparing the Content Frame

Now let's load the frames with content. We'll set up the content.htm page, which will appear in the left frame and which will allow us to click between the two pages we want to appear in the right frame. The content.htm page will be a regular HTML page set up like a table of contents. In fact, we could use a table of contents page that we already have set up and use it in the content frame. Keep in mind that this is a narrow frame, so a page designed for this frame should be designed to look good in a tall, narrow space. What's different about this page is that we need to specify where we want the pages to appear when we click on a hyperlink. Because we want the pages to appear in the frame on the right when we click on a link, we will include the TARGET attribute (TARGET="main") in the link tag. This means that when this link is clicked, the page called for will appear in the frame designated as "main." We want all of the pages to appear in the "main" frame, so we need to add the TARGET="main" attribute to all the link tags in the table of contents. If we don't specify a target in the link, the page will appear where we click—in the left frame. This is not what we want in this example, but you might want this to happen in another situation. For example, you could have a "Table of Contents Continued" link that would simply add more choices to click. You could also make the table of contents longer and have people scroll down to more page links. But let's keep things simple for now. Here's the code for the left frame, content.htm:

```
<HTML>
<BODY>
<H3>Sassy's Worldwide<BR>
Dogbite Service, Inc.</H3>
<H4>Table of Contents</H4>
<OL>
  <LI>
      <A HREF="sassy1.htm" TARGET="main">Our Founder, Sassy B. Muffin</A>
  <LI>
      <A HREF="sassy2.htm" TARGET="main">Sassy's Worldwide Dogbite Service,
Inc., Corporate Vision</A>
  <LI>
      <A HREF="sassy3.htm" TARGET="main">What Is Sassy's Worldwide Dogbite
```

```
Service, Inc., Anyway?</A>
</OL>
</BODY>
</HTML>
```

Notice that there's nothing about frames in this code. The frame coding is taken care of in the frameset page. The only frame coding you have to worry about in any HTML page that will appear in a frame is the code that determines where any links that are clicked will appear. In our example pages, the left, "content," side will have only one page in it. When a link in the left page is clicked, we want the link to appear in the right, or "main," frame, as shown in Figure 11-4.

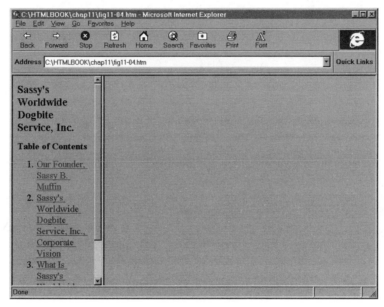

FIGURE 11-4  Here's a frameset with the table of contents loaded in the left frame.

FIGURE 11-4

```
<HTML>
</HEAD>
<FRAMESET COLS="25%, 75%">
  <FRAME SRC="content.htm">
  <FRAME SRC="">
</FRAMESET>
</HTML>
```

Preparing the "Main" Frame

The right, or "main," frame is going to contain plain HTML pages. You need to design these pages to look good in a smaller than usual window because some of the screen real estate is taken up by the table of contents frame on the left, but other than that, there's nothing special for those pages. The following is the code for the three pages called for in the table of contents. First, here's the code for sassy1.htm:

```
<HTML>
<BODY>
<CENTER>
<H1>Our Founder</H1>
<IMG SRC="sassy.gif">
<H4>Sassy's Blueberry Muffin</H4>
</CENTER>
The truth always comes out. Sassy B. Muffin is a dog. She is, however,
distinctly well qualified to hold her positions as president and CEO of Sassy's
Worldwide Dogbite Service, Inc., and vice president of security for NCT Web
Magazine. For the past eight years, Sassy has operated Sassy's Worldwide Dog
Bite Service, Inc. (NASDAQ: SDOGBITE). As the founder and majority stockholder,
she has shepherded the company from a small, local service to a worldwide
network of dogs providing contract dog biting by wire.
</BODY>
</HTML>
```

Here's the code for sassy2.htm:

```
<HTML>
<BODY>
<CENTER>
<H1>Sassy's Worldwide Dogbite Service, Inc., Corporate Vision</H1>
When we bite 'em, they stay bit.
</CENTER>
</BODY>
</HTML>
```

Here's the code for sassy3.htm:

```
<HTML>
<BODY>
```

```
<H1>What Is Sassy's Worldwide Dogbite Service, Inc., Anyway?</H1>
Just as you can order flowers for someone in a distant city by phone, you can
also arrange for someone far away to be bit by a dog. No one is beyond the reach
of our clever canine agents. We specialize in gaining quick access to
politicians and cult leaders.
</BODY>
</HTML>
```

The resulting first page is shown in Figure 11-5. There is no hidden frame coding in these pages. One thing this means is that you could convert an entire Web site to a frame-based Web site without a lot of trouble.

FIGURE 11-5

Here's the final result with the first page loaded.

FIGURE 11-5

```
<HTML>
<FRAMESET COLS="25%, 75%">
  <FRAME SRC="content.htm">
  <FRAME SRC="sassy1.htm" NAME="main">
</FRAMESET>
</HTML>
```

This is not rocket science. Remember that frames are like tables except that the cell content is not in the same file that sets up the table structure. The relationship between the frames and the pages in our example is shown in Figure 11-6.

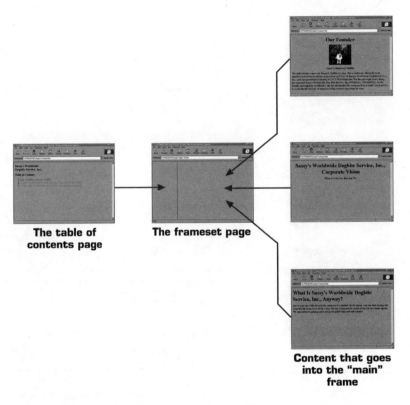

The table of
contents page

The frameset page

Content that goes
into the "main"
frame

FIGURE 11-6

The frameset page describes the structure of the frames. The content
of each frame is a separate regular HTML file.

FIGURE 11-6

```
<HTML>
<FRAMESET COLS="25%, 75%">
  <FRAME SRC="content.htm">
  <FRAME SRC="sassy1.htm" NAME="main">
```

```
</FRAMESET>
<NOFRAMES>
<H3>Sassy's Worldwide<BR>
Dogbite Service, Inc.</H3>
<H4>Table of Contents</H4>
<OL>
  <LI><A HREF="/sassy1.htm" TARGET="main">Our Founder, Sassy B. Muffin</A>
  <LI><A HREF="/sassy2.htm" TARGET="main">Sassy's Worldwide Dogbite
Service, Inc., Corporate Vision</A>
  <LI><A HREF="/sassy3.htm" TARGET="main">What Is Sassy's Worldwide Dogbite
Service, Inc., Anyway?</A>
</OL>
</NOFRAMES>
</HTML>
```

Adding the <NOFRAMES> Tag

Many viewers of your frame pages will have browsers that don't do frames. Some of your viewers will be confused by the frame setup and might get lost. They might end up with cascading sets of frames within frames within frames, as when you put two mirrors opposite each other and gaze into a descending corridor of dizzying images. Or, worse yet, some viewers might be people who simply can't stand frames. For all of these reasons, it's wise to have a no-frames version of your main navigational pages available. If someone comes to one of your frameset pages with a browser that doesn't do frames, anything you have on that frameset page between the <NOFRAMES> </NOFRAMES> tags will look hunky-dory to them—their browser will ignore all the frame stuff. (This is why you want to be sure you include your <BODY></BODY> tags.) You might have to lay things out a bit differently for that part of the frameset page, but it's no worse than what you were doing before you decided to descend into the madness of frames. In fact, you can probably just plug in your old preframes code.

You might also want to add a No Frames button on your frame pages that points to a nonframe variation of your navigational pages. This approach makes common sense and is easy to do.

Just in case you're not sure about this <NOFRAMES> stuff, here's the sample frameset page with a usable <NOFRAMES> section added at the bottom, as shown in Figure 11-7 on the next page.

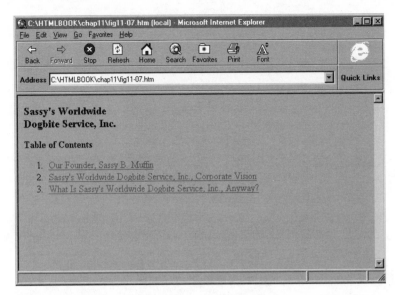

FIGURE 11-7

Here's how the sample frame page would appear for someone using a non-frame-capable browser viewing the <NOFRAMES> alternative.

FIGURE 11-7

```
<HTML>
<FRAMESET COLS="25%, 75%">
  <FRAME SRC="/content.htm">
  <FRAME SRC="/sassy1.htm" NAME="main">
</FRAMESET>
<BODY>
<NOFRAMES>
<H3>Sassy's Worldwide<BR>
Dogbite Service, Inc.</H3>
<H4>Table of Contents</H4>
<OL>
  <LI>
      <A HREF="sassy1.htm" TARGET="main">Our Founder, Sassy B. Muffin</A>
  <LI>
      <A HREF="sassy2.htm" TARGET="main">Sassy's Worldwide Dogbite Service,
Inc., Corporate Vision</A>
```

```
<LI>
    <A HREF="sassy3.htm" TARGET="main">What Is Sassy's Worldwide Dogbite
Service, Inc., Anyway?</A>
</OL>
</NOFRAMES>
</BODY>
</HTML>
```

Keep in mind that a frame-capable browser will ignore anything inside the <NOFRAMES> </NOFRAMES> tags. A non-frame-capable browser will ignore anything inside the <FRAMESET> </FRAMESET> tags. You can put the NOFRAME code at the top of the page or at the bottom.

Frame-Specific Tags and Attributes

We can explore the fine points of laying out frameset pages by examining the available frame-specific tags and attributes.

The <FRAMESET> Tag

The <FRAMESET> tags are wrapped around everything that makes up the description of the frame layout. The number of frames, their sizes, and their orientation (horizontal or vertical) is the kind of information that appears between these tags. The <FRAMESET> tag has only two possible attributes: ROWS=, which defines how many rows there will be, and COLS=, which defines how many columns there will be. You don't put a <BODY> tag before or within the <FRAMESET> tags, although you can put a <BODY> tag inside the <NOFRAMES> tag at the bottom of a frameset page. None of the tags or attributes that can appear between <BODY> tags can appear between <FRAMESET> tags. The only tags that can appear between <FRAMESET> and </FRAMESET> are <FRAME>, <FRAMESET>, and <NOFRAMES>. That keeps things simple. Most of the interesting things happen with the <FRAME> tags and their attributes. If you want to get fancy, however, <FRAMESET> tags can be nested within <FRAMESET> tags, just like <TABLE> tags can be nested within <TABLE> tags.

The ROWS= and COLS= attributes behave much the same way. Keep in mind that you should have a set of <FRAME> tags for every row and column mentioned in the <FRAMESET> tag.

The ROWS= Attribute

As you might imagine, the ROWS= attribute of the <FRAMESET> tag defines the number and size of rows to appear on the page. The number of rows defined in the <FRAMESET> tag must be matched by a corresponding number of <FRAME> tags. To the right of the = sign, you can specify the size of each row in either pixels, percentage of the screen, or relative values (essentially, whatever is left over). Don't forget to use quotes and commas, and put a space between the values. For example, the following creates a screen with three rows: the top row 20 pixels wide, the middle row 80 pixels wide, and the bottom row 20 pixels wide:

```
<FRAMESET ROWS="20, 80, 20">
```

This <FRAMESET> tag creates a screen with the top row filling 10 percent of the screen, the middle row filling 60 percent of the screen, and the bottom row filling the remaining 30 percent of the screen.

```
<FRAMESET ROWS="10%, 60%, 30%">
```

To get snazzier, you can use relative values in combination with the fixed percentage or pixel values. For example, the following tag creates a screen with the top row 20 pixels high, the middle row 80 pixels high, and the bottom row taking up any space left over.

```
<FRAMESET ROWS="20, 80, *">
```

Now suppose you do this:

```
<FRAMESET ROWS="20, 2*, *">
```

By putting a value in front of the * sign, you are allowing that particular row (the middle row, in this case) to take up twice as much of the remaining space as the bottom row. Keep in mind that these are relative measurements—if the screen size changes, the row sizes will change. This is actually a good thing in many cases because you cannot always be sure how big a monitor or what screen resolution your viewers will be using.

The COLS= Attribute

Columns work the same as rows do. The same attributes work for both.

TIP

IF YOU SPECIFY MORE ROWS AND COLUMNS IN THE <FRAMESET> TAG THAN YOU HAVE <FRAME> TAGS FOR, YOU GET A BLANK FRAME, MUCH LIKE IN A TABLE WHEN YOU DON'T SORT OUT YOUR <COLSPAN> AND <ROWSPAN> TAGS PROPERLY.

TIP

IF YOU HAVE MORE <FRAME> TAGS THAN YOU HAVE SPECIFIED IN THE <FRAMESET> TAG, YOU GET ALL YOUR ROWS OR COLUMNS, BUT THE SIZES OF THE LEFT-OVERS WILL NOT BE WHAT YOU EXPECT.

The <FRAME> Tag

The <FRAME> tag defines exactly what the frame is going to be shaped like and how it will behave. You don't use a closing tag with the <FRAME> tag because it can contain nothing. The <FRAME> tag does all its work with attributes. There are only six possible attributes for the <FRAME> tag: NAME=, MARGINWIDTH=, MARGINHEIGHT=, SCROLLING=, NORESIZE, and SRC=.

The NAME= Attribute

TIP

AS YOU MAKE FRAMES AND DEFINE THEM IN YOUR FRAME-SET PAGE, REMEMBER THAT YOU'RE WORKING FROM LEFT TO RIGHT ON THE SCREEN—NOT UP AND DOWN.

If you want pages to appear in a particular frame when the link to them is clicked, you need to name that frame so that the pages will know where to appear. In the preceding examples, we named the big frame on the right "main," and that's where we directed our pages to appear when they are selected from the table of contents in the left frame. It is a "target" frame. You don't have to name frames that won't be acting as targets. For example, you could use this:

```
<FRAME SRC="yourfile.htm" NAME="main">
```

Target names must begin with an alphanumeric character. Keep your target names simple so your head won't explode trying to keep track of them. You can reuse the same target names in different framesets. You will point links in other documents or frames to appear in the named frame when clicked:

```
<A HREF="http://www.wow.com" TARGET="main">Click here.</A>
```

When a viewer clicks on the text "Click here," the page called for will appear in the "main" frame.

We're trying to be organized here, and this is a list of attributes that are usable with the <FRAME> tag, so we won't go into great detail about targets yet. Look for more on targets later in this chapter, including the exciting *magic* targets.

The MARGINWIDTH= Attribute

MARGINWIDTH= acts much like CELLPADDING= with tables. It controls the amount of horizontal space between the frame contents and the frame walls. A value of 1 is as low as you can go. You can't specify 0. Setting a value for MARGINWIDTH= is not required, and frames default to a value of about 6 if left to themselves. An example of MARGINWIDTH= is shown in Figure 11-8 on the following page.

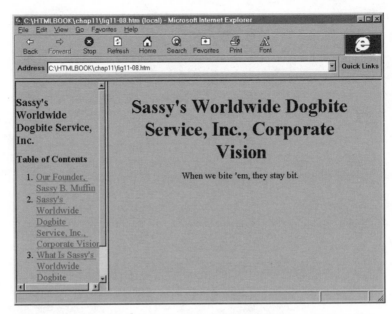

FIGURE 11-8

Typical use of MARGINWIDTH= and MARGINHEIGHT= attributes. Note that in the left frame, the margin is blown.

FIGURE 11-8

```
<HTML>
<FRAMESET COLS="25%, 75%">
   <FRAME MARGINHEIGHT="30" SRC="content.htm">
   <FRAME MARGINHEIGHT="30" MARGINWIDTH="30" SRC="sassy2.htm">
</FRAMESET>
</HTML>
```

The MARGINHEIGHT= Attribute

MARGINHEIGHT= works the same as MARGINWIDTH=. It controls the top and bottom margins of a frame. An example is shown in Figure 11-8.

The SCROLLING= Attribute

TIP

IF YOU'RE GOING TO USE
MARGINWIDTH=, USE
MARGINHEIGHT= TOO.
USING ONLY MARGIN-
WIDTH= SEEMS TO
MAKE THE VERTI-
CAL MARGINS
DEFAULT
TO 1.

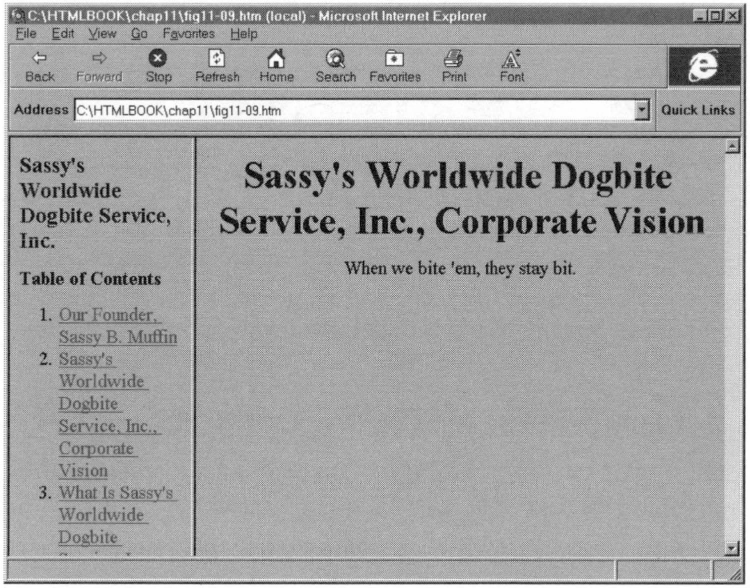

Do you want viewers to be able to scroll around in the frame? There are times when it is nice to deny this pleasure to your viewers. Your choices are SCROLLING=YES, SCROLLING=NO, SCROLLING=AUTO, and nothing specified. Using SCROLLING=YES means there will always be scroll bars in the frame, even if they are not needed. Using SCROLLING=NO means there will never be scroll bars shown, even if you need them. The document will simply be chopped off if the screen is sized so that scroll bars are needed and you specifically requested that none appear. The attribute SCROLLING=AUTO means the browser will decide whether scroll bars are necessary based on the screen size. If you don't specify any SCROLLING attribute, the effect is the same as SCROLLING=AUTO. Examples of SCROLLING= are shown in Figure 11-9.

FIGURE 11-9

*The **SCROLLING=NO** attribute was used in the left frame (it might have been better set to =YES), and **SCROLLING=YES** was used in the right frame.*

FIGURE 11-9

```
<HTML>
<FRAMESET COLS="25%, 75%">
  <FRAME SCROLLING=NO SRC="content.htm">
  <FRAME SCROLLING=YES SRC="sassy2.htm">
</FRAMESET>
</HTML>
```

The **NORESIZE** Attribute

Most of the time, a user can grab a frame wall with the mouse and size the frame. This is usually a good thing, but sometimes you might not want to let them do that. It's then you want to use the NORESIZE attribute. Keep in mind that all the borders of a frame for which you specify NORESIZE become immovable—adjacent frames might become nonresizeable as well. Use with care.

The **SRC=** Attribute

SRC= is an attribute used in the FRAME tag that says which page will appear in which frame when a particular frameset page is delivered. If you don't specify an SRC= attribute for each frame, you'll run into problems. Even if one frame is to be filled based on selections made in another frame, you should at least specify a starting page for each frame. If you don't specify a starting page and the URL for a frame, the frame will appear blank, but you might end up spawning extra copies of the browser or other unexpected results.

The **TARGET=** Attribute

Let's use our simple table of contents frames example to understand the TARGET= attribute. When a viewer clicks on one of the table of contents listings in the left frame, we want that page to show up in the right frame and the table of contents to remain unchanged in the left frame. To make this happen, we simply need to specify the TARGET frame for them to appear in when clicked on. We do this in the links on the left. This is why we named each frame in our frameset page. The frame on the right is named "main" so that we can simply add TARGET="main" to the link and the page will appear in the "main" frame, as shown in Figure 11-10.

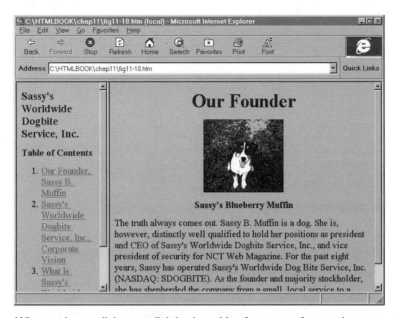

FIGURE 11-10 *When a viewer clicks on a link in the table of contents frame, the page called for appears in the "main" frame target.*

FIGURE 11-10

```
<HTML>
<HEAD>
</HEAD>
<BODY>
<H3>Sassy's Worldwide<BR>
Dogbite Service, Inc.</H3>
<H4>Table of Contents</H4>
<OL>
   <LI><A HREF="sassy1.htm" TARGET="main">Our Founder, Sassy B. Muffin</A>
   <LI><A HREF="sassy2.htm" TARGET="main">Sassy's Worldwide Dogbite Service,
Inc., Corporate Vision</A>
   <LI><A HREF="sassy3.htm" TARGET="main">What Is Sassy's Worldwide Dogbite
Service, Inc., Anyway?</A>
</OL>
</BODY>
</HTML>
```

Note that each anchor includes the TARGET="main" attribute, which sends the page to the "main" frame whenever it is clicked.

You can add the TARGET= attribute to several different tags. If you add it to the <BASE> tag, all links will go to the specified target frame without further instruction unless specifically mentioned otherwise further down in the page code. TARGET= can also be added to the <AREA> tag when you're using image maps, or you can add it to the <FORM> tag. Using frames for forms can be a good tool. Viewers can see a form side by side with the results of their form selections. Usually when you click on the Submit button on a form, the form disappears and the results page pops up. A frame-based form could be a useful navigational feature.

Magic Target Names

Magic target names have special uses. Be sure you really need them before you use them. Befuddling your viewers is a very strong possibility when you use magic target names.

Magic target names always start with the underscore character (_) and are the only names that can begin with that character. The frames for magic targets do not have to be named in advance in the frameset. This is another case in which you can end up spawning extra copies of the browser if you're not careful.

The "_blank" Target Name
If you set up a link with TARGET= set to the "_blank" target name, the link will always appear in a new, or "blank," window.

The "_self" Target Name
The "_self" target name forces the page selected to load in the same frame in which the link is located. If you click such a link located in the table of contents frame, the page the viewer selects will appear in that same table of contents frame. If you have set a BASE= frame for a whole document, this attribute might be a good way to override BASE=.

The "_parent" Target Name
The "_parent" target name is a dangerous target destination. Links targeted with the "_parent" target name will appear in the parent frameset document. This is a great way to cause your viewers' heads to explode in navigational confusion. Your own head might experience a few difficulties as well while you're trying to set this all up. Use with extreme caution.

TIP

EXTRA COPIES OF THE BROWSER POPPING OPEN UNEXPECTEDLY FOR A FRAME PAGE? IF YOU DO NOT PROPERLY SPECIFY A URL FOR EACH FRAME WINDOW, THIS CAN HAPPEN. THIS WILL ALSO HAPPEN IF YOU DON'T HAVE <TARGET> TAGS SET UP PROPERLY.

The "_top" Target Name

The "_top" target name forces links to open up in separate, nonframe windows. Another copy of the browser might be spawned no matter how you try to make it be otherwise.

Nested and Multiple Framesets

Although it might cause unnecessary navigational confusion, there might be times when you want to nest frames within frames. Personally, I think frames are strange enough to navigate without taking the risk of making things so complicated your viewers give up. But if you must do it, nesting frames is easy to do.

Basically, nesting frames works exactly like nesting tables. Set up your frameset page, and within a frame, set up another frameset. Remember, you don't have to use a closing frame tag. You might have noticed that there is no way to use <COLSPAN> or <ROWSPAN> with frames. Multiple, nested framesets allow you to do essentially the same thing. You could set up a column of two frames on the left of the screen and a column of three frames on the right by using two separate framesets within the overall frameset.

12: HTML UTILITIES

by Jerri Andreasen

Although hand-coding your Web pages is an excellent way to learn HTML development and gives you complete control over your page, it can become a tedious task. And what if you already have your information in another type of file? Do you need to copy and paste from your Excel spreadsheet into your plain text editor and then go through the arduous process of converting it into an HTML table? It seems like a lot of extra work when your data is already in tabular form in Microsoft Excel. Or what about the hit-and-miss process of selecting colors? Do you find yourself trying to guess what color E6C351 is and whether it's anything close to the color you want? And if it isn't, do you spend way too long tweaking the numbers until you get the right color?

Fortunately, there are HTML utilities to make these situations and others much easier. Most of these utilities are available as freeware or as low-cost shareware and can be downloaded from the Internet. You can be converting your Microsoft PowerPoint presentation to a multipage Web site in minutes.

Graphics Tools

Graphics tools can help tremendously with the drudgery of selecting colors and creating image maps. Other tasks, such as creating a transparent GIF, are covered elsewhere in this book, so this chapter will be limited to the two subjects in this section.

Color Selection Tools

There are several good color selection tools available on the Internet. The following are two and although similar, each has its own particular strengths. One of them should be able to meet your needs quite well.

HTML Color Reference

HTML Color Reference is an excellent color selection program created by Christopher Fazend. The fact that it is freeware makes it even better. Simply download it, unzip it, and run the SETUP.EXE file to completely install it. When you run HTML Color Reference, you see the window shown in Figure 12-1.

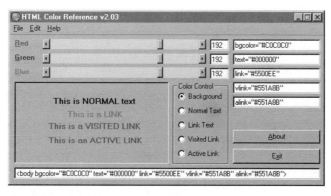

FIGURE 12-1   *The HTML Color Reference window.*

You can select a color in one of two ways. If you know the RGB value for the color you want, you can type it in the text entry boxes to the right of the red, green, and blue sliders. If you don't know the RGB value and you want to experiment with colors, you can drag the sliders or click in the bar next to the slider and the color in the sample box at the bottom will change dynamically.

HTML Color Reference lets you apply color changes to the various <BODY> tag attributes by selecting the attribute in the Color Control box. This is a quick and easy way to completely set up your <BODY> tag. Just click on each attribute in the Color Control box in turn, and set the attribute to the color you want. Once you have your background and all of your text links set to the colors you want, simply select the <BODY> tag at the bottom of the window, copy it, and then paste it directly into your HTML document. If you don't need the whole <BODY> tag, you can select and copy only the attribute you want from the text selection boxes at the right of the window.

You can download both 16-bit and 32-bit versions of the HTML Color Reference from http://www.winternet.com/~faz/HCR/.

Color Manipulation Device

Color Manipulation Device (CMD) is a $15 shareware program that is quite simple to use. After you install it, double-click on the CMD icon—it looks like a little blue frog—and you'll see a window similar to the HTML Color Reference window. You can use sliders to select the RGB value for a color, and you can select which <BODY> tag attribute to work with.

There are some differences between CMD and the HTML Color Reference. CMD does not allow you to type in the RGB value of a color, but it does have some useful features that the HTML Color Reference does not have. For example, CMD can load a background .GIF or .JPG file so that you can test your text colors on the background you will be using on your page. To do this, from the Tools menu choose Show Backgrounds in order to display a background file. Then from the Tools menu choose Load Background to select a background file for display.

You can also choose Windows Color Picker from the Tools menu to display the standard Microsoft Windows palette and color selection tool to choose a new color. Just click on the desired color, and click OK. CMD will replace the previous color of the currently selected attribute with the new color.

You can save a particular set of colors by choosing Save A Scheme from the Schemes menu. You can open a saved Scheme by choosing Open A Scheme from the Schemes menu.

If the color combination you've selected is blinding you, reset the colors to normal with the Reset Colors item from the Edit menu.

You can obtain both 16-bit and 32-bit versions of Color Manipulation Device by clicking on the "where to get it" link at the bottom of http://www.meat.com/software/cmd.html.

Image Mapping Tools

Once upon a time, the HTML developer had to code image maps entirely by hand. That meant using a graphics program to determine the coordinates of each area that was to be made clickable, or "hot" (not always an easy thing in itself), and then handwriting the references to the hot areas into a map file. And, of course, the server where the image map resided had to be set up to handle image maps properly. Today, with the advent of client-side image maps and tools to help create the map files, creating an image map is easy.

When you click on a server-side image map, the server processes the request. When you click on a client-side image map, however, the client (that is, the user's browser) processes the request. There are several benefits in having the client do the work:

- Some of the load is taken off the server, a hotly discussed topic these days.

- No image map processing program is needed on the server, so HTML developers who heretofore could not use server-side image maps can now use client-side image maps.

- Client-side image maps are not server-dependent, making them portable.

- Destination links can be shown in the status bar as the user moves the mouse over the image map.

- Client-side image maps can be created and tested locally, without requiring a server.

There are two primary image mapping tools for the Windows platform, Mapedit and MapThis! See Chapter 4 for a description of MapThis!

Mapedit

Mapedit is a $25 shareware program that makes creating client-side or server-side image maps easy. (See Chapter 4 for a discussion of client-side and server-side image maps.) When you start Mapedit, the program displays the Open/Create Map dialog box, shown in Figure 12-2.

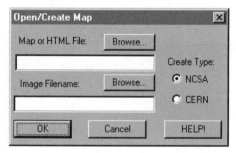

FIGURE 12-2 *The Mapedit Open/Create Map dialog box.*

This dialog box can be a bit confusing because it requests a .MAP file or an HTML file as well as an image file. How can you have a .MAP file or an HTML file if you've never created an image map before? The dialog box doesn't explain it, but Mapedit will create the .MAP file if it doesn't already exist. (Mapedit will not create an HTML file. See below for information on how to create a client-side image map.) You should specify a .MAP file if you are planning on using a server-side image map, and you need to specify an HTML file if you are planning on using a client-side image map. If you are creating a server-side image map, you must also select the correct map file type: NCSA or CERN. Most servers are NCSA-compatible. You should then enter the name of the .GIF,

.JPG, or .PNG file to be used for the image map. For client-side image maps, if you specify an existing HTML file, Mapedit will search the HTML file for inline images and prompt you to select one of them.

After you click OK in the Open/Create Map dialog box, the image you selected is loaded into the main Mapedit window and you can begin defining the hot spots and assigning URLs to them. You can use three tools to create hot spots: the rectangle, circle, and polygon tools. You select them from the Tools menu. To define a rectangular hot spot, choose the rectangle tool, click with your left mouse button where you want one corner of the hot spot, and then click again where you want the opposite corner of the hot spot to be. Using the circle tool is similar, except that the first click should be in the center of the circular hot spot and the second should be anywhere you want the edge of the circle to be. The polygon tool is a bit different. You must left-click around the perimeter of the hot spot. Once you have clicked all the points required to create the area, right-click or press the Enter key to complete the hot spot.

As soon as you define a hot spot, the Object URL dialog box pops up, as shown in Figure 12-3, letting you enter the URL for that hot spot. If you are creating a client-side image map, you will also see a field at the bottom of the dialog box where you can enter a target frame name. This is helpful if you will be using frames in your HTML document.

FIGURE 12-3 The Mapedit Object URL dialog box.

You can also specify a default URL to use when the user clicks outside your defined hot spots by choosing Edit Default URL from the File menu.

Once you have defined all of your hot spots, test the image map by choosing Test+Edit from the Tools menu. In this mode, when you click on the image map, a dialog box showing you the URL linked to that hot spot will pop up, letting you edit the URL if necessary.

Mapedit has many more features, such as adding and removing points from polygons, moving hot spots, and editing the hot spot color. You can get Mapedit from http://www.boutell.com/mapedit/ and try it free for 30 days. Be sure to register it, and send in the $25 shareware fee if you decide to keep it.

HTML Page Tools

Coding your Web pages by hand is no longer necessary. This is especially good news for Web designers who must create and maintain large sites. Creating content and keeping up with the changing state of the World Wide Web is a difficult job. This section describes a sampling of some of the newest and most sophisticated HTML page tools currently available for developing and maintaining Web sites.

Microsoft FrontPage

Microsoft FrontPage is a fast, easy way to create and manage high-quality Web sites. If you are already familiar with Microsoft Word's or Microsoft Excel's menus and toolbars, you'll be comfortable using FrontPage. It includes a Web page editor, which automatically generates the required HTML code, a conversion feature that turns images into .GIF or .JPG format, a hot spot editor that lets you quickly create an image map out of an image, a feature that creates drag-and-drop links, a forms editor, and wizards and templates to help you create your Web site. It has WebBot components that you can drop on your page to handle interactive tasks such as full-text searches, forms handling, and navigation bars. It also has advanced site management tools for maintaining your Web site. These tools include multiple views of your Web site and how the pages are all linked together, automatic updating of links when you rename or move a file, and verification and correction of broken links.

One important benefit of FrontPage is that it is designed for workgroups, enabling them to create and manage sites. It has client/server architecture, passwords, user authentication, and other security features that let group members around the world simultaneously update different pages on the same site. After you've completed your Web site, Microsoft FrontPage's one-button publishing feature will quickly set up your site so that you can host it on your own PC, on a server within your organization or company, or on an Internet server that's accessible to the whole world.

Although you can test your image maps, forms, and scripts locally when running the Personal Web Server software that comes with it, FrontPage requires that its server extensions be installed on your server to make your image maps and forms work across the Internet. This is because its image mapping process is proprietary and its CGI scripts call server extensions instead of the server CGI script processor. The extensions that are currently available for FrontPage are as follows:

- Microsoft IIS
- Personal Web Server
- O'Reilly WebSite
- NCSA
- CERN
- Apache
- Open Market Web Server
- Netscape Communications Server
- Netscape Commerce Server

For more information on Microsoft FrontPage, go to http://www.microsoft.com/FrontPage/.

Microsoft Office Internet Assistants

Microsoft has created add-ins for all of the Microsoft Office products that allow easy conversion of Office product files to HTML documents. If you use any of the Office products, you'll find it easy. For more information on the Microsoft Office Internet Tools, go to http://www.microsoft.com/MSoffice/MSOfc/it_ofc.htm.

Microsoft Word Internet Assistant

Internet Assistant for Microsoft Word is a free add-in that makes it easy to create and edit great-looking documents for the Internet and Intranets from within Microsoft Word.

If you know how to use Microsoft Word, learning to use the Word Internet Assistant will be a snap. When you install Internet Assistant, new menu commands are added to Word's existing menus. You can then save existing documents or open new Word documents as HTML. Internet Assistant automatically applies the correct HTML tags to them. The other advantages to Word Internet Assistant are that you can easily check spelling in your HTML document; use Word's AutoCorrect and AutoFormat features; quickly and easily insert links, tables, and forms; test your links within Microsoft Word; and preview your document in a Web browser.

To create an HTML document from scratch using Word Internet Assistant, follow these steps:

1. From the File menu, choose New.

2. Click Html.dot.

3. Type the text of your document. You can format your text by applying various styles such as Normal, P; Heading 1, H1; Blockquote; and Preformatted, PRE. Notice that the HTML tag appears to the right of the English version of the HTML style name (for example, H1 for Heading 1). To insert a link to another HTML document, choose HyperLink from the Insert menu. The dialog box that appears lets you type in a URL for the linked page, as well as the text for the link.

4. From the File menu, choose HTML Document Info, and type a title for your document.

5. Save the document as an HTML document.

Creating a form is as easy as choosing Form Field from the Insert menu. This is equivalent to inserting <FORM> and </FORM> tags in your document. You can insert as many forms in your document as you want, but you cannot nest one form within another. When you choose Form Field, a floating forms toolbar appears, letting you select the various form fields for insertion into your HTML document. Click the icon for the type of form field you want to add, and a dialog box will pop up to lead you through entering the information for that form field. Then type the text that you want to appear next to the form fields you just inserted, and insert Submit and Reset buttons. When you have finished creating your form, choose Protect Form on the Forms toolbar.

Creating a table is even easier than creating a form. From the Table menu, choose Insert Table. This is equivalent to inserting <TABLE> and </TABLE> tags in your document. Choose the number of rows and columns you need, and then click OK. Leave the Column Width setting as Auto. Type text in the rows and columns of your table. That's it. What could be easier? If you want to change the width of your columns, drag the column borders with the mouse. You can specify table headers by selecting the cell containing the header and choosing Cell Type from the Table menu. You can do many other things with your table, such as giving it a title or a caption, formatting the borders around the cells, and displaying certain cells (or all cells) with a background color. For more information on these and the many other features of Microsoft Word Internet Assistant, see the extensive online help file that is installed with it. You can download the Word Internet Assistant from http://www.microsoft.com/msword/internet/ia.

Microsoft Excel Internet Assistant

This no-charge add-in wizard provides Microsoft Excel users with the ability to create and distribute Microsoft Excel documents on line for viewing. It will help you convert your existing spreadsheet data to HTML format either as a separate document or as an insert in an existing one.

You must install the HTML add-in in the proper directory (usually \MSOFFICE\EXCEL\LIBRARY), start Excel, and choose Add-Ins from the Tools menu. Click on Internet Assistant Wizard in the Add-Ins dialog box. Now you're ready to start creating an HTML document.

1. Select the cells containing the data you want to convert.

2. Choose Internet Assistant Wizard from the Tools menu. Confirm that the correct cell range is listed in the text entry box at the bottom of the dialog box. Click Next.

3. Select whether to create a separate HTML file or to insert the data as a table in an existing template. Click Next.

4. If you chose to copy the table into an existing HTML document, make sure that you have typed the string ##*Table*## in the HTML document where you want the table to reside. Go to Step 6 in these instructions.

5. Enter the title of your HTML document, along with any header and footer information for the table. You can also enter your name, e-mail address, and last date the file was updated. Click Next.

6. Select whether to convert just the data or to retain rich color, font, and text formatting. Click Next.

7. Enter the path and filename for the file that you want to save.

8. Click Finish to generate an HTML document with spreadsheet data.

That's all there is to it. It takes less than five minutes from starting the installation of the Excel Internet Assistant to having an HTML document with your data ready to publish on the World Wide Web. You can download the Microsoft Excel Internet Assistant from http://www.microsoft.com/msexcel/internet/ia.

Microsoft PowerPoint 95 Internet Assistant

You can use the Internet Assistant for Microsoft PowerPoint to convert your PowerPoint 95 slides into HTML documents. It's incredibly easy to turn your slides into Web pages. Just choose Export As HTML from the File menu in PowerPoint 95 (the Internet Assistant won't work with PowerPoint 4.0 or earlier versions), type a name for your project, and click OK. The Internet Assistant will maintain your layout and images as well as automatically set up links to jump from one slide to the next (or to another HTML document).

The Internet Assistant creates a new set of linked HTML documents from your presentation. Each page is actually a client-side image map with graphical controls at the bottom that link to the next and previous slides. Two versions of each slide are created, one graphic and one text, so that you can have one version with all the colors, graphics, and structure of your presentation and another version that is faster both to load and to jump between pages. You can also use the text version for Web browsers that can't view graphics.

To export your presentation as a set of HTML documents, follow these steps:

1. Open the PowerPoint presentation you want to convert.

2. When you save the presentation as an HTML document, the Internet Assistant will automatically create links between the slides, just as you have the jumps set between slides in your PowerPoint presentation. If you want to create links to other slides or HTML documents, you must import or create a graphic object on the page where you want to create the link and then choose Interactive Settings from the Tools menu to define the link. The Internet Assistant automatically makes the object into a hot spot on the client-side image map.

3. From the File menu, choose Export As HTML.

4. Set the following options in the HTML Save Options dialog box.

   - Output style. Choosing Grayscale will create black-and-white slides, and choosing Color will create color slides.

   - Output format. JPEG is better for continuous tone images, such as photographs; GIF is better for bitmapped images such as icons or clip art. Both GIF and JPEG formats include compression, but JPEG has the potential of significantly degrading your image quality if too high a compression ratio is selected (see the following option).

   - JPEG compression quality. Use the slider to set the image quality for JPEG format. A lower setting will create a smaller file, but image quality will suffer the lower you go.

   - Folder for HTML Export. Enter the name of the drive and directory in which you want to save the HTML version of your presentation.

5. Click OK.

The Internet Assistant for Microsoft PowerPoint 95 can be downloaded from http://www.microsoft.com/mspowerpoint/internet/ia.

Microsoft Access Internet Assistant

The Internet Assistant for Microsoft Access for Windows 95 is a no-charge add-in for Microsoft Access for Windows 95 that lets you convert data stored in an Access database or in any other ODBC-compliant datasource into an HTML document.

To convert Access data, use these steps:

1. Choose Add-Ins from the Tools menu, and then click Internet Assistant.

2. Select one or more database objects (Tables, Queries, Form Datasheets, or Reports).

3. Choose whether or not to use a template and which template to use if you chose to use one.

4. Select the folder in which to place the HTML documents.

There are ten templates included with the Internet Assistant. You can use one of them, or you can create your own by using any HTML editor. There are two versions of each template included with Internet Assistant. One version is for datasheets, and the other is for reports. The report template filenames end in _r, so if you were to create a sales template, you would want to name the datasheet template *SALES.HTM* and the report template *sales_r.htm*. When you output datasheets and reports during the same session with Internet Assistant, select the template for datasheets. Internet Assistant automatically applies the report template to any reports you selected as long as it has the same name as the template for datasheets with the addition of the _r at the end of the filename. There are several strings you'll want to include in your template file. The Internet Assistant uses those strings to know where to insert your database objects into the HTML document.

You can download the Internet Assistant for Microsoft Access 95 at http://www.microsoft.com/msaccess/internet/ia.

Microsoft Schedule+ Internet Assistant

The Internet Assistant for Microsoft Schedule+ is a terrific way to publish your schedule information on the World Wide Web. If you're an international speaker, for instance, you can easily publish your scheduled speaking engagements so that people interested in attending a speech can see when you will be in their area.

To convert your Schedule+ appointments to an HTML document, choose Internet Assistant from the File menu to open the Internet Assistant dialog box. You can publish either your free/busy times or the times and descriptions of all of your appointments. Specify which hours of the day, as well as the number of weeks, to include in your HTML document, create a title, and add an e-mail address for a mailto: link. You can even include your private appointments. To see what your finished HTML document will look like, click the Preview HTML button. For this feature to work, you must have a browser installed on your computer. To complete your HTML document, click either the Save As HTML button or the Post To Web button. (Currently the Post To Web button is unavailable in the beta version of the Internet Assistant.)

You can download the Internet Assistant for Microsoft Schedule+ at http://www.microsoft.com/msscheduleplus/internet/ia.

Internet Explorer

Microsoft Internet Explorer is a full-featured leading-edge Web browser that fully supports tables; can display the most popular graphics formats, including .GIF (animated, transparent and non-transparent) and .JPG; has inline support for .AVI videos; allows global font sizing; and even lets the HTML developer specify a background sound for each page.

Version 3 adds even more features to the list, including support for frames, ActiveX controls and Scripting, Internet Conferencing, and style sheets.

One feature that was noticeably missing from version 2 was support for frames. Microsoft has added that in version 3, going so far as to allow borderless and floating frames and frames with custom borders. This version and its capabilities open up the color and structure design possibilities for your pages. Version 3 also includes the ability to use ActiveX controls, ActiveX Scripting, JavaScript, and Java applets on your page. Support for scripting and controls means that you'll be able to create interactive pages with movies, animation, and audio on them, and you'll be able to use any scripting language, such as Visual Basic Script or JavaScript, to produce this interactivity.

Using Internet Conferencing, you can make telephone calls over the Internet, including data calls with several people. You can remotely view and control any program, share a whiteboard, chat, and transfer files. You can even read pages authored in other languages, with its support for international character sets. You can enhance your tables by adding features such as graphic images for cell backgrounds, as well as having control over table borders. Internet Explorer Version 3 will also expand its graphic format support to include animated .GIF images as well as .BMP files.

Finally, Internet Explorer version 3 supports style sheets. A style sheet is a listing of attributes that can be applied to different elements in a document, specifying details such as font, color, margin, indents, size, and emphasis. The HTML developer can easily set and change the formatting of entire pages or Web sites using shared styles. The style sheet can be a separate document, or it can be placed in the new <STYLE> element in the <HEAD> section of an HTML document.

Microsoft Internet Explorer is available on Microsoft Plus! for Windows 95, and version 3 can be downloaded from http://www.microsoft.com/ie/iedl.htm. For more information on Internet Explorer version 3, go to http://www.microsoft.com/ie/default.htm.

TrueType Fonts on the Web

Use of fonts on the Web has been the bane of many a Web designer's existence. As designers have gained more control over the structure of the Web page, the desire to have control over the font displayed on a page has increased. It can be heartbreaking to labor over the layout of a Web page only to see that lovingly crafted design ruined by an inappropriate font. Microsoft kept this frustration in mind when it developed the Internet Explorer Web browser. Microsoft added the <FONT FACE> extension tag to HTML. Web designers can now use this tag to specify a preferred and alternate font for the text in their HTML documents. Currently Internet Explorer is the only browser to support this tag; other browsers ignore it and render text in the default font.

The format of the <FONT FACE> extension tag is as follows:

```
<FONT FACE="preferred font name, second choice, third choice"></FONT>
```

If the first font choice is not installed on the client computer, the second choice will be used, and then the third, and so on until a match is found. If no match is found, the browser's default font is used.

Any TrueType or Postscript Type 1 font can be used, but since it is much more likely that a user will have at least the basic TrueType fonts installed with Windows, and you can't be sure that they have purchased and installed Adobe Type Manager, it's best to include at least one TrueType font in your list. Because all of the most popular Web browsers support TrueType fonts and the TrueType Font File Format is a publicly available font specification (meaning fonts can be created with no royalties due to either Apple or Microsoft), thousands of TrueType fonts exist, many of which are free. For these reasons, TrueType fonts are an excellent choice for use with the <FONT FACE> tag.

If that isn't enough to convince you to use TrueType fonts, Microsoft has made several TrueType fonts available that you can download and install free of charge. Designers can then specify these fonts, knowing that they are freely and easily available to all Web surfers. The following fonts can be downloaded from http://www.microsoft.com/truetype/fontpack/win.htm:

Arial	Courier New (Bold)
Arial (Bold)	Courier New (Italic)
Arial (Italic)	Courier New (Bold Italic)
Arial (Bold Italic)	Impact
Arial Black	Times New Roman
Comic Sans MS	Times New Roman (Bold)
Comic Sans MS (Bold)	Times New Roman (Italic)
Courier New	Times New Roman (Bold Italic)

You probably already have versions of Times New Roman, Courier New, and Arial installed on your Windows system. The only difference between the Web versions of these fonts and the ones you already have is that these downloadable fonts contain more characters. These characters will be fully accessible with future versions of Microsoft Internet Explorer.

Here is a list of other TrueType fonts that are typically installed on a user's machine and where they would have been installed from.

Fonts supplied with Windows 95, Windows 3.1*x*, and Windows NT are as follows:

Arial	Courier New (Italic)
Arial (Bold)	Courier New (Bold Italic)
Arial (Italic)	Times New Roman
Arial (Bold Italic)	Times New Roman (Bold)
Courier New	Times New Roman (Italic)
Courier New (Bold)	Times New Roman (Bold Italic)

In addition, the WingDings and Symbol fonts are also supplied. However, except when you need a special character, it's probably best not to specify them within Web pages.

Fonts supplied with the Microsoft Plus! Pack are as follows:

Book Antiqua	Calisto MT
News Gothic MT	Copperplate Gothic Bold
News Gothic MT (Bold)	Copperplate Gothic Light
News Gothic MT (Italic)	Comic Sans MS
OCR A Extended	Lucida Sans Unicode
Abadi MT Condensed Light	Lucida Handwriting

Fonts supplied with Microsoft Office 95, Office NT, and Office 4.3 are as follows:

Algerian	Footlight MT Light
Book Antiqua	Garamond
Book Antiqua (Bold)	Garamond (Bold)
Book Antiqua (Italic)	Garamond (Italic)
Book Antiqua (Bold Italic)	Century Gothic
Arial Narrow	Haettenschweiler
Arial Black	Impact

Arial Rounded Bold	Kino MT
Bookman Old Style	Wide Latin
Bookman Old Style (Bold)	MS LineDraw
Bookman Old Style (Italic)	Matura MT Script Capitals
Bookman Old Style (Bold Italic)	Playbill
Braggadocio	Century Schoolbook
Britannic Bold	Century Schoolbook (Bold)
Brush Script MT	Century Schoolbook (Italic)
Colonna MT	Century Schoolbook (Bold Italic)
Desdemona	

Greek Symbols, Iconic Symbols, Typographic, Math, and Multinational are also included with Microsoft Office.

Once you begin to use the HTML utilities described in this chapter, you'll find that your Web page development goes much faster and is much less tedious than coding entirely by hand. You might even find it fun to create tables and choose colors.

Jerri Andreasen is a freelance Web site designer currently working at Microsoft, where she designs Web pages for a large internal site and provides technical support to other Web site designers.

13.

ACTIVEX

by Lin A. Laurie

How do you harness the energy and innovation that abound on the World Wide Web? How do you add animation, sound, video, interactivity, and customized content to your Web pages? Microsoft's answer to this question is in using ActiveX; Microsoft Visual Basic, Scripting Edition (VB Script); and Internet Explorer 3.0.

So, what do you get when you take OLE (an object-oriented technology designed for creating, managing, and accessing object-based components across process and machine boundaries) and repackage it to download automatically from a server, function device-independently, operate without requiring that the object's authoring program be installed on each user's machine, and run in HTML code? In a nutshell, that's ActiveX.

ActiveX is an API built on Win32 and OLE that lets developers enable their applications for the Internet. Supported by Internet Explorer 3.0, ActiveX adapts Visual Basic–like objects (in .OCX files) to the Web and throws in its own Internet Server API (ISAPI). Using OLE Automation and a pluggable scripting engine such as VB Script, you can add interactive features to your Web pages with just a little programming. (In this usage, "pluggable" means you can insert the code for the script inside your HTML code and identify the code, and it will run as if it were one of the codes supported by your browser.) This chapter is for the more advanced Web page developer. The technology covered is so new that it is still evolving as this book is being printed. For the most current information on ActiveX, VB Script, and Internet Explorer, access Microsoft's Web site at http://www.microsoft.com. This chapter covers ActiveX technology, looks at how to implement it using VB Script and HTML, and discusses some of the ActiveX objects and controls currently available.

What ActiveX Means to You

Imagine a future where depositories of independent and innovative objects (in .OCX files) exist, scattered across the Internet. Various independent object-authoring vendors own these depositories and sell an inventory of pluggable objects from them over the net as they are needed. Let's say that you want to include an interactive order-processing capability in your Web page or add a killer 3-D movie to your application. You would purchase the ActiveX program controls and their associated usage rights to either function from one of these object depositories. You would then write the HTML and VB Script code that would transfer variables to and from the ActiveX object and then use the HTML code to create your own Web page. Then you would install the HTML program for your Web page on a network server, and it would run whenever a user clicked on the hyperlink that activated the ActiveX object.

For instance, let's say that your 3-D movie object was created using Microsoft's SoftImage (a 3-D authoring tool). But your users don't own a copy of SoftImage. You could embed the VB Script code to call the object (3-D movie) in your HTML code, install the object on the network server that has your Web page with the code that activates the object, enable it to download automatically to the user's machine (unless it already exists there from an earlier use), and then have it execute, without requiring that SoftImage be located anywhere (on the server or the client).

Or, for an online ordering system, you would purchase the ActiveX object from the object-authoring vendor. Along with the object, you'd receive a list of parameters (data) that the object needs in order to perform its function (order processing). You'd need to use VB Script or another scripting tool to pass the needed parameters to the object. You could validate form data, automatically generate custom Web pages, and even write games as objects that run using VB Script to control them. The object would use the data to output information back to the Web page. Information such as the item amount, order total, tax, and so on could be calculated by the object and transferred back to the VB Script, which would then pass it to the HTML code, which would then display the calculated information on a Web page. The scripting language would take care of the input and output tasks to the object, passing them back to the HTML code, which would display them on the Web page, while the object would handle the calculations and any other internal processing needed to calculate the fields you'd need for valid order processing. Since most accounting applications, such as order processing, can only be done a finite number of ways, these applications would make good use of the pluggable-object technology and leave developers free to become involved in the more creative aspects of application development such as adding multimedia interactive experiences to their Web pages with Virtual Reality Modeling Language (VRML).

As a developer, you'll find abundant opportunities to purchase from these futuristic code depositories controls (custom sliders, list boxes, dialog boxes, buttons, and so on) that you can plug into ActiveX objects created in any number of languages. (You can create ActiveX objects in C++, or Java applets in JavaScript, for instance.) Your objects can have a unique or a uniform look, depending on the pluggable controls you use when you develop them. Then, when plugged into an HTML-coded Web page and viewed with Internet Explorer 3.0 or another browser that supports them, they can be used in ways you might not have imagined when creating them.

Developing controls and objects is a business opportunity you might consider. In the future, expect to see an increased need for these pluggable components (controls and objects). Since coding these components is more labor-intensive than plugging them into HTML code, this is where the challenge will exist and your innovation can truly be called into play.

Internet Explorer 3.0 and ActiveX

Internet Explorer 3.0 has a key role to play because it supports ActiveX, JavaScript, VB Script, and other pluggable scripting engines. By enhancing your Web pages for Internet Explorer 3.0, you can treat your users to state-of-the-art interactivity.

Internet Explorer 3.0 has an open and extensible architecture so that everyone can plug their components into it, regardless of the language, tool, data format, or protocol used to create them. It accomplishes this plugability using custom controls made available through ActiveX.

Microsoft has big plans for Internet Explorer 3.0—incorporating it into Windows 95 and using it to replace its Windows Explorer as a navigation tool. The Microsoft concept is to use Internet Explorer 3.0 as an interface for the Internet, for a corporate intranet, and for the contents of your hard drive.

Microsoft is also adding support for the HTML extension for frames. Frames allow Web page developers to segment the screen real estate into functionally independent panes. Internet Explorer 3.0 brings some new standards to the arena by introducing its own HTML extensions, including a FACE parameter for the existing <FONT> tag to let Web designers control the look of their Web page typography by specifying one or more alternative fonts.

Plug-ins, ActiveX, and Java are three of a kind—interactivity tools. Microsoft plans to provide support for all three of these tools by disguising Java applets and plug-ins (with wrappers) to imitate ActiveX controls.

Internet Component Download

The mechanism for downloading and installing ActiveX objects on an Internet user's system is called Internet Component Download technology and is used internally by Microsoft Internet Explorer to handle ActiveX components inserted in HTML pages.

TIP

ALTHOUGH ACTIVEX IS INSTALLED WITH INTERNET EXPLORER 3.0, ALL OF ITS CONTROLS ARE NOT.

The following description of this technology is not inclusive, but it will help you understand what happens on both the server and the client when a user clicks on a Web page that contains an ActiveX component.

Microsoft has created a new system API named GoGetClassObjectFromURL to safely download ActiveX components. Other safety needs can be met by using the WinVerifyTrust API or by using a high-level "Setup" ActiveX control. Currently the Internet Component Download will not download anything except ActiveX objects. It also downloads components into a permanent storage directory, where they sit. However, in a future release Microsoft plans to convert this storage directory to a temporary cache that discards unpopular components (when you've closed the browser).

To package an ActiveX object for downloading, you must use the <OBJECT> tag in HTML and choose one of three packaging schemes: Portable Executables (as .OCX or .DLL files), Cabinet files (as .CAB files), or stand-alone (as .INF files).

The Portable Executable Packaging Scheme

This approach uses a single executable file (such as an .OCX or a .DLL) that is downloaded, installed, and registered all at once. It is the simplest way to package a single-file ActiveX object. This packaging scheme does not use file compression, and it is not platform-independent except when used with the HTTP control.

The Cabinet Files Packaging Scheme

This approach uses a file that can contain one or more files (thus it is called a cabinet), all of which are downloaded together in a compressed cabinet file. It also is not platform-independent except when it is used with the HTTP control.

The Stand-Alone .INF Files Packaging Scheme

This approach uses a file that contains the specifications for other files that need to be downloaded and set up in order for an .OCX to run. The .INF file contains URLs pointing to files that should be downloaded. This packaging scheme can provide platform independence by listing files for various platforms, and it does not require the HTTP control. You should include an .INF file in your cabinet file specifications.

TIP

WHEN YOU EMBED AN ACTIVEX CONTROL ON A PAGE, USE THE **OBJECT** ATTRIBUTE TO SPECIFY AN ALTERNATIVE OBJECT TO DISPLAY WHEN THE CONTROL IS NOT FOUND.

Creating a Package

After defining your package scheme, you will need to create your package using a script or one of the tools in the Microsoft ActiveX Developer's Kit (MADK).

The download process is complicated, but it consists of the following general steps:

1. Download the necessary files (.CAB, .INF, or executable) using URL monikers.

2. Call the WinVerifyTrust API to ensure that all downloaded files are safe to install. Part of this API will ask the user whether he or she wants to install the files before proceeding to install them on the user's computer.

TIP

Don't assume that everyone who views your page will have the ActiveX control on their machines. Use the **CODEBASE** attribute to point to a location where the ActiveX control can be found.

3. Use the /regserver command-line argument for .EXE files and DLLRegisterServer() for other executables (such as .DLL and .OCX files) to self-register all ActiveX components.

4. Add registry entries to track downloaded code.

5. Call GoGetClassObjectFromURL to get the *rclsid* (Class ID) of the object to be installed.

6. Store the downloaded files in the windows\system\occache directory. Currently the path is hard-coded. In future releases of Internet Explorer, you will be able to use a registry setting or a Control Panel applet to choose the directory. Also, note that at the current time, downloads are stored permanently. In future releases, you will be able to specify which components should be deleted at the end of your Web session or when you turn off your computer.

Downloading ActiveX code from the Internet also is complex. This section can provide only an overview of the process that will give you a general understanding of what occurs. For additional information about this process, review the most recent postings on this subject at http://www.microsoft.com or on MSN (The Microsoft Network).

Security and ActiveX

Although .OCXs let users enjoy and interact with their computers flexibly and powerfully, they also provide a method of destroying data on your server. Unfortunately, there are people just waiting to write the next great virus using .OCX technology. Fortunately, Microsoft has taken steps to help ensure that what you're downloading is safe.

Because .OCXs can access your hardware directly, an .OCX control has the potential to do nasty things, such as formatting your hard drive. To help prevent such malicious vandalism, Microsoft is establishing a certification program that will enable you to have your .OCX certified as safe.

Before you download an .OCX that has been certified, you'll be prompted with a message saying something like, "The application you are about to download has been certified by Vendor ABC and is compliant with the Microsoft Certification guidelines. Continue?" Conversely, when you try to download an .OCX control that is not certified, a warning message will appear, telling you that what you are about to do may be unsafe. You will be able to cancel before any damage can occur.

OLE Document Objects

Although HTML code provides a single standard for documents and navigation support, it does not provide the ability to publish on the Web in any format, regardless of tools, a document that is visible to a user who doesn't own the application used to author it. Enter ActiveX documents, objects that let you publish documents in your favorite format and ensure that the viewing code for the object is available to your reader. Using hyperlinks inside your ActiveX documents, you can add navigation capability as well.

In technical terms, OLE Document Objects are a set of OLE interfaces built on top of the standard OLE in-place activation interfaces that are used in OLE objects today. A document server owns the entire client area of the document container in which it is running. What this means in layman's terms is that when an ActiveX-enabled browser such as Internet Explorer 3.0 tries to view one of these documents, it downloads the document's server container to the user's computer (after asking permission) and runs it. The container then takes over the browser's entire client area and displays the file. To end users, the process is seamless, and they continue to use the same tool to view the document that they used to browse the Internet.

OLE Scripting

Microsoft's goal from the very beginning of OLE development has been to allow software developers to become more productive by creating reusable software modules. With ActiveX, Microsoft has expanded that goal from including OLE technology across the enterprise to the largest network of all—the Internet.

With OLE Scripting, you can call reusable software modules written in any supported language and not need to learn a lot about programming. Let's say you want to run a mapping program to map a URL to an Automation object (components that allow you to extend the functionality of your script but don't require a Windows interface) with thread-safe communication to any automation server with simple syntax. Thread-safe communication is a safe instance of execution of an object, meaning that while one user's object is being executed by the server, a second client cannot interrupt the execution to use the same object. When multithreading occurs, separate instances of the object are created, each with a separate thread to the object from the client. For example, suppose you had an Automation object named myobject, a method named mymethod, and two parameters, param1 and param2. The following code demonstrates how you would execute the method through a URL name to return data in the form of a particular Web page. Because it is going through an Internet information server (IIS), the example uses the HTTP protocol and extends it by simply pointing the URL at the object. The example shows the simplicity of communicating with your OLE object using OLE Scripting.

```
http://machine/path/myobject.mymethod?param1=data1&param2=data2
```

You can use any language to create OLE applications so long as the language complies with the OLE Scripting interface. The OLE Scripting specification has the following characteristics:

- Applications can easily locate a script engine and run a script, but they don't need to know anything about the syntax, grammar, and execution model of the script itself.

- Events that are triggered from components within the application (such as OLE controls) are caught by the script engine and can have scripts associated with them.

- The script engine runs the application's space as a service, not the other way around.

- Script engine overhead should be negligible.

- The script engine should be able to customize base application objects. (Brett Morrison, *PPI Technology White Paper: OLE, Java, or Both?* [1996 Pinnacle Publishing, Inc.] p. 10.)

VB Script and ActiveX

The VB Script language is an upwardly compatible subset of Visual Basic that adds scripting capabilities to Web pages viewed with Internet Explorer 3.0 or other browsers that support the same standards. It will run in HTML without requiring the host to create or support other integration code, as opposed to languages such as CGI, which require integration code in order to execute. In technical terms, we say it is a component that is used by a host such as a browser or other application without requiring the presence of other scripting components.

VB Script is a safe language, having had any "unsafe" operations removed—that is, it does not include Visual Basic development components such as an editor, a debugger, a project manager, or a source code controller. It can be used on any hardware platform as a batch-automation language to provide scripting capability.

The classic example of VB Script uses HTML's <INSERT> tag—currently under review by the World Wide Web Consortium for inclusion into the official HTML specification. <INSERT> allows you to embed any kind of object in a browser. In the following example, we insert an .OCX control:

```
<INSERT>
    CLSID = {"ACME OCX control"}
    OLEcontrol.forecolor = true
    OLEcontrol.animate
    javaapplet.forecolor = olecontrol.forecolor
<\INSERT>
```

This example shows how easy it is to write a few lines of VB Script code that can communicate with your external program. The <INSERT> tag might seem to be a replacement for the IMG tag, but IMG is still useful for backward compatibility because the parameters to it are dynamic instead of being built into the definition. For example, the following code inserts an .AVI file if the browser supports that format; otherwise, it uses the backward-compatible IMG tag to insert a compatible image into a Web page:

```
<INSERT DATA=interview.avi
TYPE="application/avi">
<PARAM NAME=LOOP VALUE=INFINITE>
<IMG SRC="still.gif" ALT="Interview with Customer">
</INSERT>
```

Here's an example of an <INSERT> tag that loads a Java applet by referencing a Java class:

```
<INSERT CODE="BounceItem.class" WIDTH=500 HEIGHT=300>
</INSERT>
```

You can also use the <INSERT> tag by specifying an application name in its CLASSID section. Although we have become accustomed to thinking of CLASSID as an integer, it can actually be anything. The browser can then interpret CLASSID to locate the code for the class by interrogating the OLE registry or downloading it somehow by using the URL name:

```
<INSERT
CLASSID="Word.Basic"
CODE="http://ole.acme.com/apps/Word"
WIDTH=400
HEIGHT=75
ALIGN=BASELINE
>
<PARAM NAME=TEXT VALUE="This is the OLE Viewer">
</INSERT>
```

The key advantage of this technology is that the browser is only the front end of the application. In other words, there aren't any particular hoops to jump through for Internet applications. A well-designed OLE application doesn't care who it's communicating with. When you build an application that uses Internet Explorer (or any other browser supporting ActiveX) as its user interface, you're building an application that can have Visual Basic, Visual C++, Access, or any other OLE and Visual Basic–enabled hosting development tool as its front end.

ActiveX Controls

The controls described in this section are the only ones currently supported by ActiveX and released by Microsoft with the ActiveX SDK. At some future point, more controls might be included in the package. In addition, these controls are included in the Internet ActiveX Control Pack and are designed to assist you in creating powerful Internet applications based on the current base Internet protocols.

File Transfer Protocol (Client)

File Transfer Protocol (FTP) is a popular standard network protocol that is used to transfer files over networks. The FTP Client control allows developers to use Microsoft programs such as Access, Visual Basic, and Visual FoxPro to easily implement FTP in their applications.

HTML Control (Client)

The HTML control provides parsing and layout of HTML data as well as a scrollable view of the selected page.

HTTP Control (Client)

The HTTP (Hypertext Transport Protocol) control implements the HTTP client based on the HTTP specification.

NNTP Control (Client)

The NNTP (Network News Transfer) client control allows you to connect to a news server, retrieve a list of available newsgroups and their descriptions, enter a newsgroup, get lists of articles, and get any article. This control implements the basic client NNTP.

POP (Post Office Protocol) Control (Client)

The POP control provides access to Internet mail servers using the POP3 protocol. Internet mail developers and system integrators can use this control to retrieve mail from UNIX servers and other servers supporting the POP3 protocol.

SMTP (Simple Mail Transfer Protocol) Control (Client)

The SMTP control provides a reusable component that gives applications access to SMTP mail servers and mail posting capabilities.

WinSock TCP (Transmission Control Protocol) Control (Client and Server)

The WinSock TCP control is a connection-based control and is analogous to a telephone on which the user must establish a connection before proceeding.

WinSock UDP (User Datagram Protocol) Control (Client and Server)

The WinSock UDP control is a connectionless control and is analogous to a radio. The computer sending data can only "broadcast" without establishing a connection, and the receiving computer need not respond.

 NOTE: Both the WinSock TCP and the WinSock UDP controls allow data to be exchanged in both directions.

Using VB Scripts to Run ActiveX Objects

This section describes additional controls created by Microsoft or its partners for use with Windows 95 and Internet Explorer 3.0. These objects add sound, video, and interactivity to your Web pages. Some of these controls are actually authoring controls that let you create objects. Others are controls that allow you to pass parameters to them before displaying an outcome. For instance, you can define the type, color, legend text, and other elements for a pie chart. ActiveX receives the parameters you pass it and uses the .OCX to create a chart of the type you specified.

ActiveMovie

ActiveMovie Stream is an add-on toolkit that works with Internet Explorer 3.0. You can use it to play ActiveMovie streaming format (.ASF) files over low bandwidth networks such as the Internet. These are files that send (stream) sound, pictures, and URLs over the Internet in real time. The ActiveMovie streaming format is an open and extendable data-independent format used to archive, annotate, index, and transmit synchronized multimedia content. More specifically, an .ASF file allows multiple data objects (objects such as audio objects, video objects, still images, events, URLs, HTML pages, and programs) to be combined and stored in a single synchronized multimedia stream. You can incorporate these encapsulated objects into your HTML code so that they are viewable and executable from any HTTP server. In addition, the format permits progressive rendering and image stacking for rapid replay.

ActiveMovie Stream's encapsulation allows you to efficiently synchronize and store existing popular media types and formats such as MPEG, .AVI, .WAV, and Apple QuickTime on a variety of servers. You can transmit .ASF data over a variety of protocols and networks, including TCP/IP, IPX/SPX, UDP, RTP, and ATM, with some limitations. For instance, because of bandwidth limitations and Internet data loss, you might find that the playback quality is adversely affected. However, you can use error-correction information in your files to compensate for network data loss and "jitter." Another limitation is that .ASF files cannot stream through corporate firewalls.

ActiveMusic

This control offers you the ability to create music within and across pages in a Web site. The ActiveMusic control provides an interface between the AudioActive engine and Internet Explorer 3.0. It manages file transfers, can sense page transitions, and can be called only from VB Script programs. It is not an interface for compiled Visual Basic, C, or C++ programs.

Think of AudioActive as an intelligent music system that knows how to deliver the techniques of a musician in software. In a sense, it's like being able to put a living, breathing composer inside a computer and being able to ask that composer to write music that responds to programs as they unfold without subjecting the composer to the often cramped, dusty conditions and sharp, pointy things inside a computer.

Currently the following functionality is being added to the ActiveMusic control:

- Continuous controller support
- Polychord support
- Optimization of 32-bit DLL
- COM implementation of 32-bit DLL
- OCX implementation for online usage
- Integration of the RenderActive synthesis engine

For an example of how ActiveMusic works, see the Sonic Pizza sample in the ActiveX Gallery at http://www.microsoft.com.

ActiveVRML

ActiveVRML (Active Virtual Reality Modeling Language) is a new control that lets you create interactive animation in a simple and intuitive manner. For instance, ActiveVRML frees you from complex programming of events, multithreading, sampling, and frame generation. It supports the following media types:

MEDIA TYPE	DESCRIPTION
3_D Geometry	Supports importation, aggregation, and transformation. Also supports texture mapping of interactive animated images, manipulation of color and opacity, and embedding of sounds and lights.
Images	Provides infinite resolution and extent images. Supports importation, 2-D transformation, opacity manipulation, and image overlaying. Also supports rendering an image from a 3-D model and rendering an image from rich text. Even geometric and image renderings have infinite resolution and extent since discretizational and cropping are left to the display setup, which is always left implicit.
Sounds	Provides rudimentary support for importing, manipulating, and mixing sounds. Also, provides sonic rendering of 3-D models (you can listen as well as watch). Conceptually, ActiveVRML supports infinite sampling rate and sample precision.
Montages	Supports composite 2½-D images in multilayered cel animation.
2-D and 3-D Transforms	Supports translate, scale, rotate, shear, identity, composition, inversion, and matrix-based construction. Support can be extended to nonlinear deformations.
Colors	Supports various constants, construction and deconstruction in RGB, and HSL color spaces.
Text	Supports rudimentary text, including formatted text—color, font family, and optionally bold and italic.
Miscellaneous	Supports numbers, characters, and strings.

You can use existing material, available on the Internet, as a starting point in developing interactive animations because ActiveVRML supports so many media types. Then type in definitions, texture mapping characteristics, scaling requirements, color requirements, behaviors, sound requirements, reactive behaviors, competing events, repetition, event varieties, and so on. For instance, the code to import an existing item into an earth.gif image is:

```
sphere = first(import("sphere.wrl"));
earthMap = first(import("earth-map.gif"))
```

To apply an earth-type texture to earthmap, you would type in the following code:

```
unitEarth = texture(earthmap, sphere);
```

As you can see from these examples, the coding conventions for ActiveVRML are simple. The naming and composing processes are completely independent, so the author can choose how many names to introduce and where to introduce them, based on individual style and reusability plans.

To embed the ActiveVRML viewer control on an HTML page, you need to use the <OBJECT> tag and know the GUID value of the viewer control's CLASSID value. The following is an example of how you would do this. Note that you would use the CLASSID value as shown here in your own example.

```
<OBJECT CLASSID="{389C2960-3640-11CF-9294-00AA00B8A733}" WIDTH=50 HEIGHT=50>
</OBJECT>
```

Properties

When you add the viewer control to a form, you must set properties on the control that indicate which ActiveVRML script, or .AVR file, is to be used and which expression is to be displayed. For example, assume "http://www.MyStore.com/Merchandise/shelf.avr" contains the following ActiveVRML script:

```
myGeo, ptMin, ptMax = import("cube.wrl");
model = renderedImage(myGeo, defaultCamera);
```

The ActiveVRML control supports the DataPath and Expression properties. (For this example, DataPath="http://www.MyStore.com/Merchandise/shelf.avr" and Expression="model".) You must set these two properties before the ActiveVRML viewer control will display anything.

When you embed the viewer control in a Visual Basic form, you can set the viewer's properties by using the Visual Basic properties window or by right-clicking on the viewer control and selecting ActiveVRML Viewer Properties. In the latter case, you'll see a property page dialog box for the viewer control.

DataPath property: This property indicates the URL location of the ActiveVRML file to be used. This is a string value. The following are examples:

```
http://www.MyStore.com/Merchandise/shelf.avr
c:\merchandise\shelf.avr
\\myserver\merchandise\shelf.avr
```

Expression property: This property indicates which expression exposed by the ActiveVRML script is to be displayed by the viewer. This is a string value.

Environment property: This property sets a name space for the model. This is a string value and can be left empty.

Border property: This Boolean property indicates whether the viewer control should display an inset border. The default value is True. If the value is set to False, no border is drawn.

Frozen property: This property indicates whether subsequent changes to the DataPath, Expression, or Environment properties will cause the viewer to refresh the display. The default value of this Boolean property is set to False. This property is useful in cases where you want to modify one or more of the DataPath, Expression, or Environment properties while an ActiveVRML script is being viewed. Because the viewer normally refreshes the display when any one of these properties is changed, setting the Frozen property to True will keep the viewer from attempting to display the new item. When all the desired properties have been set, changing the Frozen property to False will force the browser to redisplay the new item.

Setting Properties Under Internet Explorer

With the ActiveVRML control embedded in Internet Explorer, you need to use the <PARAM> tag to set the control properties. The following example sets some control properties:

```
<OBJECT CLASSID="{389C2960-3640-11CF-9294-00AA00B8A733}" WIDTH=50 HEIGHT=50>
<PARAM NAME="DataPath" VALUE="http://www.ASite.com/avrml/myown.avr">
<PARAM NAME="Expression" VALUE="myImage">
<PARAM NAME="Border" VALUE=False>
</OBJECT>
```

Animated Button Control

The Animated Button control displays various frame sequences of an .AVI file, depending on the button state, and uses the Windows Animation Common Control. The .AVI file must be RLE-compressed or 8-bit compressed. RLE (Run-Length Encoding) is a standard form of bitmap compression used by many graphics tools in Microsoft Windows and consumes significantly less memory than ordinary bitmaps without significant display delay. Another form of bitmap compression is 8-bit compression. You need to make sure that the starting frame of any particular sequence is a keyframe (a limitation based on Windows Animation Common Control). The palette of the file must match the palette used by Internet Explorer. Currently this means that the Windows halftone palette is returned by the CreateHalftonePalette API. In the future, more palettes may be supported.

The Animated Button control can be in any of the following four states:

- DOWN, when the control receives a left mouse button click.

- FOCUS, when the control gets focus. (Focus is the ability to receive user input through the mouse or the keyboard. When an object has focus, it can receive input from a user.)

- MOUSEOVER, when the mouse pointer moves over the control.

- DEFAULT, when both the mouse cursor and the focus are not on the control.

All the states are mutually exclusive. This can be confusing because the mouse pointer can move over the control but can still have focus. However, there is a hierarchical precedence. DOWN has precedence over all the other states, and DEFAULT has the least precedence. MOUSEOVER has precedence over FOCUS. So if a control has a FOCUS state and the mouse moves over it, the state changes to the MOUSEOVER state.

The Animated Button control has the following properties associated with it:

URL: The URL location of the AVI file to be used.

DefaultFrStart: The start frame for the DEFAULT state.

DefaultFrEnd: The end frame for the DEFAULT state.

MouseoverFrStart: The start frame for the MOUSEOVER state.

MouseoverFrEnd: The end frame for the MOUSEOVER state.

FocusFrStart: The start frame for the FOCUS state.

FocusFrEnd: The end frame for the FOCUS state.

DownFrStart: The start frame for the DOWN state.

DownFrEnd: The end frame for the DOWN state.

The Animated Button control has the following method associated with it:

AboutBox: Displays the About box.

The Animated Button control has the following events associated with it:

ButtonEvent_Click: Fired when the button is clicked.

ButtonEvent_DblClick: Fired when a double click occurs.

ButtonEvent_Focus: Fired when the button gets focus.

ButtonEvent_Enter: Fired when the mouse pointer enters the button area.

ButtonEvent_Leave: Fired when the mouse pointer leaves the button area.

The HTML code to insert the Animated Button control in this page is as follows:

```
<OBJECT
CODEBASE="http://ohserv/ie/download/activex/ieanbtn.ocx#Version=4.70.0.1085"
    ID=anbtn
    CLASSID="clsid:0482B100-739C-11CF-A3A9-00A0C9034920"
    WIDTH=300
    HEIGHT=200
    ALIGN=CENTER
    HSPACE=0
    VSPACE=0
```

(continued)

```
>
<PARAM NAME="defaultfrstart" VALUE="0">
<PARAM NAME="defaultfrend" VALUE="7">
<PARAM NAME="mouseoverfrstart" VALUE="8">
<PARAM NAME="mouseoverfrend" VALUE="15">
<PARAM NAME="focusfrstart" VALUE="16">
<PARAM NAME="focusfrend" VALUE="23">
<PARAM NAME="downfrstart" VALUE="24">
<PARAM NAME="downfrend" VALUE="34">
<PARAM NAME="URL" VALUE="http://ohserv/win95.avi">
</OBJECT>
```

Chart Control

The Chart control (IECHART) lets you draw and define various chart types. You can use Chart to define the following chart types:

- Pie chart

- Point chart

- Line chart

- Area chart

- Bar chart

- Column chart

- Stocks chart

The Chart control supports only one method—AboutBox—and no events. To insert the Chart control into a Web page, follow the examples listed later in this section. Pass the parameter values for chart elements, such as color, grid, and legend, to the object, and watch as the Chart is created using ActiveX. For more complex chart usage, you can use VB Script to add timing values to your chart.

The following code inserts a chart into HTML code. Both objects are ActiveX objects. Notice how the CODEBASE command indicates the site of the control object (.OCX file).

```
<OBJECT
         CLASSID="{FC25B780-75BE-11CF-8B01-444553540000}"
         CODEBASE="http://www.microsoft.com/ie/download/activex/
iegrad.ocx#Version=4,70,0,1082"
         ID=chart1
         WIDTH=300
         HEIGHT=150
         ALIGN=center
         HSPACE=0
         VSPACE=0
   >
   <PARAM NAME="_extentX" VALUE="300">
   <PARAM NAME="_extentY" VALUE="150">
   <PARAM NAME="ChartStyle" VALUE="0">
   <PARAM NAME="ChartType" VALUE="0">
   <PARAM NAME="hgridStyle" VALUE="0">
   <PARAM NAME="vgridStyle" VALUE="0">
   <PARAM NAME="colorscheme" VALUE="1">
   <PARAM NAME="rows" VALUE="4">
   <PARAM NAME="columns" VALUE="4">
   <PARAM NAME="data[0][0]" VALUE="30">
   <PARAM NAME="data[0][1]" VALUE="60">
   <PARAM NAME="data[0][2]" VALUE="20">
   <PARAM NAME="data[0][3]" VALUE="40">
   <PARAM NAME="data[1][0]" VALUE="31">
   <PARAM NAME="data[1][1]" VALUE="61">
   <PARAM NAME="data[1][2]" VALUE="21">
   <PARAM NAME="data[1][3]" VALUE="41">
   <PARAM NAME="data[2][0]" VALUE="32">
   <PARAM NAME="data[2][1]" VALUE="62">
   <PARAM NAME="data[2][2]" VALUE="22">
   <PARAM NAME="data[2][3]" VALUE="42">
   <PARAM NAME="data[3][0]" VALUE="33">
   <PARAM NAME="data[3][1]" VALUE="63">
   <PARAM NAME="data[3][2]" VALUE="23">
   <PARAM NAME="data[3][3]" VALUE="43">
```

(continued)

```
        </OBJECT>
<OBJECT ID=timer CLASSID="{59CCB4A0-727D-11CF-AC36-00AA00A47DD2}">
<PARAM NAME="TimeOut" VALUE="750">
<PARAM NAME="enable" VALUE="1">
</OBJECT>
<SCRIPT LANGUAGE="VBS">
sub timer_time
    i = chart1.chartstyle
    chart1.chartstyle = chart1.chartstyle + 1
    if i = chart1.chartstyle then
        chart1.chartstyle = 0
        i = chart1.charttype
        chart1.charttype = chart1.charttype + 1
        if i = chart1.charttype then
            chart1.charttype = 0
            chart1.chartstyle = 0
        end if
    end if
end sub
</SCRIPT>
```

The boldface lines show how VB Script is incorporated into the HTML code. In the example, the script executes a subroutine named timer_time.

Comic Chat

Comic Chat is a new kind of graphical chat program developed by Microsoft. In recent years, a number of graphical chat programs have appeared for online services and the Internet. Comic Chat's approach varies from other graphical chat programs in that it uses a visual representation of conversations based on comic conventions. A comic strip unfolds, showing the various participants in the conversation as comic characters and their utterances in word balloons, as users type in text. To keep the users focused more on chatting and less on controlling their characters, Comic Chat automates a number of processes. It automatically chooses a default gesture and expression based on the text that is typed. It determines who should be in each panel and where they should be. There is no need to wander around looking for people to participate in a conversation. If somebody speaks to a user, the user need not turn around and try to find the speaker.

Comic Chat runs on Windows 95. It uses the Internet Relay Chat (IRC) protocol, the most popular chat protocol on the Internet, and it runs on standard IRC servers.

Gradient Control

This control shades the specified area with a range of colors, making a gradual transition from a specified color to another specified color. You can choose two different colors or a range of shades within a color. You can also specify the direction in which the gradation should occur and the gradation starting and ending coordinates.

Properties

The Gradient control has the following properties.

StartColor: The StartColor property determines the color with which the transition starts.

EndColor: The EndColor property determines the color with which the transition ends.

Direction: The Direction property determines the direction in which the color moves. It takes one of the following values:

VALUE	DIRECTION
0	The color transition is horizontal.
1	The color transition is vertical.
2	The color transition is toward the center.
3	The color transition is toward a corner.
4	The color transition is across, diagonally down.
5	The color transition is across, diagonally up.
6	The color transition is around the point specified in the StartPoint property.
7	The color transition is across the line joining the StartPoint and EndPoint properties.

StartPoint: The StartPoint property determines the coordinates of a starting point, in the format (x,y).

EndPoint: The EndPoint property determines the coordinates of an ending point, in the format (x,y).

Methods
The Gradient control has the following method.

AboutBox: This method produces the About Gradient Control box.

Events
The Gradient control has no events.

The code to insert a graded color in a square block is as follows:

```
<CENTER>
<FONT SIZE=5><B>Gradient Control</B></FONT>
</CENTER>
<BR>
This control shades the area with a range of colors, making the transition from
a specified color to another specified color.
<HR>
The following is a Gradient object.
<BR>
<OBJECT
ID=iegrad1
TYPE="application/x-oleobject"
CLASSID="clsid:017C99A0-8637-11CF-A3A9-00A0C9034920"
CODEBASE="http://www.microsoft.com/ie/download/activex/
iegrad.ocx#Version=4,70,0,1082"
WIDTH=50
HEIGHT=50
>
<PARAM NAME="StartColor" VALUE="#0000ff">
<PARAM NAME="EndColor" VALUE="#000000">
<PARAM NAME="Direction" VALUE = "4">
</OBJECT>
```

Intrinsic Controls

There are several intrinsic, or common, controls that come with Internet Explorer 3.0. Controls such as buttons, check boxes, combo boxes, list boxes, and passwords are included in the ActiveX SDK and are installed during Internet Explorer 3.0 setup. These controls are found in HTMLCTL.OCX, which is copied to the hard drive and registered during setup. You use standard HTML forms tags and values to implement these controls.

The following controls are found in HTMLCTL.OCX:

CONTROL	TAG
ButtonCtl Object	INPUT TYPE=BUTTON
CheckboxCtl Object	INPUT TYPE=CHECKBOX
ComboCtl Object	SELECT MULTIPLE
ListCtl Object	SELECT
PasswordCtl Object	INPUT TYPE=PASSWORD
RadioCtl Object	INPUT TYPE=RADIO
TextAreaCtl Object	TEXTAREA
TextCtl Object	INPUT NAME

Label Control

The Label control displays text at a given angle and supports the Click event.

The HTML code to insert the Label control into a Web page at 270 degrees is as follows:

```
<OBJECT
        CLASSID="clsid:{99B42120-6EC7-11CF-A6C7-00AA00A47DD2}"
        ID=sprlbl1
        WIDTH=150
```

(continued)

```
                    HEIGHT=500
                    VSPACE=0
                    ALIGN=left
        >
        <PARAM NAME="_extentX" VALUE="14">
        <PARAM NAME="_extentY" VALUE="14">
        <PARAM NAME="angle" VALUE="270">
        <PARAM NAME="alignment" VALUE="2">
        <PARAM NAME="BackStyle" VALUE="0">
        <PARAM NAME="caption" VALUE="Properties">
        <PARAM NAME="FontName" VALUE="Times New Roman">
        <PARAM NAME="FontSize" VALUE="130">
        </OBJECT>
```

New Item Control

You can use the New Item control to highlight new items on a Web page. Up to a specified date, it displays the selected image. After that date, it does not continue to display itself or the item.

The HTML to insert the New Item control in a Web page is as follows:

```
<OBJECT
        ID=ienewb
        TYPE="application/x-oleobject"
        CLASSID="clsid:{642B65C0-7374-11CF-A3A9-00A0C9034920}"
        WIDTH=20
        HEIGHT=10
>
<PARAM NAME="date" VALUE="5/1/1996">
<PARAM NAME="image" VALUE="/ie/images/new.gif">
</OBJECT>
```

The "date" parameter specifies the ending date—the date after which you don't want the item displayed. The image parameter defines the image that you want to display.

Popup Menu Control

The Popup Menu control displays a popup menu whenever it is enabled. The Popup Menu control is invoked by calling the method PopUp.

PARAM Tag
The Popup Menu control uses the <PARAM> tag with the following attribute.

Menuitem[]: This tag produces the menu item to be displayed.

Methods
The Popup Menu control has the following methods.

AboutBox: This method displays information about the menu.

PopUp([in] int x, [in] int y): This method pops up the menu. If no value is passed, the current mouse pointer position is used for displaying the popup menu.

Clear(): This method clears all the menu items.

RemoveItem([in] int index): This method removes the specified item. If the menu item does not exist, nothing is done.

AddItem([in] String, [in/optional] int index): This method adds the passed menu item to the menu at the specified index. If no index is passed, the item is appended to the end.

Events
The Popup Menu control has the following event.

Click(int item): The item clicked is one of the parameters passed.

HTML Code
The HTML code to insert the Popup Menu control in this page is as follows:

```
<OBJECT
    CODEBASE="http://www.microsoft.com/ie/download/activex/
iemenu.ocx#Version=4,70,0,1082"
    ID=iemenu1
```

(continued)

```
        CLASSID="clsid:0482B100-739C-11CF-A3A9-00A0C9034920"
        WIDTH=1
        HEIGHT=1
        ALIGN=left
        HSPACE=0
        VSPACE=0
    >
    <PARAM NAME="Menuitem[0]" VALUE="This is the first item">
    <PARAM NAME="Menuitem[1]" VALUE="This is the second item">
    <PARAM NAME="Menuitem[2]" VALUE="This is the third item">
    <PARAM NAME="Menuitem[3]" VALUE="No way this is the fifth item">
    <PARAM NAME="Menuitem[4]" VALUE="This is the fifth item">
    </OBJECT>

<SCRIPT LANGUAGE="VBScript">
sub Iepop1_Click(ByVal x)
    Alert "Menu click on item:  "&x
    Randomize
    call Iepop1.RemoveItem(x)
    call Iepop1.AddItem("Added Me", x)
    call Iepop1.PopUp(Rnd*640,Rnd*480)
end sub
sub timer1_timer
    Alert "Got timer"
    timer1.Enabled = False
    call Iepop1.PopUp()
end sub
</SCRIPT>
```

Preloader Control

Preloader is an invisible control, in that the user does nothing and the code controls what image downloads behind the image the user is currently viewing. Preloader lets you specify an image to be downloaded to the Internet Explorer cache after a user decides that he or she wants to load that image. Downloading to the cache takes less time than downloading to disk, especially with large images, giving your Web page the appearance of more efficient operation.

Here is the code to use to preload an object using Preloader.

```
<OBJECT
        ID=movie
        CLASSID="clsid:16E349E0-702C-11CF-A3A9-00A0C9034920"
        CODEBASE="http://ohserv/ie/download/activex/ieprld.ocx"
        WIDTH=1
        HEIGHT=1
>
<PARAM NAME="URL" VALUE="http://ohserv/win95.avi">
<PARAM NAME="enable" VALUE="1">
</OBJECT>
```

Label Control

You can use the Label control to display text at a given angle and along curves that you define. It supports CLICK, CHANGE, MOUSEDOWN, MOUSEOVER, and MOUSEUP events. This control operates like WordArt.

Caption
This specifies the text to be displayed.

Angle
This specifies in degrees the counterclockwise rotation of the given text.

Alignment
This specifies the alignment of the text in the control. Alignment takes the following values.

0: Alignment is to the left.

1: Alignment is to the right.

2: Alignment is centered.

3: Alignment is to the top.

4: Alignment is to the bottom.

BackStyle

This controls the background. Backstyle takes the following values.

0: The background is transparent.

1: The background is opaque.

FontName

This is the name of a TrueType font.

FontSize

This is the size of the font.

FontItalic

This is a flag for italicized text.

FontBold

This is a flag for bold text.

FontUnderline

This is a flag for underlined text.

FontStrikeout

This is a flag for strikeout text.

Mode

This specifies which mode the text should be rendered in. Mode takes the following values.

0: The mode is normal (the same as the Label control).

1: The mode is normal text with rotation.

2: This value applies the user-specified lines while rendering without rotation.

3: This value applies the user-specified lines while rendering with rotation.

To specify the two lines along which the text will be shown, use <PARAM> tags such as TopPoints, TopXY, BotPoints, and BotXY. You can use this feature in VB Script because it supports proper-ties such as TopPoints, TopIndex, TopXY, BotPoints, BotIndex, and BotXY. You can also use a property page (an OLE function that occurs when a Properties window in Visual Basic is encountered) with this control.

HTML Code

The following HTML code inserts the Label control (IELABEL.OCX) into your Web page in a vertical rendering of 270 degrees.

```
<OBJECT
    CLASSID="clsid:99B42120-6EC7-11CF-A6C7-00AA00A47DD2"
    CODEBASE="http://ohserv/ie/download/activex/ielabel.ocx#version=4
        ID=sprlbl1
        WIDTH=150
        HEIGHT=150
        VSPACE=0
        ALIGN=LEFT
>
<PARAM NAME="Angle" VALUE="270">
<PARAM NAME="Alignment" VALUE="2">
<PARAM NAME="BackStyle" VALUE="0">
<PARAM NAME="Caption" VALUE="Properties">
<PARAM NAME="FontName" VALUE="Times New Roman">
<PARAM NAME="FontSize" VALUE="60">
</OBJECT>
```

Timer Control

The Timer control evokes events on a periodic basis and is an invisible control at run time.

The following HTML code inserts the Timer control (IETIMER.OCX) into your Web page so that when you click on a button, you toggle between enabled and disabled states. When enabled, you can use the Timer control to wait before executing a command, or to automatically execute a command or run an application at a designated interval.

```
<OBJECT
    CLASSID="clsid:59CCB4A0-727D-11CF-AC36-00AA00A47DD2"
    CODEBASE="http://ohserv/ie/download/activex/ietimer.ocx#version=4,70,0,1085"
```

(continued)

```
        ID=timer1
        ALIGN=MIDDLE
>
<PARAM NAME="Interval" VALUE="200">
<PARAM NAME="Enabled" VALUE="True">
</OBJECT>
<OBJECT
        CLASSID="clsid:59CCB4A0-727D-11CF-AC36-00AA00A47DD2"
        CODEBASE="http://ohserv/ie/download/activex/ietimer.ocx#version=4,70,0,1085"
        ID=timer2
        ALIGN=MIDDLE
>
<PARAM NAME="Interval" VALUE="1000">
<PARAM NAME="Enabled" VALUE="True">
</OBJECT>

<SCRIPT LANGUAGE="VBSCRIPT">
Sub BtnToggle_OnClick
        Timer1.Enabled = Not Timer1.Enabled
        Timer2.Enabled = Not Timer2.Enabled
End Sub

sub timer1_timer
        label.Angle = (label.Angle + 5) mod 360
end sub
sub timer2_timer
        cool.forecolor = rnd() * 16777216
end sub
</SCRIPT>
```

ActiveX and VB Script Examples

The following information provides you with some dos and don'ts for using VB Script with ActiveX components. It also provides working examples of the VB Script code in its current implementation. The examples are based on two working ActiveX demo applications from Microsoft:

Volcano Coffee Company and Sonic Pizza. These examples are packaged with the ActiveX SDK code, and the most up-to-date version can be downloaded from MSN or at http://www.microsoft.com. Before we get to the samples, however, let's look at some common misunderstandings that developers have when using this new technology.

Some Common Misunderstandings

Contrary to what you might have heard, VB Script will not be able to perform file I/O (input and output) or access hardware directly, and it will live and run within a browser. In the current version, in order to be "safe," any code that could potentially cause damage to a user's computer has been disabled. When security on the Internet is no longer a big issue, this safety feature may no longer be necessary.

Many developers have trouble understanding that objects are not simple variables. In all flavors of Visual Basic, including VB Script, you must use special operators when dealing with objects. For example, you will get an error when you try to execute the following code:

```
<SCRIPT LANGUAGE="VBSCRIPT">
Sub Button1_OnClick
     if x = empty then
       msgbox "x is empty"
     end if
     if addrbook = empty then
       msgbox "no addrbook"
     end if
End Sub
Sub Button2_OnClick
     if x = empty then
       msgbox "x is empty"
     end if
     if addrselector = empty then
       msgbox "no addrselector"
     end if
End Sub
</SCRIPT>
```

As a comparison, use the Is operator, and to perform an assignment, use Set as in the following code:

```
Dim X
    Set X = SomeOtherObj
    If X Is Nothing Then
        'The assignment didn't work
    Else
        X.method
    End If
```

If X is an object, use a line of code like this:

```
If X = empty Then
```

This amounts to saying the following:

```
If X.Defaultproperty = 0 Then
```

This is because "empty" has no meaning. (Visual Basic thinks it is a variable you've just created.) If the object in question does not have a default property, you will get an error stating that the object doesn't support this property or method.

Coding with ActiveX

Now let's look at some sample code. The following section uses the Volcano Coffee Company demo program to illustrate how to combine HTML 3.0, VB Script, and ActiveX objects into a working Web page that serves as an online catalog and ordering system. The opening screen is shown in Figure 13-1.

The Volcano Coffee Company Web page is built using frames. Each frame has been coded into a separate HTML file and pulled together from a master HTML file. The following code is in the master HTML file (VOLCANO3.HTM). This file describes each frame, names the frames "lefty" and "righty," and codes the sources of the other frame files so that they can be run from the master program. In addition, it loads a dynamic source, which loops an infinite number of times.

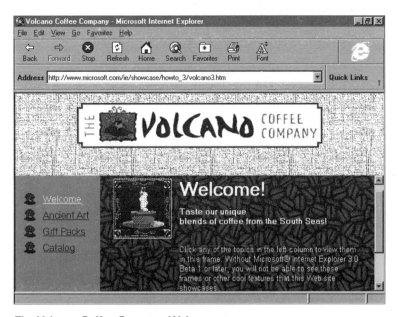

FIGURE 13-1 *The Volcano Coffee Company Welcome screen.*

This code displays the cup in the upper left corner of the Welcome screen and causes the cup to loop continuously. Notice that the code that indicates the sound loop is not used until later, when the Welcome frame (righty) is actually created.

If you have Internet access, you can display the most current version of this demo at http://www.microsoft.com/ie/showcase/howto_3/volcano3.htm.

```
<HEAD>
<TITLE> Volcano Coffee Company</TITLE>
</HEAD>
<FRAMESET ROWS="137,65%" FRAMEBORDER=0 FRAMESPACING=0>
        <FRAME SRC="/ie/showcase/howto3/masthead.htm" SCROLLING="no" NORESIZE>
        <FRAMESET COLS="145,*">
        <FRAME NAME="lefty"
SRC="/ie/showcase/howto_3/contents.htm"
SCROLLING="no" NORESIZE SCROLL=NO>
```

(continued)

```
        <FRAME NAME="righty"
SRC="/ie/showcase/howto_3/welcome.htm"
SCROLLING="yes" NORESIZE>
        </FRAMESET>
</FRAMESET>

<NOFRAMES>

<BODY TOPMARGIN="0"  BACKGROUND="/ie/images/canvas2.gif" BGPROPERTIES=FIXED
LINK="#000000" VLINK="#000000">
<BGSOUND SRC="/ie/audio/drmshort.wav" LOOP=3>
<CENTER>
<TABLE BORDER=0 CELLSPACING=0 CELLPADDING=0>
<TR VALIGN="top">
<TD><IMG SRC="/ie/images/masthead.gif" HSPACE=5 ALT="The Volcano Coffee Company"
WIDTH=424 HEIGHT=75>
</TD>
</TR>
</TABLE>
<P>
<P>
<CENTER>
<TABLE BORDER=1 BORDERCOLOR="BLACK" BGCOLOR="#FFFCC" WIDTH=90%  CELLPADDING=3
CELLSPACING=3>

<TR BGCOLOR="#D36D32" ALIGN=LEFT VALIGN=TOP>
<TD ROWSPAN=2><IMG DYNSRC="/ie/AVI/cup.avi"
SRC="/ie/avi/cupalt.gif" HSPACE=2 LOOP=INFINITE WIDTH=100
HEIGHT=100 ALIGN=LEFT></TD>
<TD><FONT FACE="HELV" SIZE=6 COLOR="#F3D2A6"><B>Welcome!</B></FONT>
</TD>
</TR>

<TR BGCOLOR="#D36D32">
<TD VALIGN=TOP><FONT FACE="HELV" SIZE=3 COLOR="#F3D2A6"><B>Taste our unique</B>
<BR>
blends of coffee from the South Seas!</FONT>
</TD>
</TR>
```

```
<TR BGCOLOR="#D36D32">
<TD COLSPAN=2><IMG SRC="/ie/images/volbttn.gif" ALIGN=MIDDLE WIDTH=24 HEIGHT=24
HSPACE=6><A HREF="/ie/showcase/howto_3/welcome.htm"><FONT FACE="HELV"
SIZE=3>Welcome</FONT></A>
<BR>
</TD>
</TR>

<TR BGCOLOR="#D36D32">
<TD COLSPAN=2><IMG SRC="/ie/images/volbttn.gif" ALIGN=MIDDLE WIDTH=24 HEIGHT=24
HSPACE=6>
<A HREF="/ie/showcase/howto_3/ancient.htm"><FONT FACE="HELV" SIZE=3>Ancient
Art</FONT></A>
<BR>
</TD>
</TR>

<TR BGCOLOR="#D36D32">
<TD COLSPAN=2><IMG SRC="/ie/images/volbttn.gif" ALIGN=MIDDLE WIDTH=24 HEIGHT=24
HSPACE=6>
<A HREF="/ie/showcase/howto_3/catalog.htm"><FONT FACE="HELV" SIZE=3>Catalog
</FONT></A>
<BR>
</TD>
</TR>

<TR>
<TD COLSPAN=2><FONT FACE="HELV" SIZE=2 Color="#black">Because you are viewing
this page in Internet Explorer 2.0, you cannot see how the browser window is
divided into frames or see other cool features of Microsoft Internet Explorer
3.0. You can:
<BR>
<P>
<IMG SRC="/ie/images/volbttn.gif" ALIGN=MIDDLE WIDTH=24 HEIGHT=24 HSPACE=6>View
the showcase page for <A HREF="/ie/showcase/howto/iedemo.htm">Microsoft Internet
Explorer 2.0</A>
<BR>
```

(continued)

```
<P>
<IMG SRC="/ie/images/volbttn.gif" ALIGN=MIDDLE WIDTH=24 HEIGHT=24 HSPACE=6>View
the demo that explains the <A HREF="/ie/showcase/howto_3/pdcdemo.htm">Microsoft
Internet Explorer 3.0 showcase pages.</A>
<BR>
<P>
<IMG SRC="/ie/images/volbttn.gif" ALIGN=MIDDLE WIDTH=24 HEIGHT=24
HSPACE=6>Download a beta version of <A HREF="/intdev/sdk/"><B>Microsoft Internet
Explorer 3.0. including the Microsoft ActiveX(tm) Developers Kit.</B></A></FONT>
</TD>
</TR>
</TABLE>
</CENTER>
</CENTER>
</BODY>
</NOFRAMES>
</HTML>
```

The masthead is called into place by some additional code. The following code shows how the masthead was placed as part of the Welcome screen:

```
<HTML>
<HEAD>
<TITLE>The Volcano Coffee Company</TITLE>
</HEAD>
<BODY BACKGROUND="/ie/images/canvas2.gif"  BGPROPERTIES=FIXED>
<BGSOUND SRC="/ie/audio/drmshort.wav" LOOP=3>
<CENTER>
<TABLE BORDER=0 CELLSPACING=0 CELLPADDING=0>
<TR VALIGN="top"><TD>
<IMG SRC="/ie/images/masthead.gif" HSPACE=5 ALT="The Volcano Coffee Company"
WIDTH=424 HEIGHT=75>
</TD>
</TR>
</TABLE>
</CENTER>
</BODY>
</HTML>
```

Here is the code to create the table of contents frame. Of particular note are the boldface lines that describe where to place the next frame ("righty"), where to get the next frame's .HTM file, and what to print on its masthead.

```html
<HTML>
<HEAD>
<TITLE>Contents - Volcano Coffee Company </TITLE>
<META NAME="GENERATOR" CONTENT="Internet Assistant for Microsoft Word 2.0z Beta">
</HEAD>
<BODY BGCOLOR="#D36D32" LEFTMARGIN=10 TOPMARGIN=10 LINK="#000000" VLINK="#F3D2A6">
<BASEFONT SIZE=2 FACE="HELV">
<BR>
<TABLE WIDTH=140 CELLPADDING=0 CELLSPACING=3>
<TR>
<TD><IMG SRC="/ie/images/volbttn.gif" ALIGN=MIDDLE WIDTH=24 HEIGHT=24></TD>
<TD><A TARGET="righty" HREF="/ie/showcase/howto_3/welcome.htm">
<FONT SIZE=3>Welcome<BR></TD></FONT></A>
</TR>
<TR>
<TD><IMG SRC="/ie/images/volbttn.gif" ALIGN=MIDDLE WIDTH=24 HEIGHT=24></TD>
<TD><A TARGET="righty" HREF="/ie/showcase/howto_3/ancient.htm">
<FONT SIZE=3>Ancient Art<BR></TD></FONT></A>
</TR>
<TR>
<TD><IMG SRC="/ie/images/volbttn.gif" ALIGN=MIDDLE WIDTH=24 HEIGHT=24></TD>
<TD><A TARGET="righty" HREF="/ie/showcase/howto_3/giftpack.htm">
<FONT SIZE=3> Gift Packs<BR></TD></FONT></A>
</TR>
<TR>
<TD><IMG SRC="/ie/images/volbttn.gif" ALIGN=MIDDLE WIDTH=24 HEIGHT=24></TD>
<TD><A target="righty" HREF="/ie/showcase/howto_3/catalog.htm">
<FONT SIZE=3>Catalog<BR></TD></FONT></A>
</TR>
<TR>
<TD><IMG SRC="/ie/images/volbttn.gif" ALIGN=MIDDLE WIDTH=24 HEIGHT=24></TD>
<TD><A target="righty" HREF="/ie/showcase/howto_3/coffee.htm">
<FONT SIZE=3>Brew A Cup!</FONT></A><BR></TD>
```

(continued)

```
    </TR>
  </TABLE>
</BODY>
</HTML>
```

If you follow the code, you can see where HTML targets the frame and where it places the text.

The second Web page is called the Ancient Art of Coffee Brewing (see Figure 13-2). This is only a frame change, but it incorporates Marquee text (text that scrolls across the screen). This is a new feature for Internet Explorer 3.0 and HTML 3.0 and is not supported in other browsers. If you view the HTML code in another browser, you might see a black bar where the text would normally be displayed.

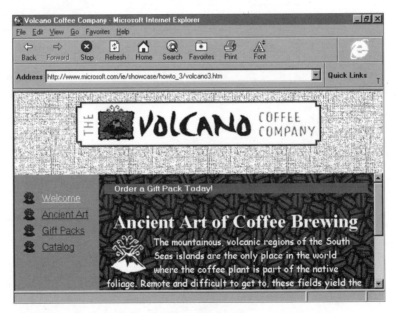

FIGURE 13-2 *The Ancient Art of Coffee Brewing frame.*

Here is the code for the frame that displays the Ancient Art of Coffee Brewing frame:

```
<HTML>
<HEAD>
```

```
<TITLE>HTML document for the World Wide Web</TITLE>
<META NAME="GENERATOR" CONTENT="Internet Assistant for Microsoft Word 2.0z
Beta">
</HEAD>
<BODY BACKGROUND="/products/ie/images/beans.gif" BGPROPERTIES=FIXED>
<A HREF="/ie/showcase/howto_3/giftpack.htm"><FONT FACE="HELV" SIZE=2
COLOR="F3D2A6"><B><Marquee WIDTH=100% DIRECTION=LEFT ALIGN=MIDDLE BORDER=0
BGCOLOR="#8F237D">
Order a Gift Pack Today!
</MARQUEE></A></FONT></B>
<BR>
<BR>
<BR>
<TABLE BORDER=0>
<CAPTION> <FONT FACE="Brush Script MT Italic" SIZE=4 COLOR="#F3D2A6">
<B><H1>Ancient Art of Coffee Brewing</H1></B></FONT></CAPTION>
<TR>
<TD VALIGN=TOP><IMG SRC="/products/ie/images/volctan.gif" ALIGN=LEFT HSPACE=6
HEIGHT=66 WIDTH=65> <FONT FACE="Comic Sans MS" COLOR="#F3D2A6">The mountainous,
volcanic regions of the South Seas islands are the only place
in the world where the coffee plant is part of the native foliage.
Remote and difficult to get to, these fields yield
the plumpest, most flavor-filled coffee beans in the world. Harvested
by hand by the Mo'a Mana tribe, these are the beans used exclusively
by The Volcano Coffee Company for its unique and aromatic coffee
blends. Our select Limited Edition roasts are available in our cafes
and by the pound throughout the area for your drinking pleasure.</FONT></TD>
</TABLE>
</BODY>
</HTML>
```

Notice the code to add marquee text to your frame:

```
<A HREF="/ie/showcase/howto_3/giftpack.htm">
<FONT FACE="HELV" SIZE=2 COLOR="F3D2A6"><B>
<MARQUEE WIDTH=100% DIRECTION=LEFT ALIGN=MIDDLE BORDER=0 BGCOLOR="#8F237D">
Order a Gift Pack Today!
</MARQUEE></A></FONT></B>
```

You can determine the direction, font, font size, alignment, border, and background color for your marquee text. You place the text you want to appear on the marquee on a separate line without any HTML coding.

The Design a Gift Pack Web page (see Figure 13-3) is one of the trickier pages of the Volcano Coffee Company demo. It uses VB Script to generate the HTML code for the page, indicates when items are ordered, and totals the order. Notice the fourth line of code, which indicates that a scripting language is being used. However, it isn't until later in the code that VB Script is actually used.

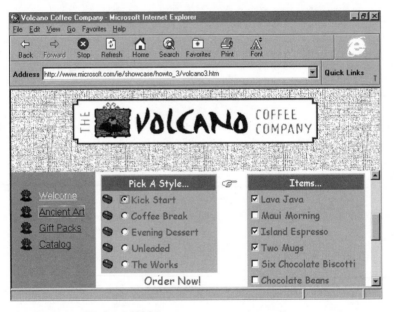

FIGURE 13-3 *The Design a Gift Pack Web page.*

```
<HTML>
<HEAD><TITLE>Design a Gift Pack</TITLE></HEAD>
<BODY BGCOLOR="#FFFCC">
<SCRIPT LANGUAGE="VBSCRIPT">
</SCRIPT>
<FONT FACE="Comic Sans MS" COLOR="8F237D" SIZE=2>
```

```
<CENTER>
<TABLE>
<CAPTION><FONT SIZE=6>Design a Gift Pack<P></FONT></CAPTION>
<TR><FONT FACE="Comic Sans MS" COLOR="8F237D" SIZE=2>
<TD>
South Sea Blends!
<P>
Hand-Crafted Mugs!
</TD>
<TD> <IMG SRC="/ie/images/giftpack.GIF" WIDTH=143 HEIGHT=151 ALIGN=MIDDLE></TD>
<TD> Chocolate Biscotti!
<P>Order Now!</TD>
</TR></FONT>
</TABLE>
</CENTER>
<BR>
<FONT FACE="Comic Sans MS" SIZE=2 COLOR="8F237D">
```

The following is the code for displaying the basket style:

```
<TABLE BGCOLOR="C9A177" WIDTH=200 ALIGN=LEFT>
    <TR><TD BGCOLOR="8F237D" ALIGN=CENTER><FONT COLOR="FFFFCC">Pick A Style...</
FONT></TD></TR>
    <TR><TD><IMG SRC="/ie/images/beanicon.GIF" WIDTH=18 HEIGHT=16 ALT="*"
ALIGN=CENTER> <INPUT TYPE=RADIO NAME=R ONCLICK="KickStart_onClick">Kick
Start</TD></TR>
    <TR><TD><IMG SRC="/ie/images/beanicon.GIF" WIDTH=18 HEIGHT=16 ALT="*"
ALIGN=CENTER> <INPUT TYPE=RADIO NAME=R ONCLICK="Coffeebreak_onClick">Coffee
Break</TD></TR>
    <TR><TD><IMG SRC="/ie/images/beanicon.GIF" WIDTH=18 HEIGHT=16 ALT="*"
ALIGN=CENTER> <INPUT TYPE=RADIO NAME=R ONCLICK="Evening_onClick">Evening
Dessert </TD></TR>
    <TR><TD><IMG SRC="/ie/images/beanicon.GIF" WIDTH=18 HEIGHT=16 ALT="*"
ALIGN=CENTER> <INPUT TYPE=RADIO NAME=R
ONCLICK="Unleaded_onClick">Unleaded</TD></TR>
    <TR><TD><IMG SRC="/ie/images/beanicon.GIF" WIDTH=18 HEIGHT=16 ALT="*"
ALIGN=CENTER> <INPUT TYPE=RADIO NAME=R ONCLICK="TheWorks_onClick">The
Works</TD></TR>
</TABLE>
</FONT>
```

The preceding code uses the ONCLICK method for determining when each image displays a selected radio button.

The following code describes the items you can select for your box. In the style box, radio buttons were used. In this portion of the screen, check boxes are used. You can choose any type you'd like for your own code. Notice that you can also designate font and font size and the color of both the font and the table background.

```
<FONT FACE="Comic Sans MS" SIZE=2 COLOR="8F237D">
<TABLE BGCOLOR="C9A177" WIDTH=200 ALIGN=RIGHT>
    <TR><TD BGCOLOR="8F237D" ALIGN=CENTER><FONT COLOR="FFFFCC">Items...</FONT>
</TD></TR>
    <TR><TD><INPUT TYPE=CHECKBOX NAME=Lavajava ONCLICK=SetTotalCost>Lava Java
</TD></TR>
    <TR><TD><INPUT TYPE=CHECKBOX NAME=Mauimorn ONCLICK=SetTotalCost>Maui Morning
</TD></TR>
    <TR><TD><INPUT TYPE=CHECKBOX NAME=Island ONCLICK=SetTotalCost>Island Espresso
</TD></TR>
    <TR><TD><INPUT TYPE=CHECKBOX NAME=Mugs ONCLICK=SetTotalCost>Two Mugs
</TD></TR>
    <TR><TD><INPUT TYPE=CHECKBOX NAME=Biscotti ONCLICK=SetTotalCost>Six Chocolate Biscotti
</TD></TR>
    <TR><TD><INPUT TYPE=CHECKBOX NAME=Beans ONCLICK=SetTotalCost>Chocolate Beans
</TD></TR>
</TABLE>
</FONT>
```

The following code uses the WingDings font to display hands in the marquee border. (The F character in WingDings is a hand.) You can play with this to display other WingDings characters if you like.

```
<FONT FACE="WINGDINGS" SIZE=6>
    <MARQUEE WIDTH=50 DIRECTION=RIGHT ALIGN=MIDDLE BGCOLOR=WHITE>F</MARQUEE>
</FONT>
<BR>
    <CENTER>
        <BR><FONT SIZE=4>Order Now!</FONT>
        <BR><BR>
```

```
</CENTER>
 <P>
<BR><BR><BR><BR>
<P>
<P>
<BR><BR>
        <FONT SIZE=2>
<I> The cost for a Gift Pack is $10.00 </I><BR>
<I> Each additional item is $5.00 </I>
<P>
 <CENTER>
<INPUT TYPE=SUBMIT VALUE="Order" NAME="Order">

<P>
    Description: <INPUT NAME=Text1 SIZE=60><BR>
    Total = <INPUT NAME=Sum VALUE="$0.00" SIZE=8><BR>
</CENTER>
<BR>
</FONT>
```

The following code is the VB Script used to control what happens when you click the Order button. If you add other items, the program will recalculate the order total and display a new total.

```
<SCRIPT LANGUAGE="VBSCRIPT">
'------------------------------------------------
'-- SetTotalCost
'--
'-- This method will set the total cost of the
'-- gift pack.
'--
'------------------------------------------------
sub SetTotalCost
    '----------
    '-- Get total number of items.
    '----------
    total = Lavajava.checked + Mauimorn.checked    + Island.checked + _
            Mugs.checked    + Biscotti.checked + Beans.checked
```

(continued)

```
        '----------
        '-- The price of a gift pack is $10... then add the number of
        '-- items.
        '----------
        sum.value = "$" + CStr(10 + (total * 5)) + ".00"
    end sub


    '--------------------------------------------------
    '-- When the user clicks the order button,
    '-- submit the order and alert the user that their
    '-- order will be arriving soon...
    '--------------------------------------------------
    sub Order_onClick
        '----------
        '-- Make sure the total cost is set and
        '-- give the user a nice message.
        '----------
        SetTotalCost
        text1.value = "Thank you, your gift pack will arrive in two days."
    end sub


    '--------------------------------------------------
    '-- KICK START GIFT PACK
    '--
    '--    A Kick Start contains Lava Java, Maui Morning, and Two Mugs.
    '--------------------------------------------------
    sub KickStart_onClick
        Lavajava.checked    = True
        Mauimorn.checked    = False
        Island.checked      = True
        Mugs.checked        = True
        Biscotti.checked    = False
        Beans.checked       = False
        text1.value         = "Our pick-me-up package. Great on Monday mornings."

        SetTotalCost
    end sub
```

```
'--------------------------------------------------
'-- Coffee Break Gift Pack
'--
'--    A Coffee Break gift pack contains Maui Morning, Two Mugs, and Biscotti.
'--------------------------------------------------
sub Coffeebreak_onClick
    Lavajava.checked    = False
    Mauimorn.checked    = True
    Island.checked      = False
    Mugs.checked        = True
    Biscotti.checked    = True
    Beans.checked       = False
    text1.value         = "Relax before going back to work."

    SetTotalCost
end sub


'--------------------------------------------------
'-- Evening Dessert Gift Pack
'--
'--
    An Evening Dessert gift pack contains Island Espresso, Two Mugs, Biscotti, and Beans.
'--------------------------------------------------
sub Evening_onClick
    Lavajava.checked    = False
    Mauimorn.checked    = False
    Island.checked      = True
    Mugs.checked        = True
    Biscotti.checked    = True
    Beans.checked       = True
    text1.value         = "Savor our sweet desserts over a cup of espresso with a friend."

    SetTotalCost
end sub


'--------------------------------------------------
'-- Unleaded Gift Pack
```

(continued)

```
'--
'--
An Unleaded gift pack contains decaffeinated Lava Java, Island Espresso, and Two Mugs.
'--------------------------------------------------
sub Unleaded_onClick
    Lavajava.checked   = True
    Mauimorn.checked   = False
    Island.checked     = True
    Mugs.checked       = True
    Biscotti.checked   = False
    Beans.checked      = False
    text1.value        = "Our decaffeinated versions of Volcano's best brews."

    SetTotalCost
end sub


'--------------------------------------------------
'-- The Works Gift Pack
'--
'--    A gift pack with the works contains everything.
'--------------------------------------------------
sub TheWorks_onClick
    Lavajava.checked   = True
    Mauimorn.checked   = True
    Island.checked     = True
    Mugs.checked       = True
    Biscotti.checked   = True
    Beans.checked      = True
    text1.value = "Splurge and purchase our most popular gift pack."
    SetTotalCost
end sub
</SCRIPT>
</FONT>
</BODY>
</HTML>
```

The last page of the Volcano Coffee Company demo is the catalog. Unfortunately, placing it in a frame instead of displaying it on a full Web page made taking a good screen shot more difficult, so in Figure 13-4, you can see the part of the frame that contains the catalog. This frame contains two dynamic objects that perform actions when you pass your mouse cursor over the objects. Object 1 is a coffeepot that makes perking sounds as it pours coffee. The coffee level changes as the sounds are played. Object 2 is a volcano that erupts when you pass your mouse pointer over it. Both objects make the catalog page more interesting and certainly more playful. They provide additional ambience to customers and make the ordering experience more enjoyable. How could you use this type of object in your own Web pages? Only your imagination limits you.

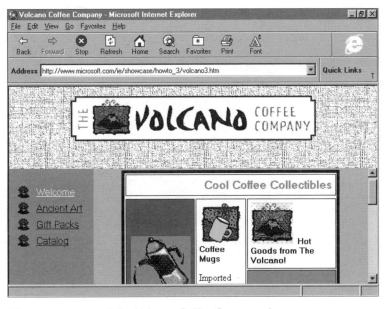

FIGURE 13-4 *The catalog page of the Volcano Coffee Company demo.*

The following code creates the catalog frame of the Volcano Coffee Company demo. The code contains table cells within the frame to create the individual boxes for each item.

```
<HTML>
<HEAD>
<TITLE>Volcano Coffee Company Catalog</TITLE>
```

(continued)

```
<META NAME="GENERATOR" CONTENT="Internet Assistant for Microsoft Word 2.0z
Beta">
</HEAD>
<BODY BGCOLOR=C9A177>
<CENTER>
```

The following code creates a table within the Catalog frame, "Cool Coffee Collectibles."

```
<TABLE WIDTH=80% HEIGHT=80% BGCOLOR=#FFFCC CELLSPACING=2 CELLPADDING=5
RULES=BASIC FRAME=BOX BORDER=5 BORDERCOLOR=BLACK>
<THEAD>
<TR ALIGN=center BGCOLOR=#FFFFFF>
     <TH COLSPAN=4 ALIGN=RIGHT> <FONT FACE="HELV" COLOR=#D36D32 SIZE=4>Cool
Coffee Collectibles</FONT></TH></TR></THEAD>
```

Below is the code for the first box, "Coffee Press." This box contains a dynamic source file, POUR.AVI, which performs movement and generates sounds when you move your mouse cursor over the image.

```
<TBODY><TR>
     <TD HEIGHT=1 COLSPAN=3 BGCOLOR=#D36D32 ></TD></TR>
<TR VALIGN=TOP>
     <TD VALIGN=MIDDLE ALIGN=CENTER BGCOLOR=#8F237D ROWSPAN=2><IMG DYNSRC="/ie/
avi/pour.avi" SRC="/ie/avi/pour.gif" START=MOUSEOVER,FILEOPEN HSPACE=2 WIDTH=102
HEIGHT=100><FONT FACE="HELV" SIZE=2>
     <P><H5> Coffee Press</H5>Brew your coffee at the table! </FONT><FONT
FACE="HELV" SIZE=1><P><B>Catalog #65-986 $39.95 each </B></TD></FONT>
     <TD VALIGN=TOP ROWSPAN=2><IMG SRC="/ie/images/mug.gif" ALIGN=LEFT HSPACE=2
WIDTH=72 HEIGHT=69> <FONT FACE="HELV" SIZE=2><H5> Coffee Mugs</H5></FONT>
     <P>Imported from Brazil, these mugs are perfect for lattes. Pick from three
festive colors: canary yellow, peacock blue, and aqua green. Dishwasher safe.
     <P> <FONT FACE="HELV" SIZE=1><b>Catalog #65-897 Six for $36.00</b></TD>
     </FONT>
```

The following code designates the second dynamic image, VOLCANO.AVI, which erupts when you pass your mouse cursor over it. It also creates the table cell with the text for this box.

```
     <TD VALIGN=TOP> <IMG DYNSRC="/ie/avi/volcano.avi" START=MOUSEOVER,FILEOPEN
HSPACE=2 WIDTH=72 HEIGHT=70><FONT FACE="HELV" SIZE=2><b>Hot Goods from The
```

```
Volcano!</b></FONT></TD></TR>
<TR>
```

Here is the code for the box that contains the text "Volcano Coffee Co." As you can see, it is simple to create boxes within a frame. You can designate each "box," or table cell, with a different background color, font, and text.

```
    <TD BGCOLOR="#D36D32" ROWSPAN=2><FONT COLOR="#FFFCC" FACE="HELV"
SIZE=4><B> <BR>Volcano Coffee Co.<BR>
123 Lava Street<BR>
Honolulu, HI 99999-1234<P>
1-800-999-9999</B></FONT><BR>   </TD></TR>
<TBODY>
<TR>
    <TD COLSPAN=2 ROWSPAN=2> <IMG SRC="/ie/images/grinder.gif" WIDTH=71 HEIGHT=72
ALIGN=RIGHT> <FONT FACE="HELV" SIZE=2><H5>Hand Grinder</H5>
    <P>Smell the aromas of the South Seas when you grind your Volcano Coffee beans
by hand in this classic oak grinder. </FONT>
    <P><FONT FACE="HELV" SIZE=1><B>Catalog #54-268 $35.50 each</B></TD></FONT>
```

Here is the code for the box that contains the text "Call Today!"

```
<TR>
    <TD ALIGN=CENTER BGCOLOR="#FFFFFF"><FONT COLOR="#D36D32" FACE="HELV"
SIZE=4><B> Call Today! </B></FONT></TD></TR>
</TBODY>
</TABLE>
</CENTER>
</BODY>
</HTML>
```

It isn't difficult to create exciting Web pages, full of interactivity, sound, video clips, and dynamic objects using VB Script and ActiveX objects. Although this chapter could not be all-inclusive, it is meant to give you a glimpse into the exciting future of Web page interactivity and to show you that it isn't as hard as you might think to incorporate it into your own Web pages. Technology is changing rapidly. As I write this, many developers at companies all over the world are thinking of new ways to help you add excitement to your Web pages. The Web is our future, and only those farsighted developers know what direction that future is headed. Technology is coming, and it will be pulling you in its wake. So hang on for the ride, and enjoy the experience. Good luck!

 NOTE: You can use the Web to locate many companies currently offering ActiveX code depositories. You can also use the Web to browse http://www.microsoft.com for the latest information about VB Script and ActiveX controls. This is a rapidly changing technology, and Web content is dynamic enough to keep up with the changes. Use Yahoo or another search facility to locate pages on the VB Script and ActiveX topics.

Lin Laurie is owner of WinPro Online Press and is a technical writer, editor, and Web page developer in Seattle, Washington. She is the former editor of the WinHelp Journal *and does occasional presentations on online help and Web page development. You can reach her at (206) 784-5821 or at linlaurie@msn.com.*

● INDEX

D

dashes, 38
decimal point, 61
default, for drop-down lists, 45–47
Definition List (<DL>) tag, 14, 15–16
digital audio, 112–13, 114, 115
digital video, 119–20
DINGBAT= attribute (<LI> tag), 20–22
DIRECTION= attribute (<MARQUEE> tag), 36
DLL files, 210, 211
<DL> (Definition List) tag, 14, 15–16
DP= (Decimal Point) attribute, 61
drop-down lists, default for, 45–47
DSP Group, 119
DXF files, 90
dynamic range, 113–14

E

em spaces, 38
en spaces, 38, 60–61
environment variables, 157–58
Example (<XMP>) tag, 38
Excel. *See* Microsoft Excel Internet Assistant
EXE files, 211

F

f2mail.cgi file, 164–67
FACE= attribute (<FONT> tag), 25, 28–29, 202–3
file formats
   audio, 117–18
   graphics, 90
   video, 120–21
flush left alignment, 4, 64

flush right alignment, 4–5, 64
fonts
   coloring, 27–28
   overriding browsers, 25–29
   using TrueType in Web pages, 202–5
<FONT> tag
   COLOR= attribute, 27–28
   FACE= attribute, 25, 28–29, 202–3
   SIZE= attribute, 25, 26
forms
   and CGI scripts, 159–62
   data collection alternatives, 47–50
   default for drop-down lists, 45–47
   lining up display elements, 40–42
   overview, 40
   sample data mailer, 164–67
   tables for display elements, 42–45
   using CGI programs, 49–50
   using handling services, 48
<FORM> tag
   ACTION= attribute, 47, 48
   METHOD= attribute, 159
   TARGET= attribute, 188
frames
   creating, 172–81
   creating with CELLSPACING= attribute, 73
   how they work, 171–72
   and non-frame-capable browsers, 179–81
   overview, 168–69, 178
   preparing content frame, 174–75
   preparing frameset, 172–74
   preparing "main" frame, 176–79
   and terminology, 169
   when to use, 170–71
framesets
   creating, 172–74
   defined, 171–72, 178
   multiple, 189
   nested, 181, 189

<FRAMESET> tag
   COLS= attribute, 182
   overview, 172–74, 181
   ROWS= attribute, 182
<FRAME> tag
   MARGINHEIGHT= attribute, 184
   MARGINWIDTH= attribute, 183–84
   NAME= attribute, 183
   NORESIZE attribute, 186
   overview, 168, 183
   SCROLLING= attribute, 185–86
   SRC= attribute, 186
   TARGET= attribute, 186–89
frequency response, 114–15
FrontPage, 195–96
FTP Client control, 215

G

GIF files
   87a vs. 89a, 91
   and inline animation, 129
   interlaced, 93–94
   making transparent, 91–92
   and NOSHADE attribute, 33
   as part of double background, 33, 80, 107–8
   using as backgrounds, 80, 102–4
GoGetClassObjectFromURL API, 209, 211
Gradient control, 227–28
gradient fill backgrounds, 108–9
graphic chat programs, 226–27
graphics
   adding borders, 11, 12–13
   adding space around, 11–12, 12–13
   as backgrounds, 80, 102–4
   bounding boxes for, 86–88
   centering, 5–7
   file formats, 90
   image maps, 94–98

tables, *continued*
blank cells, 62
centering, 63
color in, 80–85
creating margin outside, 59
creating text columns, 75–78
for form elements, 42
headers for, 55–56
overview, 52
setting margins inside cells, 62–63
spacing of cells, 70–73
spanning cells, 57–58
spanning rows, 58
specifying cells in rows, 54–55
specifying cell width, 59–60
specifying colors in cells, 54, 80–83
specifying rows, 53
specifying row width, 59–60
specifying width, 59–60
using boxes as frames, 73–74
using to position text and graphics, 78–79
wrapping text, 56
<TABLE> tag
BORDER= attribute, 69–70
BORDERCOLOR= attribute, 83–84
BORDERDARK= attribute, 84–85
BORDERLIGHT= attribute, 84–85
CELLPADDING= attribute, 62–63
CELLSPACING= attribute, 70–73
COLSPEC= attribute, 61
creating frames, 73–74
creating text columns, 75–78
overview, 52
UNIT= attribute, 60–61
using to position text and graphics, 78–79
WIDTH= attribute, 59–60
TABONE attribute, 16
tabs, adding, 16
<TAB> tag, 16

tags, 3. *See also names of tags*
TARGET= attribute (<FRAME> tag)
in link tags, 174, 186–88
magic target names, 188–89
target names, 183, 188–89
<TD> (Table Data) tag
ALIGN= attribute, 63–65
BGCOLOR= attribute, 80–83
BORDERCOLOR= attribute, 83–84
BORDERDARK= attribute, 84–85
BORDERLIGHT= attribute, 84–85
COLSPAN= attribute, 57–58
NOWRAP attribute, 56
overview, 54–55
ROWSPAN= attribute, 58
VALIGN= attribute, 63, 65–66
text
aligning, 4–5
centering, 5–7
colored, 27–28, 110–11
horizontally scrolling, 34–37
indenting, 14–16
wrapping, 7–13
TEXT= attribute (<BODY> tag), 110
text-only browsers, 87
text/plain content type, 161
<TH> (Table Header) tag
ALIGN= attribute, 63
COLSPAN= attribute, 57–58
NOWRAP attribute, 56
overview, 55–56
ROWSPAN= attribute, 58
VALIGN= attribute, 63
WIDTH= attribute, 59–60
thumbnail graphics, 99
TIFF files, 90
tiling background images, 105–7
Timer control, 235–36
titles, for tables, 67–68

TOPMARGIN= attribute (<BODY> tag), 14
transparent images
creating, 90–92
vs. regular images, 89
<TR> (Table Row) tag
ALIGN= attribute, 63–65
overview, 53
VALIGN= attribute, 63, 65–66
WIDTH= attribute, 59–60
TrueSpeech, 119
TrueType fonts, 202–5
TYPE= attribute
<OL> tag, 22–23
<UL> tag, 17–19
typography. *See also* fonts
special characters, 38

U

UL files, 117
<UL> (Unordered List) tag
new HTML 3.0 attributes, 17–19
PLAIN= attribute, 19
SRC= attribute, 20
TYPE= attribute, 17–19
Unicode, 151
UNIT= attribute (<TABLE> tag), 60–61
units of measurement, 60–61
Unordered Lists (<UL>), 17–19, 20
Unordered List (<UL>) tag, 17–19, 20
USEMAP= attribute (<IMG> tag), 96

V

VALIGN= attribute
<TD> tag, 63, 65–66
<TR> tag, 63, 65–66
VALUE= attribute (list tags), 23, 24

X

W

BRUCE MORRIS

Bruce Morris is Global Internet Manager at Gateway 2000 and Publisher of *NCT Web Magazine*.

At Gateway 2000, he founded the Internet Information Services Department, assembled a Web team, and helped create one of the most exciting commercial Web sites on the planet.

He has had numerous articles, reviews, and columns published in computer magazines, including *National Computer Tectonics, Government Computer News, GCN State and Local, Reseller Management,* and *Medio Multimedia Magazine.* He is a frequent public speaker. His background is in journalism and environmental engineering.

Bruce lives on a farm in South Dakota with his wife, Laura; four dogs; several cats; three quarterhorses; and a variety of barnyard animals. In 1990, he was Tennessee State Champion Pole Bender and Reserve World Champion Amateur Pole Bender. He is a graduate of Woodstock and other 60s renaissance events. He enjoys scuba diving, blues guitar, red wine, and fast horses and is a frequent flyer with over 250,000 yearly miles.

The manuscript for this book was prepared and submitted to Microsoft Press in electronic form. Text files were prepared using Microsoft Word 7.0 for Windows 95. Pages were composed by Microsoft Press using PageMaker 6.0 for Windows 95, with text in Sabon and display type in Eurostile bold. Composed pages were delivered to the printer as electronic prepress files.

Cover Graphic Designer
Gregory Erickson

Cover Illustrator
Glenn Mitsui

Interior Graphic Designer
Pam Hidaka

Interior Graphic Artists
Travis Beaven
Paul Carew

Compositors
Candace Gearhart
Sandra Haynes

Indexer
Julie Kawabata

Make your presence felt on the Internet or within your own intranet.

U.S.A. $39.95
U.K. £37.49 [V.A.T. included]
Canada $54.95
ISBN 1-57231-304-8

This book is not about developing Web site content (although it touches on it). BUILD YOUR OWN WEB SITE shows you how to publish your content on the Internet or your corporate intranet using Microsoft® Windows NT® Server and Microsoft Internet Information Server—even if you have little or no programming or networking experience. In this helpful guide, you will find everything you need to know about:

- How the Internet or an intranet works
- Why Windows NT Server is the platform to choose
- How to calculate choices of hardware, connections, security, bandwidth, and routing
- How to set up your system, maintain security, create content, and observe Internet etiquette
- How to configure your system, deal with maintenance issues, and plan for the future
- How to become an Internet service provider

BUILD YOUR OWN WEB SITE also familiarizes you with hot new technologies such as Java and ActiveX™.

If you're ready to establish your organization on the Internet or to set up your own intranet, BUILD YOUR OWN WEB SITE is the smart place to start.

Microsoft Press

Microsoft Press® books are available wherever quality books are sold and through CompuServe's Electronic Mall—**GO MSP**—or our Web page, http://www.microsoft.com/mspress/. Call **1-800-MSPRESS** for more information or to place a credit card order.* Please refer to **BBK** when placing your order. Prices subject to change.

*In Canada, contact Macmillan Canada, Attn: Microsoft Press Dept., 164 Commander Blvd., Agincourt, Ontario, Canada M1S 3C7, or call 1-800-667-1115. Outside the U.S. and Canada, write to International Coordinator, Microsoft Press, One Microsoft Way, Redmond, WA 98052-6399, or fax +1-206-936-7329.

Publish it **yourself** on your **intranet** or on the World Wide Web!

*D*iscover how Microsoft® FrontPage™ makes it fast, easy, and fun to create and manage your own Web site—on your intranet or on the World Wide Web—using content created in FrontPage, in Microsoft Office, or in other applications.

As the Internet and intranets surge in popularity, more and more people want to get in on the action by creating personal or small-business Web sites. Up to now, you've needed HTML programming expertise, or else you've been stuck using lower-end Web publishing systems that produce less-than-exciting pages.

Now, using Microsoft FrontPage, with help from INTRODUCING MICROSOFT FRONTPAGE, you can create your own great-looking, effective Web pages and put them up on your intranet or the World Wide Web—even if you have *no* previous Web publishing experience!

Packed with information, INTRODUCING MICROSOFT FRONTPAGE is the one book you shouldn't be without when you build your Web site with Microsoft FrontPage!

U.S.A.	**$24.95**
U.K.	£22.99 [V.A.T. included]
Canada	$34.95
ISBN 1-57231-338-2	

Microsoft Press® books are available wherever quality books are sold and through CompuServe's Electronic Mall—**GO MSP**—or our Web page, http://www.microsoft.com/mspress/. Call **1-800-MSPRESS** for more information or to place a credit card order.* Please refer to **BBK** when placing your order. Prices subject to change.

*In Canada, contact Macmillan Canada, Attn: Microsoft Press Dept., 164 Commander Blvd., Agincourt, Ontario, Canada M1S 3C7, or call 1-800-667-1115. Outside the U.S. and Canada, write to International Coordinator, Microsoft Press, One Microsoft Way, Redmond, WA 98052-6399, or fax +1-206-936-7329.

Microsoft®Press

 **Want to:** Find a job? Buy a car? Raise ants? Find your uncle? Study paleontology? Learn about bats? Meet casting directors? Look at pictures through the Virtual Magnifying Glass? **Well, be our guest!**

Includes the CD-ROM version with direct links to thousands of Internet sites! A simple double click of the mouse takes you *immediately* wherever you want to go!

The MICROSOFT® BOOKSHELF® INTERNET DIRECTORY is your host for thousands of Internet sites—an amazing spectrum that covers everything from activism to zoology. Unlike most other Internet directories, this book brings you only the best—the hand-picked crème de la crème, complete with descriptions of and comments on the most useful and entertaining Web sites and ftp sites (locations for downloading files) on the Internet. The wonders of the Internet await you, and the MICROSOFT BOOKSHELF INTERNET DIRECTORY is your magic carpet to a vast world of information resources.

So what are you waiting for? Get the MICROSOFT BOOKSHELF INTERNET DIRECTORY!

U.S.A.	**$35.00**
U.K.	£32.99 [V.A.T. included]
Canada	$47.95
ISBN 1-55615-947-1	

Microsoft Press® books are available wherever quality books are sold and through CompuServe's Electronic Mall—**GO MSP**—or our Web page, http://www.microsoft.com/mspress/. Call **1-800-MSPRESS** for more information or to place a credit card order.* Please refer to **BBK** when placing your order. Prices subject to change.

*In Canada, contact Macmillan Canada, Attn: Microsoft Press Dept., 164 Commander Blvd., Agincourt, Ontario, Canada M1S 3C7, or call 1-800-667-1115. Outside the U.S. and Canada, write to International Coordinator, Microsoft Press, One Microsoft Way, Redmond, WA 98052-6399, or fax +1-206-936-7329.

IMPORTANT—READ CAREFULLY BEFORE OPENING SOFTWARE PACKET(S). By opening the sealed packet(s) containing the software, you indicate your acceptance of the following Microsoft License Agreement.

MICROSOFT LICENSE AGREEMENT

(Book Companion CD)

This is a legal agreement between you (either an individual or an entity) and Microsoft Corporation. By opening the sealed software packet(s) you are agreeing to be bound by the terms of this agreement. If you do not agree to the terms of this agreement, promptly return the unopened software packet(s) and any accompanying written materials to the place you obtained them for a full refund.

MICROSOFT SOFTWARE LICENSE

1. GRANT OF LICENSE. Microsoft grants to you the right to use one copy of the Microsoft software program included with this book (the "SOFTWARE") on a single terminal connected to a single computer. The SOFTWARE is in "use" on a computer when it is loaded into the temporary memory (i.e., RAM) or installed into the permanent memory (e.g., hard disk, CD-ROM, or other storage device) of that computer. You may not network the SOFTWARE or otherwise use it on more than one computer or computer terminal at the same time.

2. COPYRIGHT. The SOFTWARE is owned by Microsoft or its suppliers and is protected by United States copyright laws and international treaty provisions. Therefore, you must treat the SOFTWARE like any other copyrighted material (e.g., a book or musical recording) except that you may either (a) make one copy of the SOFTWARE solely for backup or archival purposes, or (b) transfer the SOFTWARE to a single hard disk provided you keep the original solely for backup or archival purposes. You may not copy the written materials accompanying the SOFTWARE.

3. OTHER RESTRICTIONS. You may not rent or lease the SOFTWARE, but you may transfer the SOFTWARE and accompanying written materials on a permanent basis provided you retain no copies and the recipient agrees to the terms of this Agreement. You may not reverse engineer, decompile, or disassemble the SOFTWARE. If the SOFTWARE is an update or has been updated, any transfer must include the most recent update and all prior versions.

4. DUAL MEDIA SOFTWARE. If the SOFTWARE package contains more than one kind of disk (3.5", 5.25", and CD-ROM), then you may use only the disks appropriate for your single-user computer. You may not use the other disks on another computer or loan, rent, lease, or transfer them to another user except as part of the permanent transfer (as provided above) of all SOFTWARE and written materials.

5. SAMPLE CODE. If the SOFTWARE includes Sample Code, then Microsoft grants you a royalty-free right to reproduce and distribute the sample code of the SOFTWARE provided that you: (a) distribute the sample code only in conjunction with and as a part of your software product; (b) do not use Microsoft's or its authors' names, logos, or trademarks to market your software product; (c) include the copyright notice that appears on the SOFTWARE on your product label and as a part of the sign-on message for your software product; and (d) agree to indemnify, hold harmless, and defend Microsoft and its authors from and against any claims or lawsuits, including attorneys' fees, that arise or result from the use or distribution of your software product.

DISCLAIMER OF WARRANTY

The SOFTWARE (including instructions for its use) is provided "AS IS" WITHOUT WARRANTY OF ANY KIND. MICROSOFT FURTHER DISCLAIMS ALL IMPLIED WARRANTIES INCLUDING WITHOUT LIMITATION ANY IMPLIED WARRANTIES OF MERCHANTABILITY OR OF FITNESS FOR A PARTICULAR PURPOSE. THE ENTIRE RISK ARISING OUT OF THE USE OR PERFORMANCE OF THE SOFTWARE AND DOCUMENTATION REMAINS WITH YOU.

IN NO EVENT SHALL MICROSOFT, ITS AUTHORS, OR ANYONE ELSE INVOLVED IN THE CREATION, PRODUCTION, OR DELIVERY OF THE SOFTWARE BE LIABLE FOR ANY DAMAGES WHATSOEVER (INCLUDING, WITHOUT LIMITATION, DAMAGES FOR LOSS OF BUSINESS PROFITS, BUSINESS INTERRUPTION, LOSS OF BUSINESS INFORMATION, OR OTHER PECUNIARY LOSS) ARISING OUT OF THE USE OF OR INABILITY TO USE THE SOFTWARE OR DOCUMENTATION, EVEN IF MICROSOFT HAS BEEN ADVISED OF THE POSSIBILITY OF SUCH DAMAGES. BECAUSE SOME STATES/COUNTRIES DO NOT ALLOW THE EXCLUSION OR LIMITATION OF LIABILITY FOR CONSEQUENTIAL OR INCIDENTAL DAMAGES, THE ABOVE LIMITATION MAY NOT APPLY TO YOU.

U.S. GOVERNMENT RESTRICTED RIGHTS

The SOFTWARE and documentation are provided with RESTRICTED RIGHTS. Use, duplication, or disclosure by the Government is subject to restrictions as set forth in subparagraph (c)(1)(ii) of The Rights in Technical Data and Computer Software clause at DFARS 252.227-7013 or subparagraphs (c)(1) and (2) of the Commercial Computer Software — Restricted Rights 48 CFR 52.227-19, as applicable. Manufacturer is Microsoft Corporation, One Microsoft Way, Redmond, WA 98052-6399.

If you acquired this product in the United States, this Agreement is governed by the laws of the State of Washington.

Should you have any questions concerning this Agreement, or if you desire to contact Microsoft Press for any reason, please write: Microsoft Press, One Microsoft Way, Redmond, WA 98052-6399.

Register Today!

Return this
HTML In Action
registration card for a Microsoft Press® catalog

U.S. and Canada addresses only. Fill in information below and mail postage-free. Please mail only the bottom half of this page.

1-55615-948-XA   *HTML IN ACTION*   *Owner Registration Card*

NAME

INSTITUTION OR COMPANY NAME

ADDRESS

CITY   STATE   ZIP

Microsoft ®Press

Quality Computer Books

For a free catalog of
Microsoft Press® products, call
1-800-MSPRESS

NO POSTAGE
NECESSARY
IF MAILED
IN THE
UNITED STATES

BUSINESS REPLY MAIL

FIRST-CLASS MAIL   PERMIT NO. 108   REDMOND, WA

POSTAGE WILL BE PAID BY ADDRESSEE

MICROSOFT PRESS REGISTRATION
HTML IN ACTION
PO BOX 3019
BOTHELL   WA   98041-9946